Manga Studio Ex 5 Cookbook

Over 90 hands-on recipes to help you create digital comics, from page setup to exporting the final product

Elizabeth Staley

[PACKT]
PUBLISHING
BIRMINGHAM - MUMBAI

Manga Studio Ex 5 Cookbook

First published: September 2015

Production reference: 1220915

Published by Packt Publishing Ltd.
Livery Place
35 Livery Street
Birmingham B3 2PB, UK.

ISBN 978-1-78588-107-7

www.packtpub.com

Credits

Author
Elizabeth Staley

Reviewers
Damien Barban
Viktor Jäderlund
Kevin Nakakihara
Kyle Shold

Commissioning Editor
Swapnil Khedekar

Acquisition Editor
Reshma Raman

Content Development Editor
Shali Deeraj

Technical Editor
Tanmayee Patil

Copy Editor
Vikrant Phadke

Project Coordinator
Sanchita Mandal

Proofreader
Safis Editing

Indexer
Rekha Nair

Production Coordinator
Aparna Bhagat

Cover Work
Aparna Bhagat

Foreword

Hello there! Welcome to the party!

"Party?" you say? Yes! Whenever I use Manga Studio EX 5 to create one of my illustrations or comics, it feels like a party. That's how much I enjoy Manga Studio EX 5 (or Clip Studio Paint Pro). I turn on some classic rock and roll, open up Manga Studio, and let the creative juices flow.

If you've made it this far with Manga Studio EX 5, then you know what I'm talking about. In my opinion, there is no better tool for creating comics and graphic novels than this software. And the key to my success with Manga Studio EX 5 has been my work with Elizabeth Staley, the author of this book you just purchased.

Elizabeth Staley creates a wonderful comic called *Adrastus*, which is about a robot and the young lady destined to operate it. For the past couple of years, she and I have worked together on her comic. She writes, draws, and inks the comic. Then, I come in and add the colors and shading. It has been a great collaboration, and it has taught us both a lot about how to create better-looking comics.

I am self-taught as an artist. I also joined this party later in my life. I drew comics in my high-school and college years, but put the pencils down until I picked them up again in 2007, at the "young" age of 50. Then, I knew that to succeed in today's digital environment, I better learn new drawing techniques. I tried out a variety of drawing software packages, but it was Manga Studio that hit the mark for me. I struggled at the beginning, mostly as I was not only learning the software but also relearning how to draw.

I quickly joined Twitter and connected with a diverse group of comic creators. This led to me forming the Webcomic Alliance in 2010. This alliance is a group of artists who have decided to share the ups and downs of their forays into digital comics, or webcomics. A huge portion of this journey was made possible by Manga Studio.

When Manga Studio 5 and EX 5 were released, they changed the game significantly. Now, there was a single tool for drawing, inking, and coloring my comics and illustrations. The push was on learning even more about Manga Studio EX 5.

Enter Elizabeth Staley. Elizabeth Staley helped me discover the tools and processes in Manga Studio EX 5 that would help me improve and streamline my drawing processes. Her first book, *Mastering Manga Studio 5, Packt Publishing*, has been a big success, and now she's assembled an awesome set of "recipes" for Manga Studio EX 5. The "recipes" in this book will help you improve your drawing process over time, just as they did for me. From simple to complex, every method outlined in this book will bring you closer to becoming a Manga Studio master yourself.

The proof of this claim is the fact that I'm writing this foreword. Thanks to Manga Studio and her expert training, I was recently hired by NBC Sports to produce a set of illustrations for use in NBC's coverage of NASCAR races. Manga Studio made it possible for me to create an extremely large set of drawings (over 6 feet tall) in a short time span to meet NBC's deadlines. They were so pleased with the results that they hired me to make even more illustrations for them. Without the right tools and training, none of this would have been possible.

So, since 2007, I've grown from a "want-to-be" comic artist to a successful illustrator and comic creator. I've been hired to provide demonstrations on Manga Studio as well as illustrations for NBC Sports—all of that in 8 short years. I am also going to Manila in the Philippines to demonstrate Manga Studio EX 5 at an upcoming major comic convention in 2015. None of this would have been possible without Manga Studio and Elizabeth Staley.

Now, it's time for you to get cracking. Take each of the chapters and recipes crafted masterfully by Elizabeth Staley, and slowly add it into your drawing process. Over time, you too will see improvements in your work. Perhaps one of your drawings will be noticed by a TV network, and you'll be on your way to becoming a successful illustrator and comic creator too. Only time will tell.

Rock on!

W. Byron Wilkins
Artist/Owner of TR1 Studios, Creator of *1977 the Comic*, and Co-founder of the Webcomic Alliance
Montgomery, Illinois, USA

About the Author

Elizabeth Staley is a writer and artist currently living in western Pennsylvania, USA. When she isn't working on comics, she can be found watching crime shows and cartoons, reading comics and novels, or outdoors with her horse. She graduated with a bachelor's degree in media arts and animation in 2004. She has been working on her current web-published comic, *Adrastus*, since 2010.

She started using Manga Studio for her drawing in 2011 and hasn't looked back since. Elizabeth was involved in Smith Micro's beta test for Manga Studio 5 soon after she started using Manga Studio 4, and she has been talking about its benefits for artists ever since.

Mastering Manga Studio 5, Packt Publishing, was Elizabeth Staley's first software book, released in 2013. After a warm reception from the Manga Studio artist community, she came back to write *Manga Studio EX 5 Cookbook* in 2015. In addition to these two titles, she has also self-published two comic collections and a novel.

First, I would like to thank Smith Micro for their tireless work on Manga Studio 5 and for all the help that they provided for this book. I would also like to thank my husband, who has been a pillar of support for me during the writing process and helped me through many troublesome chapters, long nights, and bouts of tearing my hair out. As always, many thanks to the team at Packt Publishing for guiding me through the process, answering my questions, and being just as excited about the book as I've been. Also, thanks to all the Manga Studio artists out there who have encouraged me throughout the past few months with their enthusiasm for this title: this book is for all of you!

About the Reviewers

Damien Barban is a French cartoonist and storyboard artist based in Paris. He has been working for the last 13 years on movies, comics, and illustrations.

Damien has worked on many TV ads, video clips, and movies.

Viktor Jäderlund, born in 1987, is a deaf comic artist who works in Sweden. He mostly draws comics about deaf people and sign language users. But sometimes, he dreams of working on an epic comic project one day. His brain is often full of ideas of projects that he wants to do, but there is not much time for him.

When he begins one project, he is almost unstoppable. He draws at full speed. Many people are often shocked by seeing how fast Viktor can draw.

Once he completes a dream project, there is always a new one to dream of. But there's one special project that he loves, *Tidsbyrån (TimeBureau)*, which he is hoping to complete sometime in the future.

He has written and made some contributions to these books: *Dövas Dassbok* (*Deaf toilet joke book*) in 2011 and *Altcom No Borders* in 2012; contributions to the comic *Why*, *Skräpmonstret* (*The rubbish monster*) in 2012; the cover of *Ögats folk* (*The people of the eye*) in 2012, the cover of *Abe Z* in 2013; the *fanzine Kvarnby Serier* in 2013 (*Kvarnby comics*); the *Comic art school's yearbook*, *Serienördens kokbok* (*Comicbook nerd's cookbook*), in 2014; contributions to the comic *Kaktajm*, *Seger – en dövhistorisk seriebok* (*Victory – a deaf history comic book*) in 2015; *Plutonium Comics 12* in 2015; and contributions to the comic *Flight*.

To know more about Viktor, check out his website at `http://www.deafca.com/`.

Thank you all for giving me the honor of reviewing this book. It has really been fun and interesting. It is something I have never done before. So, thanks for letting me participate in this project.

Kevin Nakakihara is a digital painter who has been interested in art software since 2004. He currently manages the site `MangaStudioSensei.com`, a resource for those interested in learning more about how to navigate through Manga Studio 5 and find more sources of inspiration.

Thanks to all the people of the active Manga Studio 5 community for keeping this program on the map, and thanks to my parents for their continued support.

Kyle Shold, after graduation from The Art Institute of Seattle, went on to work in the video game industry for 10 years, illustrating backgrounds, conceptualizing environments, storyboarding, and being an art director for companies such as Humongous Entertainment, Atari, Big Top Games, and Bungie.

He then joined the Key Publishing group as the art director for *Make-Up Artist* magazine and the International Make-up Artist Trade Show (IMATS). Kyle brought a new energy and vitality into the look and feel of every aspect of Key Publishing's visual presentation. His influence is visible to this day.

He is currently a freelance illustrator and graphic designer. He works with a variety of exciting new clients, creating apparel and craft beer labels, comic books, promotional material, and much more. He resides in Vancouver, Washington state, USA, with his beautiful wife and three daughters.

Kyle's website is at `http://kyleshold.com/`.

www.PacktPub.com

Support files, eBooks, discount offers, and more

For support files and downloads related to your book, please visit www.PacktPub.com.

Did you know that Packt offers eBook versions of every book published, with PDF and ePub files available? You can upgrade to the eBook version at www.PacktPub.com and as a print book customer, you are entitled to a discount on the eBook copy. Get in touch with us at service@packtpub.com for more details.

At www.PacktPub.com, you can also read a collection of free technical articles, sign up for a range of free newsletters and receive exclusive discounts and offers on Packt books and eBooks.

PACKTLIB™

https://www2.packtpub.com/books/subscription/packtlib

Do you need instant solutions to your IT questions? PacktLib is Packt's online digital book library. Here, you can search, access, and read Packt's entire library of books.

Why subscribe?

- Fully searchable across every book published by Packt
- Copy and paste, print, and bookmark content
- On demand and accessible via a web browser

Free access for Packt account holders

If you have an account with Packt at www.PacktPub.com, you can use this to access PacktLib today and view 9 entirely free books. Simply use your login credentials for immediate access.

Table of Contents

Preface

Hello and welcome to the *Manga Studio EX 5 Cookbook*! This book is set up to give you "recipes" to complete tasks in Manga Studio EX 5—from creating pages, to using vector layers, to exporting your finished project. I hope that this book will become an invaluable resource in your library and that you'll look at it often when you can't remember the steps to do something in this amazing art software. I also hope that you'll use the techniques and tips presented in these pages to inspire you to create your own techniques and to streamline your workflow.

You may have purchased this book even though you don't have Manga Studio EX 5. Perhaps you have Manga Studio 5 and are looking to see if you should upgrade to the EX version? Thankfully, most of this book will apply to the Manga Studio 5 version of the software, but there are several exciting and time-saving features that are only available in the EX version.

If you have purchased my first book, *Mastering Manga Studio 5, Packt Publishing*, these two books work very well together!

What this book covers

Chapter 1, Creating and Manipulating Pages and Page Templates, covers everything about making new pages (files) in Manga Studio EX 5. We will learn how to make custom paper sizes, make files with multiple pages (EX only), and make page and cover templates to save time in our drawing.

Chapter 2, Customizing Brushes, teaches us all about making new brushes in Manga Studio EX 5. This includes special effect brushes, such as broken glass, clothing ruffles, and cracked rubble!

Chapter 3, Getting a Handle on Vectors, covers some of the vector tools in Manga Studio EX 5. We'll learn how to make vector layers, make marks with the brush and line tools, and edit those shapes by using the control points.

Chapter 4, Using the Layer Modes, have you ever wondered what the layer modes such as Multiply, Screen, and Darken do? This chapter will teach you all about these methods of combining layers.

Chapter 5, Making Selections and Layer Masks, includes the newest updates of Manga Studio EX 5 have included some new ways of making selections. Learn how to make layer masks, use the selection pen, and more in this chapter.

Chapter 6, Using New Rulers and Line Tools, covers the newer updates of Manga Studio EX 5, new rulers and new line tools. We'll learn how to use the Symmetry ruler, saturated lines, scattered lines, the Gloom tool, and more in this chapter.

Chapter 7, Adding and Creating Tones and Materials, shows that Manga Studio EX 5 comes with a large library of screentones and other materials, but we can also add our own! Learn how to apply existing materials to a drawing, then learn how to make your own screentones, fabric patterns, and more.

Chapter 8, Playing with Color Palettes, shows that there are many ways to store and choose colors for our drawing in Manga Studio EX 5. This chapter will teach us how to import an existing palette from another program, save color sets, create harmonious color schemes, and use the Color History palette.

Chapter 9, Creating Special Effects, covers color holds, shiny leather, lightning, and laser blasts! This chapter can get you started on some special effects to make your illustrations and comics pop!

Chapter 10, Using 3D Objects, reveals that Manga Studio EX 5 comes with many 3D elements that can be used in your work. Learn how to add 3D models to the page, move the objects and the 3D camera, customize models, and save custom 3D information as materials.

Chapter 11, Exporting the Finished Product, now that we have some comics made, it's time to take them and show them to the world- via print or the Web. This chapter will teach us about exporting pages, including how to reduce file size or change image dimensions without changing our original file.

What you need for this book

To use this book, you will need Manga Studio 5. Either the EX or the regular version will work. If you do not have EX 5 then some of the recipes in the first chapter and one recipe in the final chapter will not be accessible to you: specifically the recipes about making or exporting multiple page files.

You will also find it easiest to use this book with a drawing tablet of some sort. There are many brands and styles, from ones that replace your mouse with a pen and board that you draw on, to monitors that display your work and allow you to make changes on-screen, just like drawing with pencil and paper. The first type, without a display in it, is the cheapest type and is usually best for a beginner to digital art. The most popular brand of tablets is Wacom, but there are many others out there.

Who this book is for

This book is for intermediate users who already know a little bit about graphics software. Maybe you've used Adobe Photoshop for a while and are trying to make the switch to Manga Studio 5 EX? If you already know what layers are and can find the pencil, pen, and other tools, then you should not have any problems following along with the recipes in this book.

Sections

In this book, you will find several headings that appear frequently (*Getting ready*, *How to do it...*, *How it works...*, *There's more...*, and *See also*).

To give clear instructions on how to complete a recipe, we use these sections as follows:

Getting ready

This section tells you what to expect in the recipe, and describes how to set up any software or any preliminary settings required for the recipe.

How to do it…

This section contains the steps required to follow the recipe.

How it works…

This section usually consists of a detailed explanation of what happened in the previous section.

There's more…

This section consists of additional information about the recipe in order to make the reader more knowledgeable about the recipe.

See also

This section provides helpful links to other useful information for the recipe.

Conventions

In this book, you will find a number of text styles that distinguish between different kinds of information. Here are some examples of these styles and an explanation of their meaning.

New terms and **important words** are shown in bold. Words that you see on the screen, for example, in menus or dialog boxes, appear in the text like this: "In the **Preferences** window, click on the **Edit text** option on the left-hand-side menu."

> Warnings or important notes appear in a box like this.

> Tips and tricks appear like this.

Reader feedback

Feedback from our readers is always welcome. Let us know what you think about this book—what you liked or disliked. Reader feedback is important for us as it helps us develop titles that you will really get the most out of.

To send us general feedback, simply e-mail `feedback@packtpub.com`, and mention the book's title in the subject of your message.

If there is a topic that you have expertise in and you are interested in either writing or contributing to a book, see our author guide at `www.packtpub.com/authors`.

Customer support

Now that you are the proud owner of a Packt book, we have a number of things to help you to get the most from your purchase.

Errata

Although we have taken every care to ensure the accuracy of our content, mistakes do happen. If you find a mistake in one of our books—maybe a mistake in the text or the code—we would be grateful if you could report this to us. By doing so, you can save other readers from frustration and help us improve subsequent versions of this book. If you find any errata, please report them by visiting `http://www.packtpub.com/submit-errata`, selecting your book, clicking on the **Errata Submission Form** link, and entering the details of your errata. Once your errata are verified, your submission will be accepted and the errata will be uploaded to our website or added to any list of existing errata under the Errata section of that title.

To view the previously submitted errata, go to `https://www.packtpub.com/books/content/support` and enter the name of the book in the search field. The required information will appear under the **Errata** section.

Piracy

Piracy of copyrighted material on the Internet is an ongoing problem across all media. At Packt, we take the protection of our copyright and licenses very seriously. If you come across any illegal copies of our works in any form on the Internet, please provide us with the location address or website name immediately so that we can pursue a remedy.

Please contact us at `copyright@packtpub.com` with a link to the suspected pirated material.

We appreciate your help in protecting our authors and our ability to bring you valuable content.

Questions

If you have a problem with any aspect of this book, you can contact us at `questions@packtpub.com`, and we will do our best to address the problem.

1
Creating and Manipulating Pages and Page Templates

In this chapter, we will cover the basics of creating and managing pages in Manga Studio EX 5. We will be covering the following recipes:

- Setting up and saving a standard-sized comic page file
- Adding the story's title to the page
- Adding the author's name to the page
- Adding page numbers and folio information to the page
- Creating a multi-page file
- Setting up cover pages
- Creating two-page spreads
- Applying a framing template
- Creating a custom framing template
- Making and using cover templates
- Accessing the Page Manager
- Rearranging story pages
- Deleting story pages
- Editing the story information

- Editing the basic work settings
- Using the Story Editor to enter text
- Searching and replacing entered text

Introduction

The features of story files and the ability to create entire chapters or books all at once, rearrange the pages, and give a full overview of your comic story, set Manga Studio EX 5/ Clip Studio Paint apart from most other graphics packages. This feature will save your time both in your production stage and in editing the page, and with the new text editor, in the scripting phase as well.

Story files are only available in the EX version of Manga Studio 5. If you are using the regular version of MS5, you can still create page templates and custom page setups, but the multiple page files will not apply to you. This means that the recipes on **Story Editor**, page numbering, two-page spreads, creating cover pages, accessing the Page Manager, rearranging pages, deleting pages, story information, and making multi-page files in this chapter will not apply if you have Manga Studio 5. If you have Manga Studio EX 5, all the recipes in this chapter will work for you.

Also, if you have Manga Studio 5 instead of EX, most other recipes in the entire book will also apply. So don't feel bad if you can't follow along with a portion of this chapter; the rest of the book will still be useful. If you ever upgrade to Manga Studio EX 5, you will already know how to use these features.

If you have purchased the digital download of Manga Studio 5 or EX 5, you may have a program called **Clip Studio Paint Pro** or **Clip Studio Paint EX**. These are the same as Manga Studio 5 and Manga Studio EX 5, respectively; they just had a name change for the digital files.

A full chart of the differences between Manga Studio 4, Manga Studio 4 EX, Manga Studio 5, and Manga Studio 5 EX is available at the time of writing this book at `http://my.smithmicro.com/manga-studio-ex-5-compare.html`.

The recipes in this chapter will get you familiar with everything about making pages and using the **Story Editor** menu. Let's get started!

Setting up and saving a standard-sized comic page file

In this recipe, you're going to learn how to create a custom-sized page file and save it for future use in Manga Studio EX 5. This is invaluable when you are looking to get your comics printed after drawing them. Make sure that you first carry out research on standard printing sizes, though. If you know which printing service you want to use, check out their file setup or artwork guidelines for the dimensions you will need.

Getting ready

You will need the dimensions of the finished page that you want to print as well as any bleed information and safe area dimensions. Bleeds are standardly 0.25 inches, but check with your preferred printer to be sure.

How to do it...

Creating a page properly from the start of a project will save time later. The following directions should work for any printer that prints standard-sized American comic books—roughly 6.75 inches wide by 10.25 inches tall:

1. Click on the **New** icon or go to **File** | **New** to create a new file.
2. Change the **Unit** drop-down menu to **in** (inches).
3. Be sure that the checkbox next to **Manga draft settings** is checked.
4. Under the **Binding (finish) size** options, enter `6.75` for **Width** and `10.25` for **Height**.
5. Set the **Bleed width** value to `0.25`.
6. Under **Default border (inner) size**, enter `6.25` for **Width** and `9.75` for **Height**. Leave **X offset** and **Y offset** at `0.00`.

7. Under the **Canvas** settings, enter `7.5` as **Width** and 11.5 as **Height**. Refer to the following screenshot to understand this:

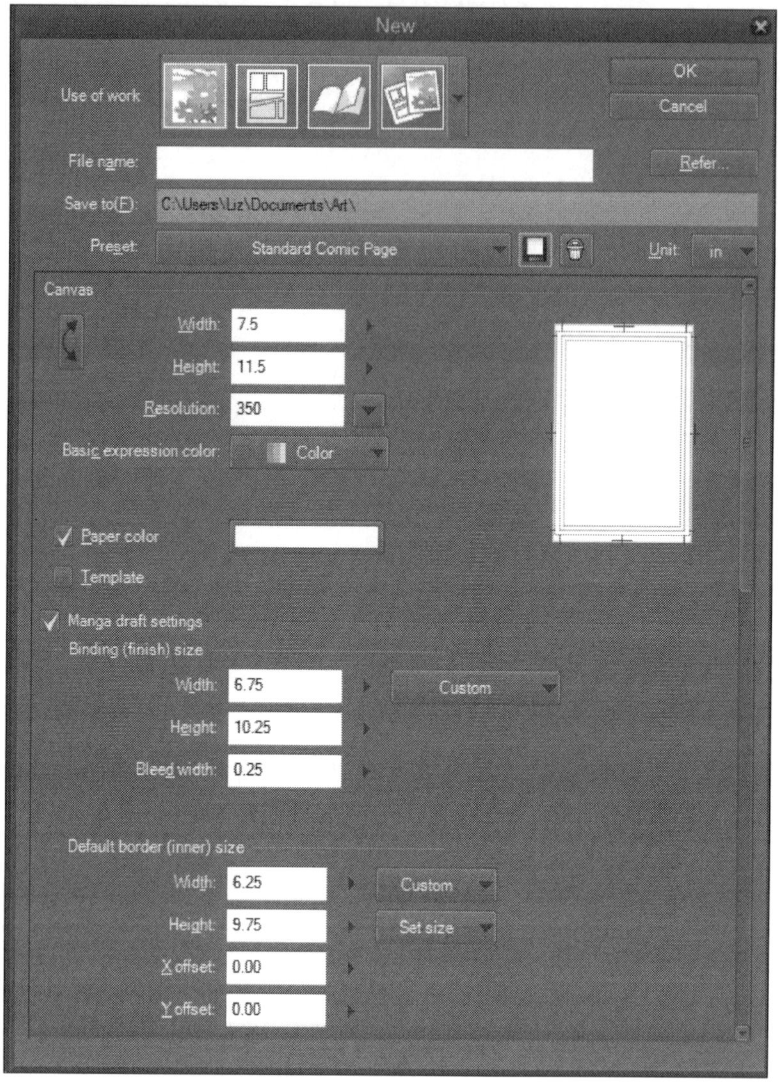

8. At the top of the **New** dialog box, click on the save icon to the right of the **Preset** drop-down menu. This will bring up the **Register to preset** window.
9. Enter `Standard Comic Page` as **Preset name**.

10. Under **Canvas setting**, be sure that the **Resolution**, **Template**, **Paper color**, and **Basic expression color(D)** boxes are all given a check mark, as shown here:

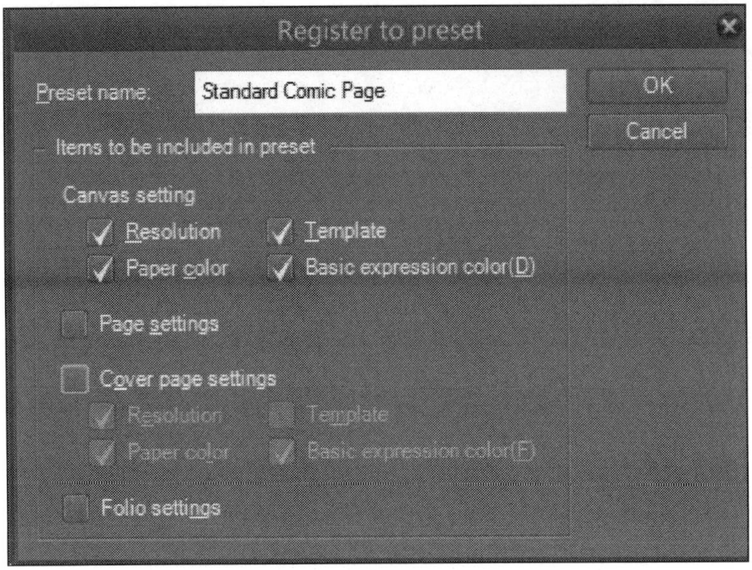

11. Click on **OK**.

How it works...

There are three parts to setting up a custom-sized page in Manga Studio EX 5:

- Setting **Binding (finish) size** (the **trim** size). The **Binding (finish) size** is the size of the finished page after the publisher has trimmed off any bleed areas. If you have a comic book sitting near you, grab it and grab a ruler. You'll find that the comic book will measure roughly 6.75 x 10.25 inches. This is the trim size of the book.
- Setting **Default border (inner) size** (the **live** area). The **Default border (inner) size** is the live area of the page. This is the area inside which any panel borders, text, or other important elements should be placed in order to ensure that they are not accidentally trimmed off in the printing process. Any artwork that goes outside of this area should extend all the way to the edge of the canvas as a bleed.

- Setting **Canvas** (**overall page size**). This is the total size of the page, including any bleed areas. Manga Studio has two bleed areas to take into consideration: one for displaying the folio information set in the program, and one for the publisher. The number set in **Bleed Width Setting** is the publisher's bleed requirement. In the case of the page we just set up, we used a .25-inch bleed all around. Manga Studio automatically calculates this and makes another crop mark at the correct measurement. The rest of the canvas is used to display story information and page numbers, if included. The following illustration will assist you with setting up more custom page sizes in the future:

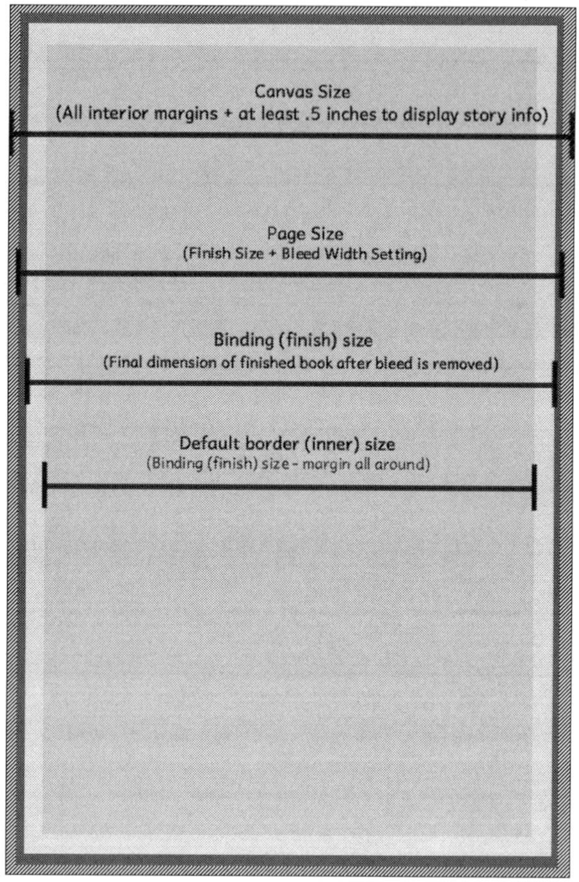

Using the **Register to preset** box, we can save our settings for this page and load it easily the next time we need to use it. We simply choose **Standard Comic Page** from the **Preset** menu, and the settings we saved will be loaded without us having to set up the page dimensions all over again.

See also

- *Creating a multi-page file*
- *Setting up cover pages*

Adding the story's title to the page

There may be times when we need or want to include the title of our comic's story on each page, either for a publisher submission or to keep track of the printed pages that we're storing at home. There are a myriad of reasons for us to mark our pages, and Manga Studio EX 5 makes this easy to do.

How to do it...

The following steps will help you add a story title to the pages of your project:

1. Create a new page by going to **File** | **New** or using the **New** icon.
2. Go to the **Story Information** section of the **New** dialog box.
3. In the **Story name** box, type the name of your story. For this example, I'll use `Living Glory Bound` as the name of the story.
4. Choose the position to display the story name using the drop-down menu to the right of the textbox.
5. If we wish to, we can check the box next to **Number of stories** and add the volume or chapter number. Let's use `1` in this case, as it's the first chapter of our story. Alternately, you can leave this box unchecked if you do not wish to display a story number.
6. If the story has a subtitle, add it in the **Subtitle** textbox. It will be displayed with the story name.

7. Click on **OK**. If there is any **Author** or **Page number** information to add, go to the relevant one of the next two recipes. The following screenshot shows how these fields should be filled in, according to the example in the preceding steps:

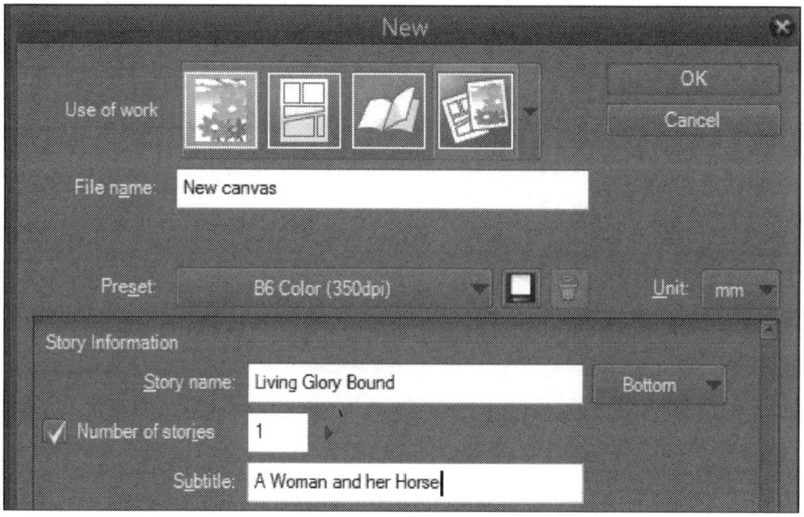

See also

- *Adding the author's name to the page*
- *Adding page numbers and folio information to the page*
- *Editing the story information*

Adding the author's name to the page

Other than adding our story's name, we can also add the name of the author or artist.

Getting ready

Before you start, have the **New** dialog window opened by going to **File** | **New** or clicking on the **New** icon in the top toolbar.

How to do it...

The following steps will teach you how to add the author's name to your project page:

1. Go to the **Story Information** section of the **New** dialog box.
2. In the **Author** textbox, type in the name to be displayed.

3. Use the drop-down menu to the right of the textbox to choose where the text will be displayed on the page, as shown in the following screenshot:

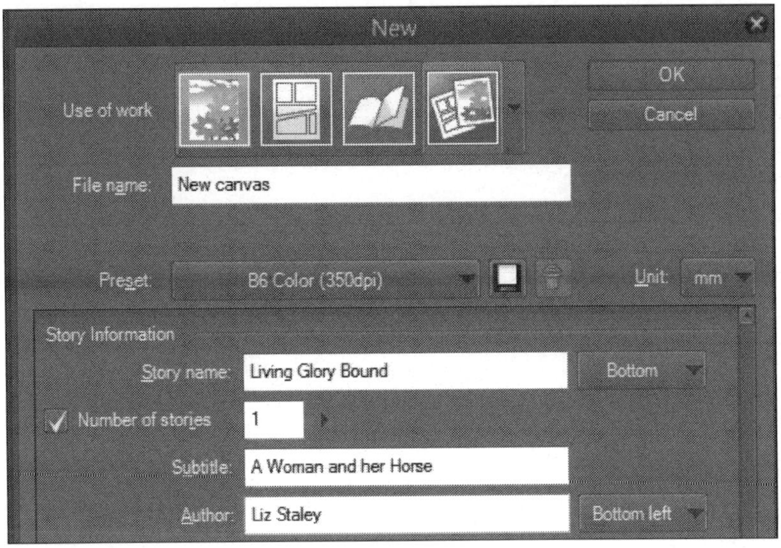

4. Click on **OK**. If there is page number information to add, go to the next recipe.

See also

- *Adding the story's title to the page*
- *Adding page numbers and folio information to the page*
- *Editing the story information*

Adding page numbers and folio information to the page

Manga Studio can automatically add page numbers to your pages. Let's see how this works and explore some different options for page numbering.

Getting ready

Before you start, have the **New** dialog window opened by going to **File** | **New** or clicking on the **New** icon in the top toolbar.

How to do it...

Follow these simple steps to add a page number to your project:

1. Go to the **Story Information** section of the **New** dialog box.
2. Make sure that the checkbox next to **Page number** is checked.
3. Use the drop-down menu to the right of the **Page number** checkbox to choose the display position.
4. Choose a number in **Start number**.

How it works...

Using the **Page number** option will display a number in Manga Studio's margin (outside of the trim area). This number will not be visible after the page has been trimmed down to the finish size.

There's more...

Manga Studio EX 5 has multiple options for page numbers. The following subsection shows you how to add folio page numbers.

Including a folio page number

Folio numbers are inside of the finish size, and so they are visible on the page after the printing is done and the bleeds have been trimmed:

1. In the **New** dialog box, go to the **Folio** section.
2. Check the box next to **Folio(P)** to turn this option on.
3. Use the drop-down menu to the right of the checkbox to choose the display position for the number.
4. Add any leading or trailing formatting for the page number in the **Format** textboxes.
5. Choose the number to begin with using the **Start number** option, either by typing the number manually in the textbox or by using the slider to the right.
6. Using the **Font** drop-down menu, select the font to use from those installed on your computer.
7. Adjust the display size of the folio page number information using the **Size** option. Again, either type the desired value in the text box or use the slider to the right by clicking on the black arrow icon.

8. Using the **Color** drop-down menu, select whether to display the text in black or white.
9. To add a contrasting outline around the page number, check the box next to **Put edges**. Black folio information will have a white border around it, and vice versa.
10. Choose the thickness of the outline using the textbox to the right of the **Put edges** option. The larger the number, the thicker the outline.
11. Click on **OK** to create the new page.

Using the **Format** boxes, we can make our page number read **Page 1 of 12**. Simply enter `Page ` in the first textbox (before the number) and ` of 12` in the textbox after the number. See the following screenshot.

> Note the extra spaces in `Page ` and ` of 12` in the preceding example. These need to be added to make the folio information read correctly. If the spaces are not added, they will not be included when the new page is generated.

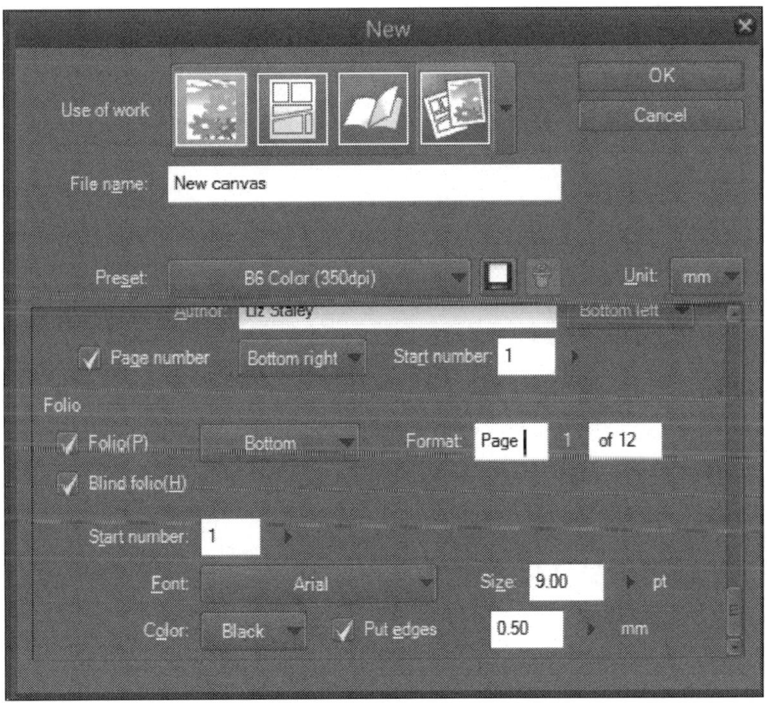

Blind folio(H) is a page number in the margin of the book. When the book is printed and bound, it will not be seen.

Check out this screenshot to learn how the story name, author information, and page numbers are displayed using information from the preceding recipes:

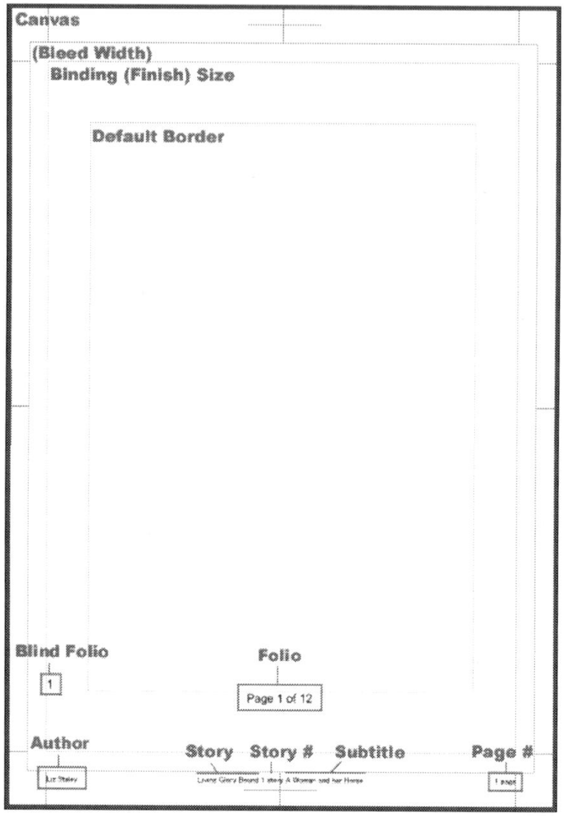

See also

- *Adding the author's name to the page*

Creating a multi-page file

Manga Studio 5 and Manga Studio EX 5 have one major difference: the EX version gives you the ability to create story files. These `.cmc` files collect a number of page files (`.lip`) and allow them to be viewed together, opened easily, and rearranged. We can think of the story file as a folder on our desk that has papers in it. You can open the folder and spread the pages inside to see them, rearrange them, and pull out the ones you don't want. Let's create a story file with 12 pages in this recipe.

Getting ready

Before you start, have the **New** dialog window opened by going to **File** | **New** or clicking on the **New** icon in the top toolbar.

How to do it...

The following steps show you how to create a file with 12 pages:

1. Find the **Multiple pages** checkbox and click on it to open the options, as shown in the following screenshot:

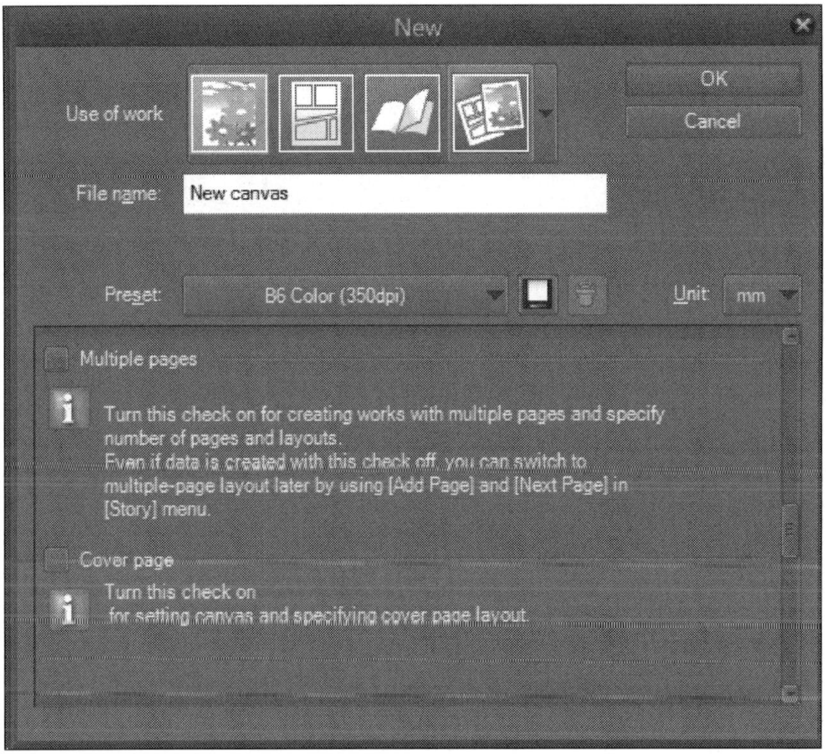

2. Next to **Number of pages:**, either enter the desired number of pages manually in the textbox, or use a preset number of pages by clicking on the black down arrow and choosing from the list.
3. Choose which side of the book the binding will be on.
4. Choose which side the starting page will be on.

5. At the top of the **New** window, enter a filename for the story to be saved under, in the **File name** textbox.
6. The **Save to(F)** box will show the currently selected folder for the file to save in. To select a different folder, click on the **Refer...** button on the right-hand side of the dialog box.

> The **Refer...** button will show only after the **Multiple pages** checkbox is activated.

7. Navigate to the desired save folder and click on **OK**. Our **New** screen should now look like what is shown in this screenshot:

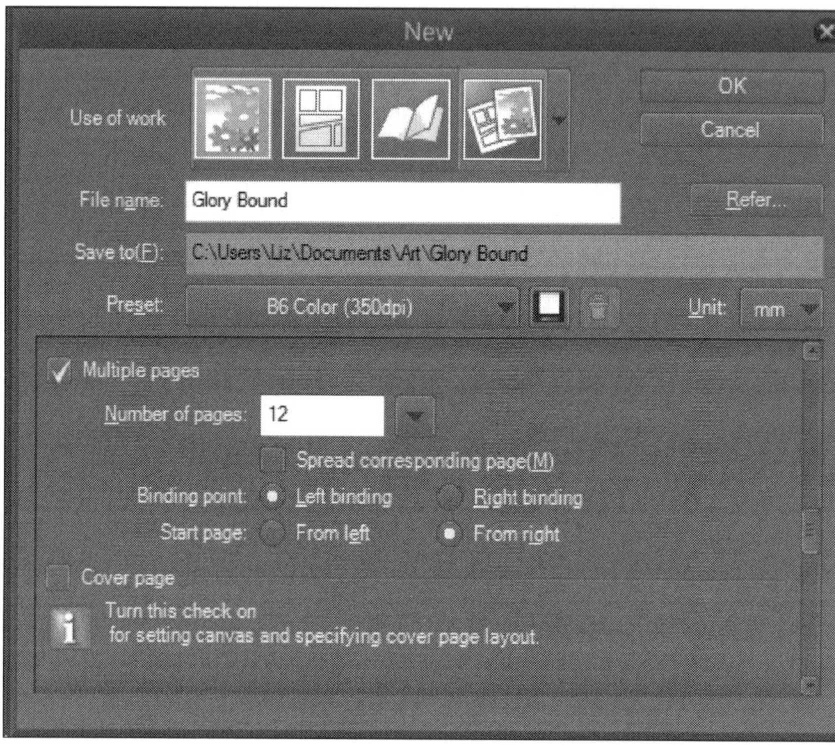

8. Click on **OK** in the **New** dialog box.

See also

- *Creating two-page spreads*

Setting up cover pages

Manga Studio EX 5 recently added options for cover pages in the multi-page file settings. This feature designates pages in your story file as covers, both back and front.

Getting ready

Again, before you start, have the **New** dialog window opened by going to **File** | **New** or clicking on the **New** icon in the top toolbar.

How to do it...

The following steps show you how to create a multi-page file with a front and a back cover page:

1. Locate the **Cover Page** checkbox and click on it to activate the options. The following screenshot shows where the checkbox is located:

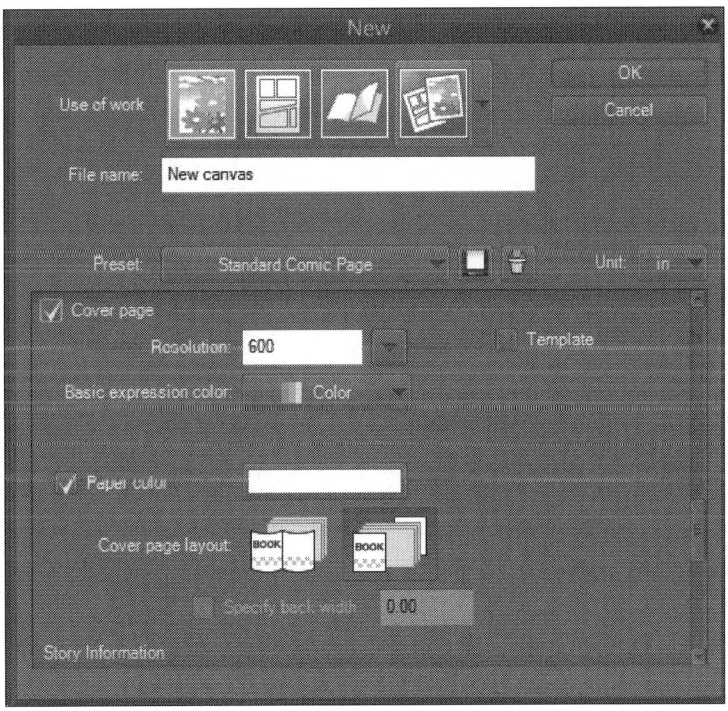

2. Select **Resolution** (dpi) for the cover pages. For this example, let's leave it at `600` dpi.
3. Select a color under **Basic expression color**. Our cover in this example will be colored at the end, so we'll leave it at **Color**. If your cover will be grayscale or pure black and white, select the applicable expression color.
4. Then, select a color under **Paper color**.
5. Next, select a layout under **Cover page layout**, either a two-page spread layout, or two separate covers.
6. If you are using a two-page spread cover page layout, use the **Specify back width** option to set the spine width, if applicable.
7. Be sure to have the **Multiple pages** option turned on and a number of pages higher than four selected.
8. Enter a filename under **File name** in the textbox at the top of the dialog window.
9. Select a folder to save the story file in.
10. Click on **OK** and wait a moment for your story file to generate.

How it works...

Manga Studio EX 5 allows us to set a different resolution for the cover pages than for the interior images. This means that if we're working on black-and-white or grayscale comic pages, we can keep them at a relatively low resolution (at least 300 dpi) and still get a nice-looking print. However, we want our cover pages to look sharp and detailed, so we can create our covers with a higher dpi without affecting our interior pages.

Within the program, we can also set the paper color. This option automatically fills a bottom layer in the page file with the chosen color. Let's say that we already know that our cover is going to have a blue background. We can choose for the paper color to be blue and then work on our cover on top of it, eliminating the need to fill the background with blue later. If we want a transparent background with no color fill at all, we can simply turn this option off by deselecting the checkbox.

> You can change the paper color of individual pages at any time by double-clicking on the **Paper** layer's thumbnail in the **Layer** palette. Choose a new color and click on **OK** to set it.

We can select to either have separate front and back covers, or have the cover pages automatically joined as a two-page spread. The two-page spread option is perfect for wraparound covers. Simply select this option when creating your new file to make a two-page spread.

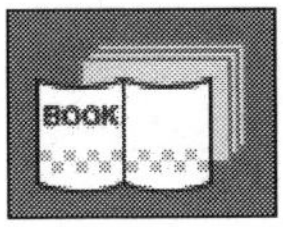

When creating a two-page spread or wraparound cover, we have the **Specify Back Width** option. This is the width of the spine of the book. For a typical monthly issue of about 30 pages, this shouldn't be needed, but for larger graphic novels, it's very handy. The spine of a larger book could have the title and author information displayed on it. Be sure to carry out some research beforehand if you are creating a large book, and account for the spine by calculating the number of pages. Your publisher or printer should be able to assist you with this.

See also

- *Creating a multi-page file*

Creating two-page spreads

Sometimes, the action of comics is so huge that it cannot be contained in one page. In these instances, we can use the two-page spread for big, attention-grabbing splash pages. Let's learn how to create them in Manga Studio EX 5.

Getting ready

Before you start, have the **New** dialog window opened by going to **File** | **New** or clicking on the **New** icon in the top toolbar.

How to do it...

The following steps show you how to create a multi-page file with two-page spreads set up:

1. Locate the **Multiple pages** option in the **New** dialog window.
2. Check the box next to **Spread corresponding page(M)**, which is located in the **Multiple pages** section, as shown in the following screenshot:

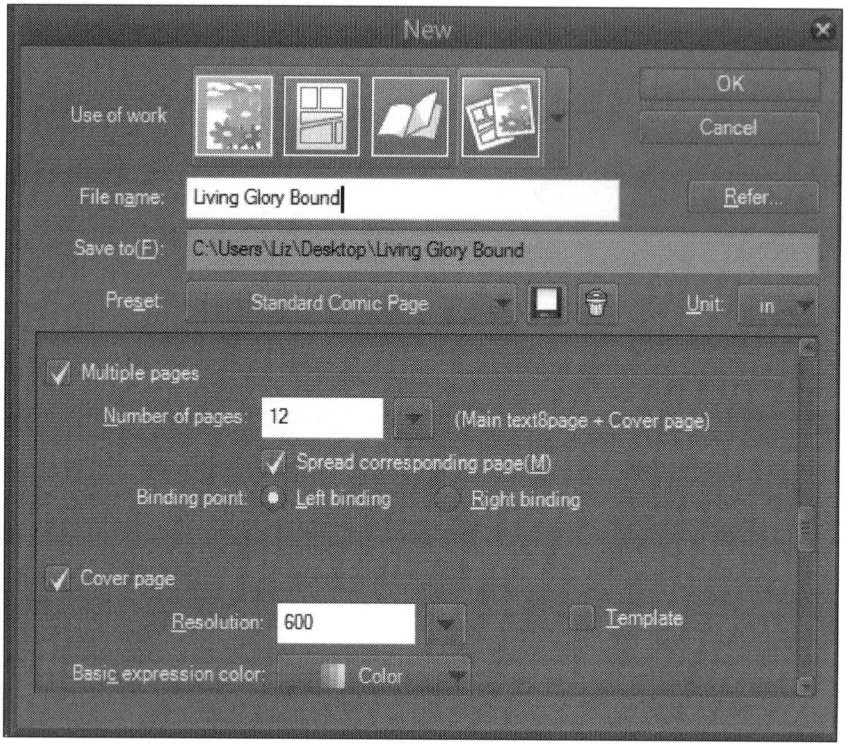

3. Make sure that the binding point is set correctly for your publisher (books that read left to right will have the binding on the left).
4. Enter a filename for your story under **File name**, and choose a destination folder to save it in.
5. Click on **OK**.

How it works...

When we turn on the **Spread corresponding page(M)** option, Manga Studio will automatically join facing pages (for example, pages 2 and 3). Once your story is generated, it will look something like this:

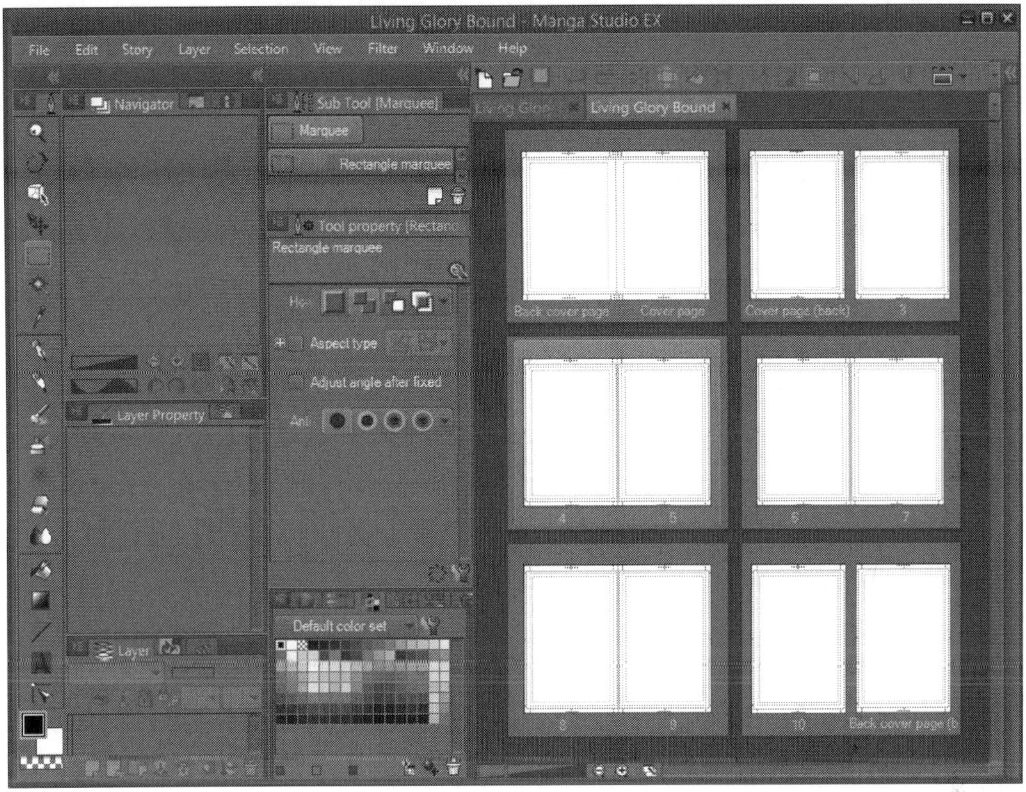

In the preceding story, the cover has been set as a two-page spread as well. The back page of the inside cover is not attached to page 3, because page 3 is the first page of our comic interior. Page 10 is the last page of our comic interior, and so it is not joined with the inside of the back cover.

There's more...

What if we've already made a story file with individual pages, but then we realize that we need to join two pages to make a splash page as we're working? Not a problem!

Creating two-page spreads in existing story files

The following instructions show you how to join two pages in an existing file into a two-page spread:

1. With your story file open, go to **Page Manager**. If **Page Manager** is not visible, go to **Story(P)** | **Page Manager(W)** to open it.
2. Locate the two pages that you wish to join. Remember that only two facing pages can be combined into a spread. Facing pages will be grouped together in boxes in **Page Manager**.
3. Click on one of the pages that you want in the two-page spread.
4. With the page still selected, go to **Story(P)** | **Combine Pages...** (alternately, in Windows, right-click on the selected page and click on **Combine Pages...** from the menu that appears).
5. An option box, as shown in the following screenshot should appear:

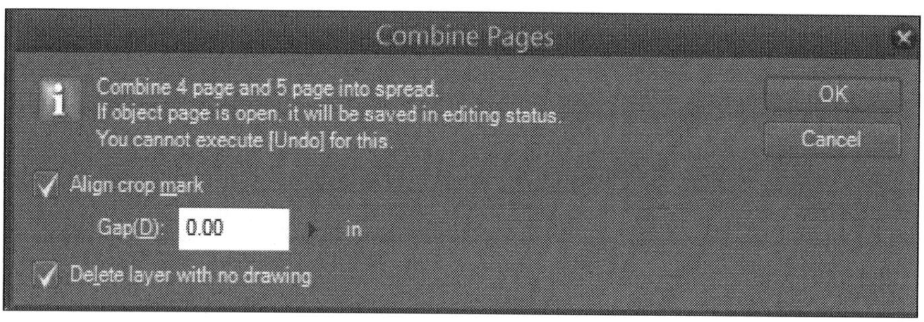

6. Set **Gap(D)** if needed. Gap means the number of joined pages that will not be visible because of the binding of the book.
7. Be absolutely certain that you want to combine the pages. As this box warns, we cannot undo this change. The pages can be split afterwards, but this operation cannot be taken away by choosing **Edit** and **Undo**!
8. Click on **OK**.

Our pages are now combined. Look at the next screenshot for the example. Note that pages **6** and **7** are still single pages, but **4** and **5** have been joined.

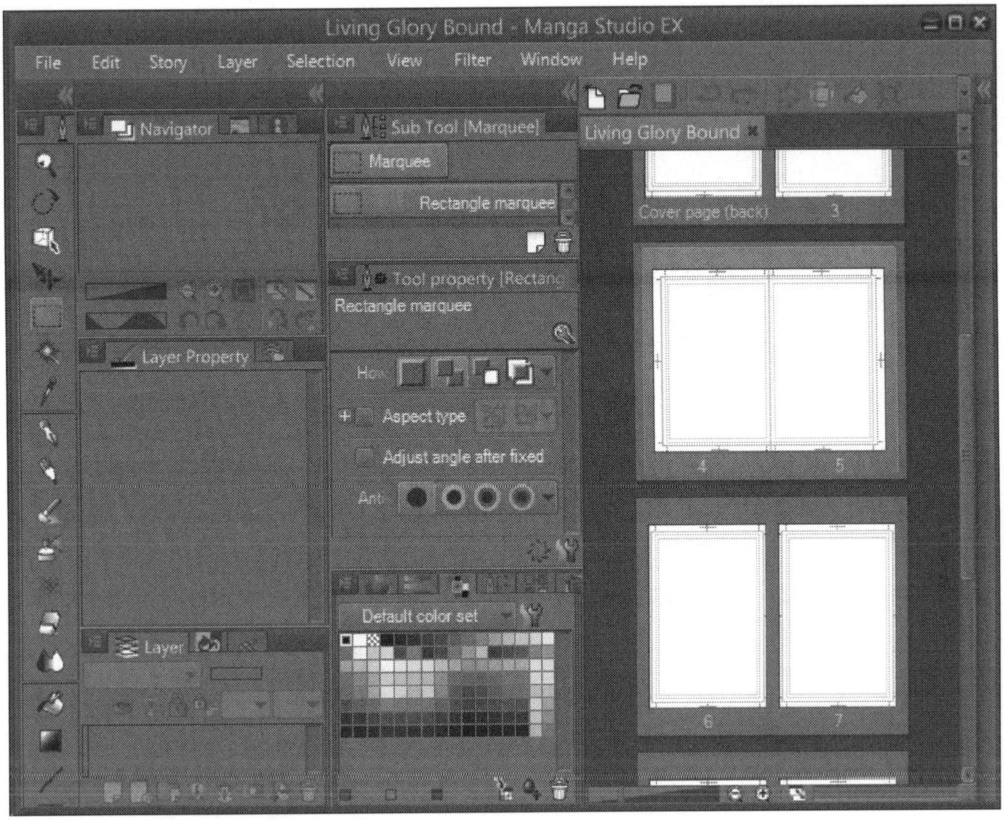

See also

- *Accessing the Page Manager*

Applying a framing template

Some comics, such as comic strips, don't necessarily vary their panel layout from page to page. We can save time in Manga Studio EX 5 by applying a framing template to all of our interior pages.

Getting ready

Before you start, have the **New** dialog window opened by going to **File** | **New** or clicking on the **New** icon in the top toolbar.

How to do it...

The following steps detail how to load a pre-existing comic template into the interior pages of a story file:

1. Under the **Canvas** options, locate the **Template** checkbox. It is shown under **Paper color** in the following screenshot:

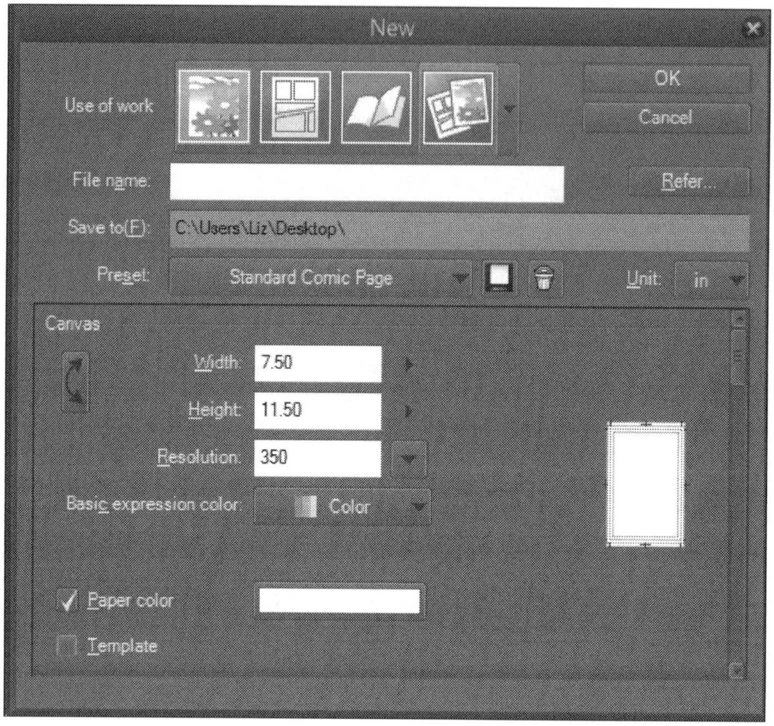

2. Check the box next to **Template** to bring up the **Template** library.
3. Select a template to use on the pages. For this recipe, let's use the template called **4 frames 2 strips**. Click on the template so that it is highlighted. Refer to the following screenshot to understand this:

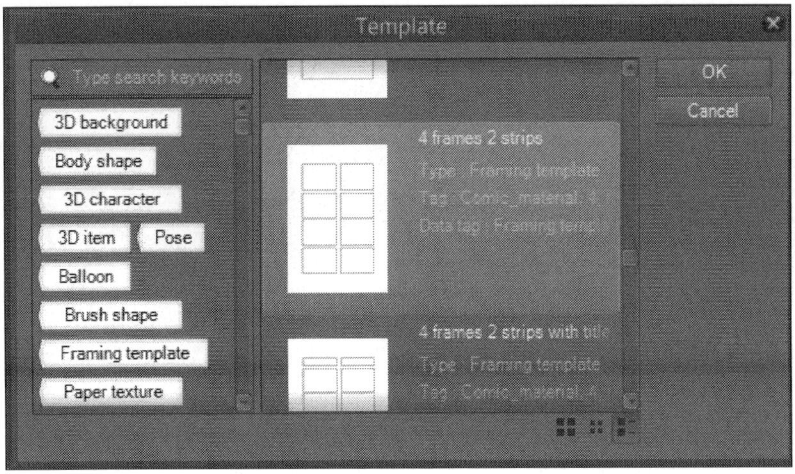

4. Click on the **OK** button to confirm the template selection.
5. Finish making the other selections for your new story file, and then click on **OK** to create it.

How it works...

The template that we select will automatically be fitted for the **Default border(inner) size** value of our page and included on each page of the story file. See the following screenshot:

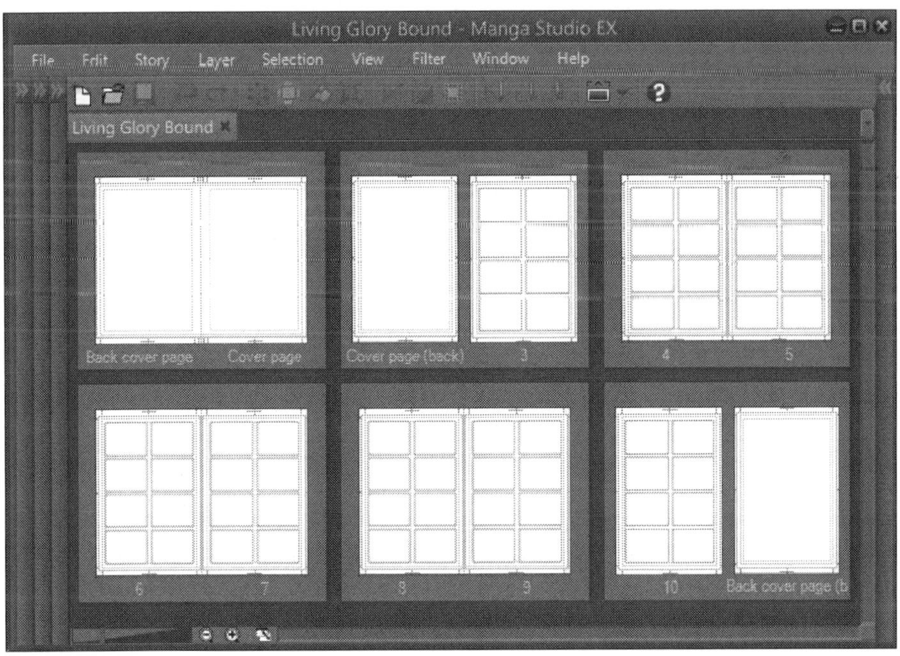

See also

- *Creating a custom framing template*
- *Creating and using cover templates*

Creating a custom framing template

In the previous recipe, we saw how to use a framing template to speed up our comic creation time when each of our comics uses the same layout. Well, what if our desired panel setup isn't available in the **Template** library? No worries! We can create it and save it in the **Template** library to use in the future.

How to do it...

Let's create a custom frame template and add it to all the interior pages of our story file with this recipe:

1. Open a blank page that includes a **Default border (inner) size** margin.
2. Create a panel layout using the panel tools.
3. Go to **Edit** | **Register Layer as Template Material**.
4. In the **Material property** window, add a descriptive material name.
5. Under **Location to save material**, navigate to **Manga material** | **Framing template** and select it as the folder to save the new template.
6. Enter search tags.

> Tag every material that you add to the materials library with a tag unique to you, such as **custom** or your name. This makes it easy to find the materials that you've created later. Just search for the tag that you've chosen. Personally, I use **custom** to tag all my new materials.

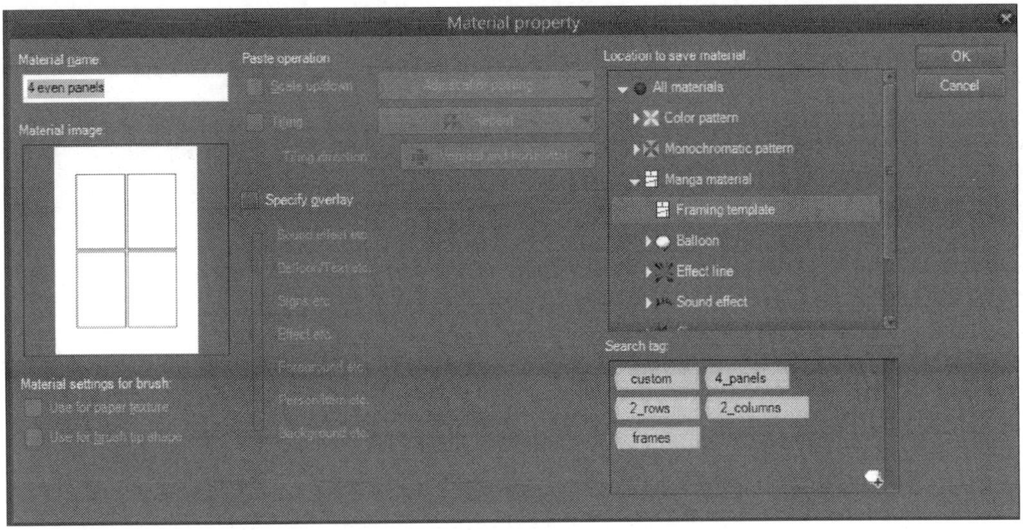

7. Click **OK**.
8. Go to **File** | **New** to start another new file.
9. Choose a page template to use that has **Default border (inner) size** in it.
10. Under the **Canvas** options, check the **Template** box.
11. Navigate to the custom framing template created earlier. Click on it to select it.

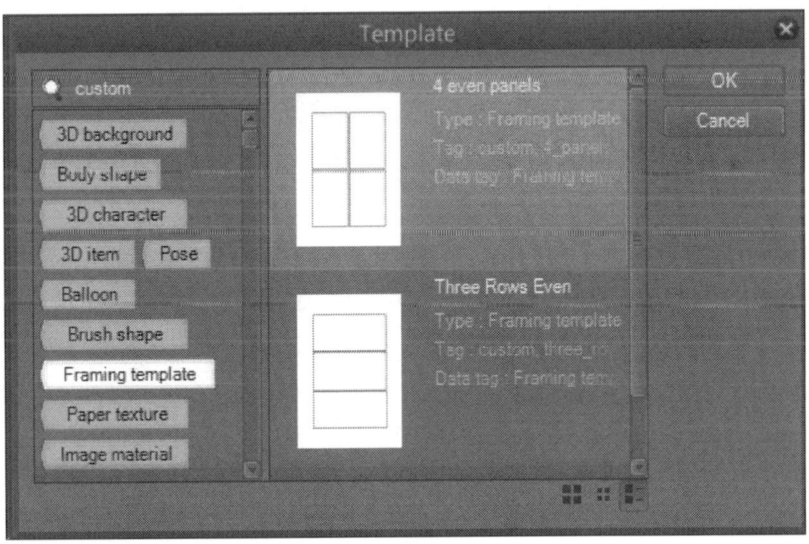

12. Click on **OK**.
13. Create a file with multiple pages.

14. Then click on **OK** to finish creating the file.

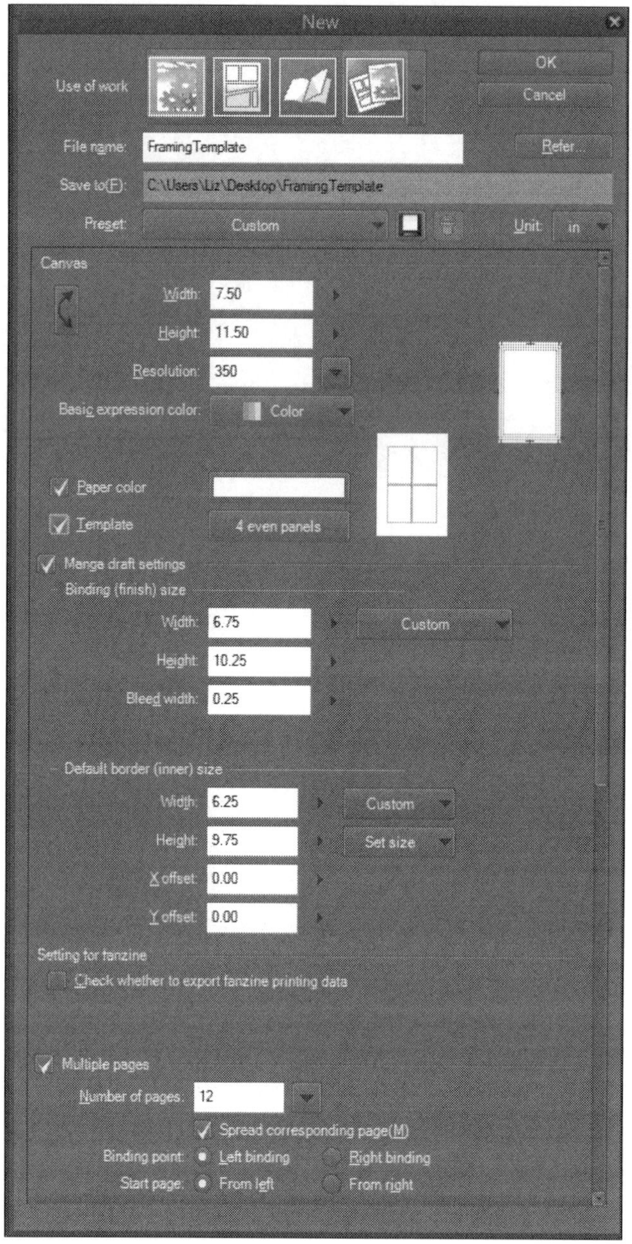

How it works...

First, we have to create our frames before we can save them as a framing template, which is why we opened a blank page to start our recipe. Having the default border gives us measurements for the center of each side of our page by looking at the crop markings.

Use the frame tools of your choice to mark the frames for the template. The easiest way for us to do this is by using the rectangle frame tool and drawing our squares.

We can also go to **Layer | New Layer | Frame Border folder(C)**. This will create a frame with the dimensions of the default inner border. Then we can use the divide frame border tool to slice out our frames. The benefit of using this tool is that the borders of our panels will line up perfectly, with even gutters all around.

Registering the layer as a template material allows us to select our new framing template on new files. However, we have to save it in the **Framing template** folder, which is in **Manga material**, to make sure that it shows up when we create a new file. Only the materials in this folder will show up while we are creating files that use a template on all pages.

Tagging the material makes it easy to find later. We should always tag our new materials when we add them to the library, because it eliminates scrolling through all the materials to find what we need.

After we've saved the template as a material, we can apply it to any new file. All our interior pages will share the same framing template, which means that we save time by putting new frames in.

See also

- *Creating and using cover templates*

Creating and using cover templates

Covers catch the reader's eye and convey information about the comic. Sure, they will tell you the title, the publisher, and perhaps the people who worked on the comic. They can also convey the subject matter and tone of the comic. Some elements of a cover will appear on each one that's made, so let's create a template to save time in our art process and apply it to our cover pages.

How to do it...

This recipe shows you how to create a cover, save it as a material, and then apply it as a template to a new file:

1. Open a blank page that has the default size (inner) margins set up.
2. Add a text or logo design for the comic title at the top of the page, resizing, rotating, or transforming as needed.
3. Add the name of the comic's author and/or artist, colorist, and so on as needed.
4. Add any other graphics that will be on each cover.
5. If a **Paper** layer is included in the current file, select it. Then delete the paper layer. The following screenshot is an example of what a cover template might include, such as comic title and logo, subtitle, author, and artist information:

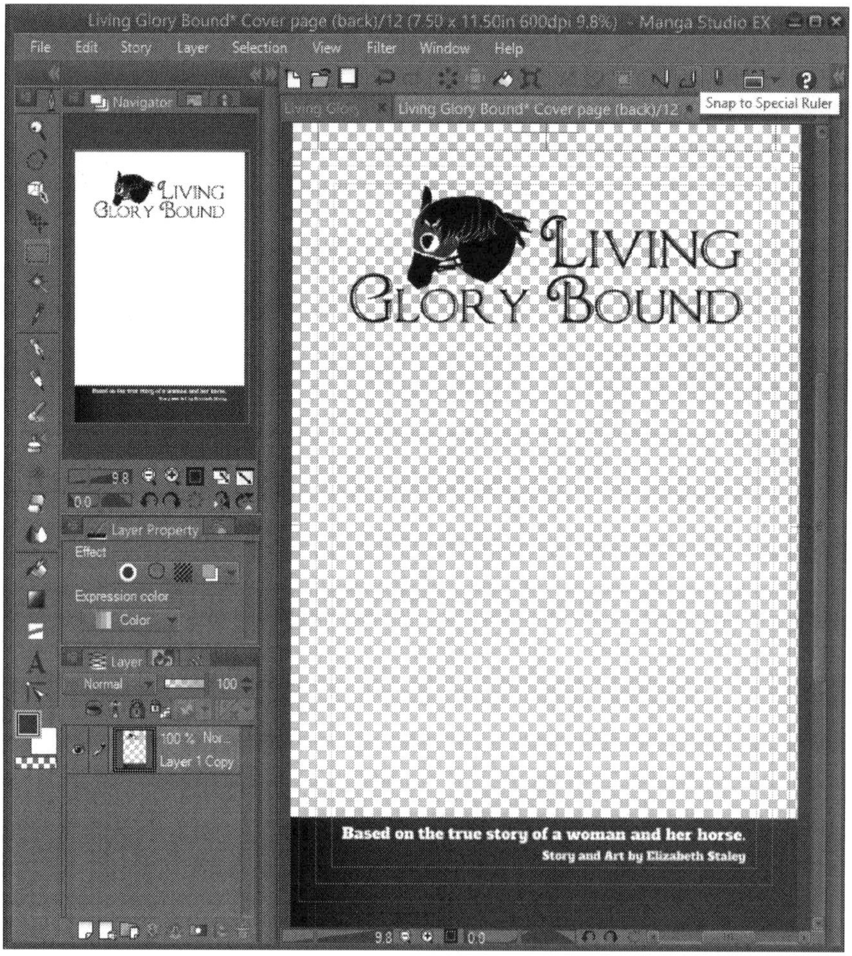

6. Go to **Edit** | **Register Layer as Template Material**.
7. In the **Material property** window, enter **Material name** (for example, `Living Glory Bound Cover Template`).
8. Check the **Material image** thumbnail to ensure that all the elements that you wish to include in the template are shown.
9. Click on the arrow to the left of **Material** under **Location to save material** to open the material categories.
10. Navigate to **Manga material** | **Framing template** and click to select it as the location to save the cover template in.
11. Enter some search tags to find the cover template easily. Refer to this screenshot for suggestions:

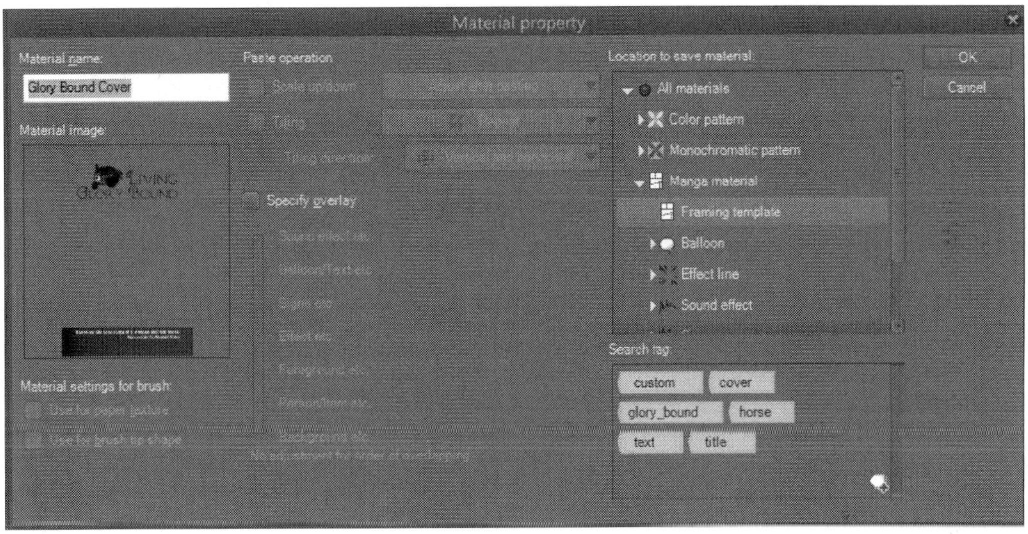

12. Click on **OK**.
13. Go to **File** | **New** and create a new story file with multiple pages and a cover page.
14. Under the **Cover page** options, click on the **Template** checkbox.

15. Locate the cover template that you just created and select it. In the following screenshot, our saved cover template is visible:

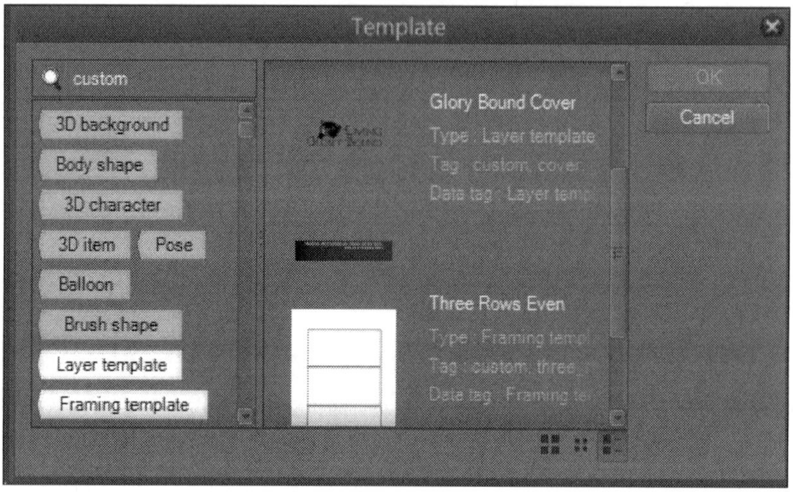

16. Click on **OK**.
17. Then click on **OK** in the **New dialog** window to create the new story file, with the template for the front cover.

How it works...

Before we can use a cover template, we have to create the cover. By laying out the title and any other elements that will be on each cover, we'll save time later on during the creation of our comic by not having to set the cover elements each time we create a new chapter or book.

By erasing the paper layer, we ensure that our template will show up in all new covers without a white background all around it. This will allow us to use other paper colors and draw directly behind the template to create our cover art.

Currently, if we want to put a different image on the front and back cover, we have to go to the back cover, delete the layer containing the template, and then add the back cover images. As of Manga Studio EX 5.0.5, there is no way to use different templates on the front and back covers. As shown in this screenshot, the two-page spread cover has the same template on both the front and the back:

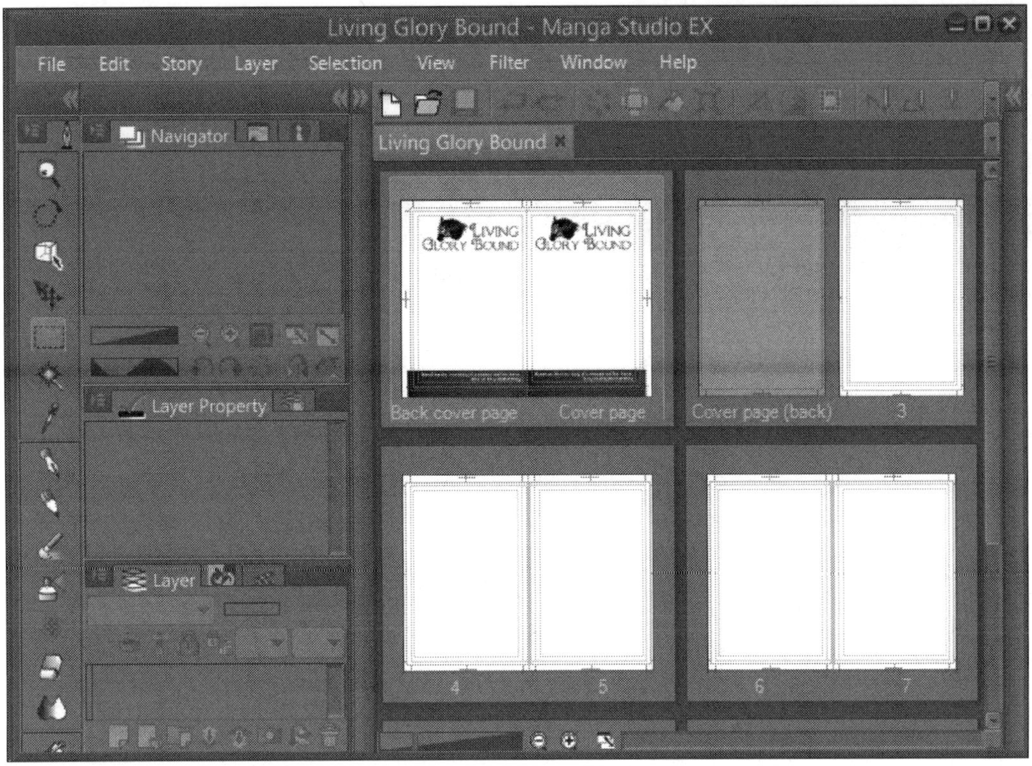

See also

- *Creating a custom framing template*
- *Setting up cover pages*

Accessing the Page Manager

The Page Manager is where we can take a look at our entire story at once, with each page in thumbnail form. Manga Studio EX 5 gives you lots of options on how to display the Page Manager, depending on the structure of your workflow.

How to do it...

The following steps show how to open **Page Manager(W)** as a **Tab** in Manga Studio EX 5:

1. Open a file with multiple pages.
2. Go to **Story(P)** | **Page Manager Layout(Q)** | **Tab**.

> If **Tab** is already checked, as shown in the following screenshot, skip this step:

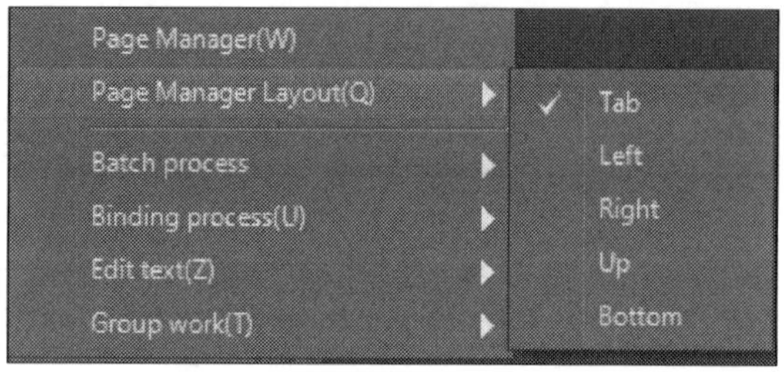

3. Now go to **Story(P)** | **Page Manager(W)** to show the Page Manager as a new tab inside of Manga Studio EX 5. Refer to this screenshot to understand what the tab will look like:

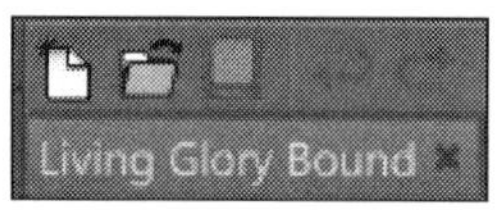

There's more...

Depending on your workflow, you may want to have the Page Manager shown in orientations other than the tab. The following subsection shows how to do this.

Viewing the Page Manager in other orientations

Follow these steps to open a Page Manager at the top of the screen:

1. Open a file with multiple pages.
2. Go to **Story** | **Page Manager Layout(Q)** | **Up** to make the Page Manager appear at the top of the Manga Studio EX 5 window.
3. If a tab Page Manager is open, close it by clicking on the **X** mark on the right-hand side of the tab.

4. Go to **Story(P)** | **Page Manager(W)** to open the new Page Manager. Here is an example of the manager set to **Up**:

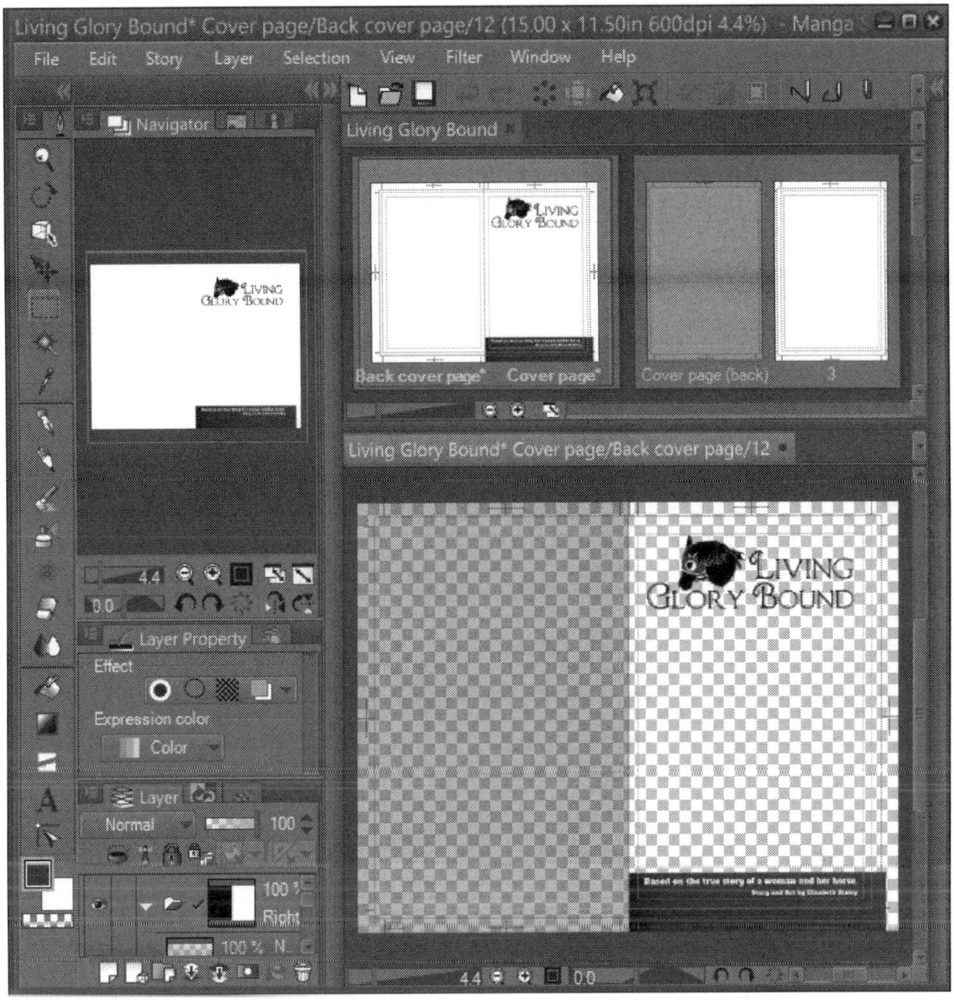

Experiment with the other Page Manager layout options to find out which layout is right for you and your workflow.

See also

- *Rearranging story pages*
- *Deleting story pages*

Rearranging story pages

Sometimes, you just realize that a page, or pages, of a comic would fit better earlier or later in the story. Manga Studio EX 5's Page Manager gives us an easy way to rearrange pages so that we can make a perfect story.

How to do it...

This recipe teaches you how to rearrange pages in a story file:

1. Open a file with multiple pages.
2. Go to **Page Manager**. If the Page Manager is not visible, go to **Story(P)** | **Page Manager(W)** to open it.
3. Locate and select the page that needs to be moved.
4. Click on the page and hold down the mouse button.
5. With the mouse button still pressed, drag the page to the new location. A red line shows where the page will be moved, as shown in the following screenshot:

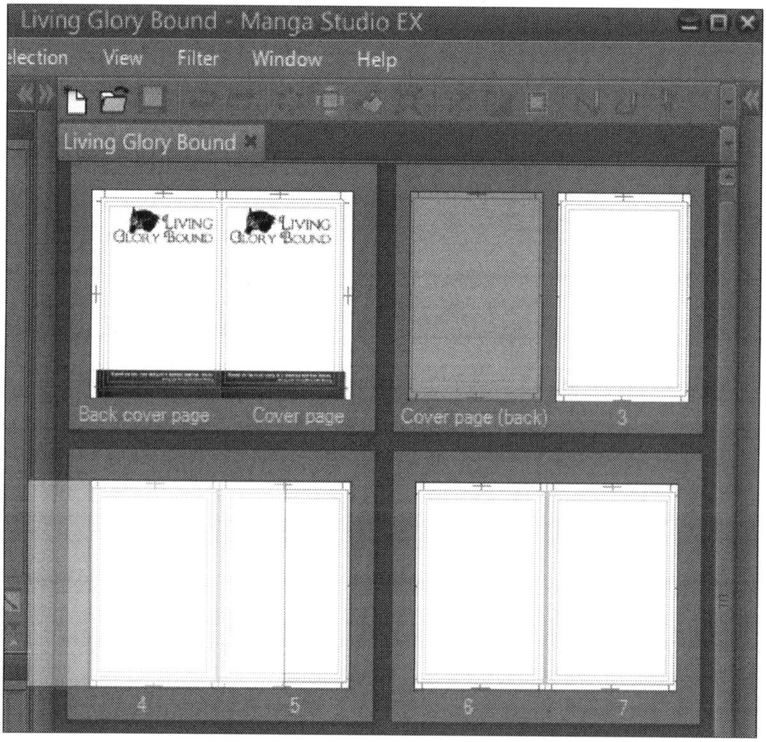

6. Release the mouse button once the new location has been reached.
7. Wait a moment as Manga Studio adjusts the story information and page numbers.

There's more...

Manga Studio EX 5 allows us to rearrange more than one page at a time.

Rearranging multiple pages

Follow these steps to change the position of multiple pages at once:

1. From the Page Manager, locate the pages that need to be moved.
2. Hold down the *Ctrl* key (PC) or *command* key (Mac) and click to select all the pages to move.
3. Once selected, hold down the mouse button and drag the pages to their new location.

See also

- *Accessing the Page Manager*
- *Deleting story pages*

Deleting story pages

Sometimes, we realize that some content no longer works in our story. This section will teach you how to delete pages that are no longer necessary in the project.

How to do it...

Follow these steps to delete a story page:

1. Open a file with multiple pages.
2. Go to **Page Manager**. If the Page Manager is not visible, go to **Story(P)** | **Page Manager(W)** to open it.
3. Locate the page to be deleted. Click on it to highlight it.
4. Go to **Story(P)** | **Delete Page** (or right-click on windows and select **Delete Page** from the menu that appears).

5. The window shown in the following screenshot will appear. If you are sure that you wish to delete the page, click on **OK**. *This operation cannot be undone, so be sure that this is the correct page!*

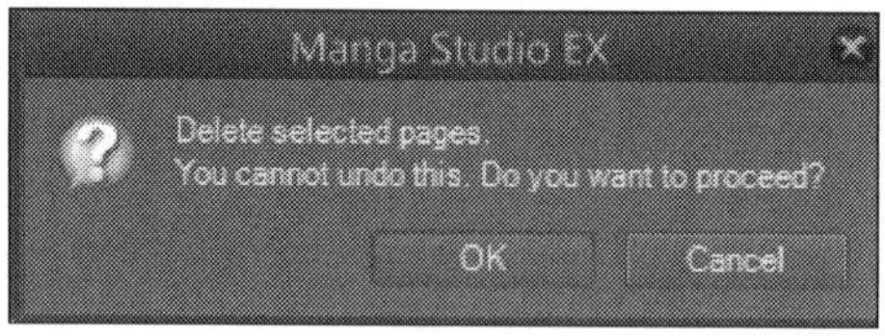

Manga Studio will update the story information and page numbers.

There's more...

We can also delete more than one page at a time. If an entire section of a story needs to be erased, we can do so very easily.

Deleting multiple pages

Follow these steps to delete more than one page from a story file at a time:

1. From **Page Manager**, locate the pages that need to be deleted.
2. Hold down the *Ctrl* key (PC) or *command* key (Mac) and click to select all the pages to delete.
3. Go to **Story(P)** | **Delete Page** (or in Windows, right-click and select **Delete Page** from the menu that appears).
4. The window that you saw in the previous section will appear to confirm the deletion. If you are sure that you wish to delete the page, click on **OK**. This operation also cannot be undone, so be sure that this is the correct page!

Manga Studio will update the story information and page numbers.

See also

- *Accessing the Page Manager*
- *Rearranging story pages*

Editing the story information

We've all done it—get halfway through a project and then notice that we spelled the title wrong! Or suddenly, we think of a better title for the graphic novel for which we just drew 150 pages, and the old title is on every page of the Manga Studio file! No need to fret; we can edit it!

How to do it...

This recipe shows us how to make changes to the story information:

1. Open a file with multiple pages.
2. Go to **Story** | **Set story information**, as shown in the following screenshot:

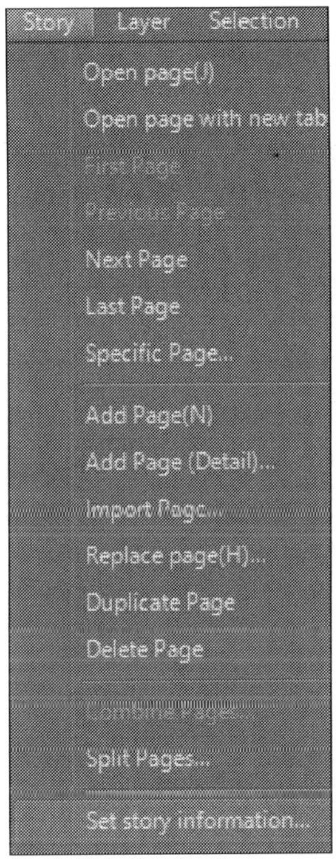

3. In the window that appears, make any changes needed to the story title, author information, folio, or blind folio information. In this screenshot, the subtitle, font, and display position of the author's name have been changed:

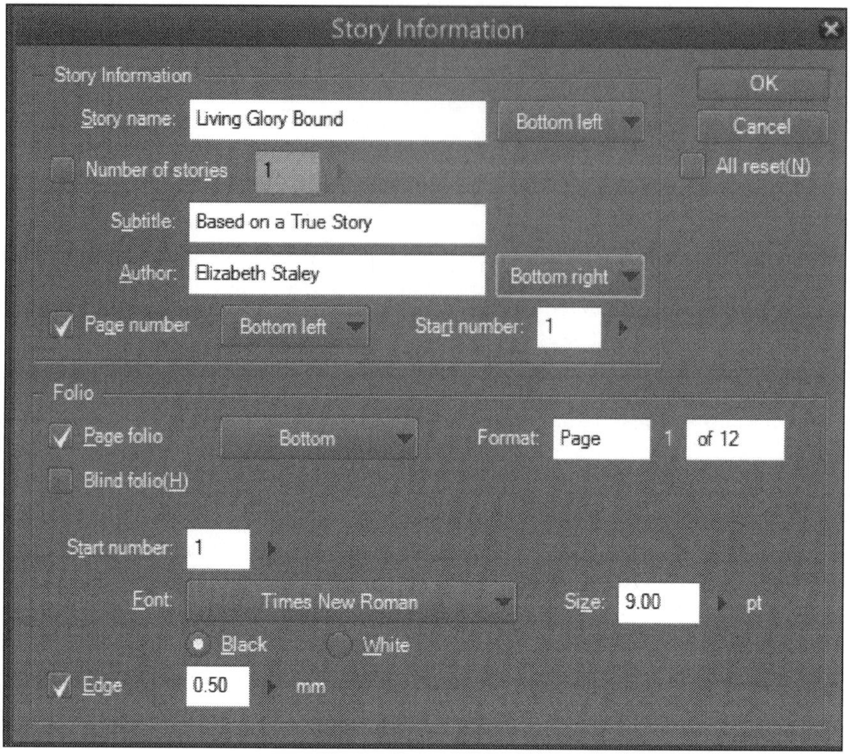

4. Click on **OK**.
5. Wait a moment for Manga Studio 5 to process the changes.

See also

- *Adding the story's title to the page*
- *Adding the author's name to the page*
- *Adding page numbers and folio information to the page*
- *Creating a multi-page file*
- *Editing the basic work settings*

Editing the basic work settings

What if we decide that we need to change our binding position, or that we don't want to use the cover page settings anymore? Not a problem! We just need to edit the basic work settings.

How to do it...

These very simple steps show us how to make changes to the basic work settings:

1. Open a file with multiple pages.
2. Go to **Story** | **Change basic work settings**. Refer to the following screenshot to know the location:

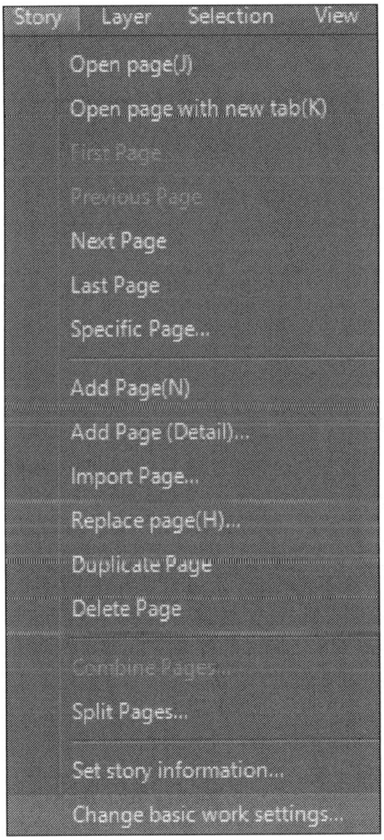

3. Update any information in the basic work settings as needed. Refer to this screenshot to understand what the basic work settings dialog box looks like:

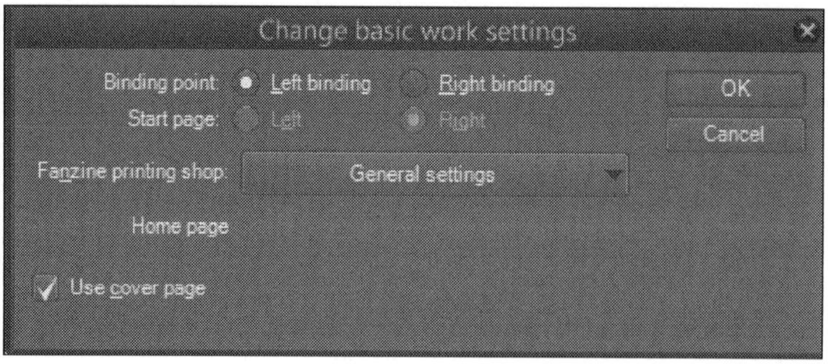

4. Click on **OK**.
5. Wait a moment for Manga Studio EX 5 to update the pages.

See also

- *Adding the story's title to the page*
- *Adding the author's name to the page*
- *Adding page numbers and folio information to the page*
- *Creating a multi-page file*
- *Editing the story information*

Using the Story Editor to enter text

Creating a comic (usually) means putting in text for dialog, narration, and other story indicators (words such as "Meanwhile..." or "The Next Day..."). With Manga Studio EX 5's **Story Editor**, we can input all our dialogs and other text quickly, all from one screen, and make them show up on our page files. With just a little editing once the text is in the page files, we'll have our text all laid out and be ready to draw.

Getting ready

First, we need to create a multi-page file. We will also need a comic script (or at least an idea of some text to include in our pages).

How to do it...

Let's learn how to use the **Story Editor** in this recipe:

1. Go to **File** | **Preferences**.
2. In the **Preferences** window, click on the **Edit text** option on the left-hand-side menu.
3. Under **New text property**, set the drop-down menu to **Selected text tool property**.

> To view the entered text in the font being used for the comic, select it from the font drop-down menus under **View**.

4. Click on **OK** to save the preferences.

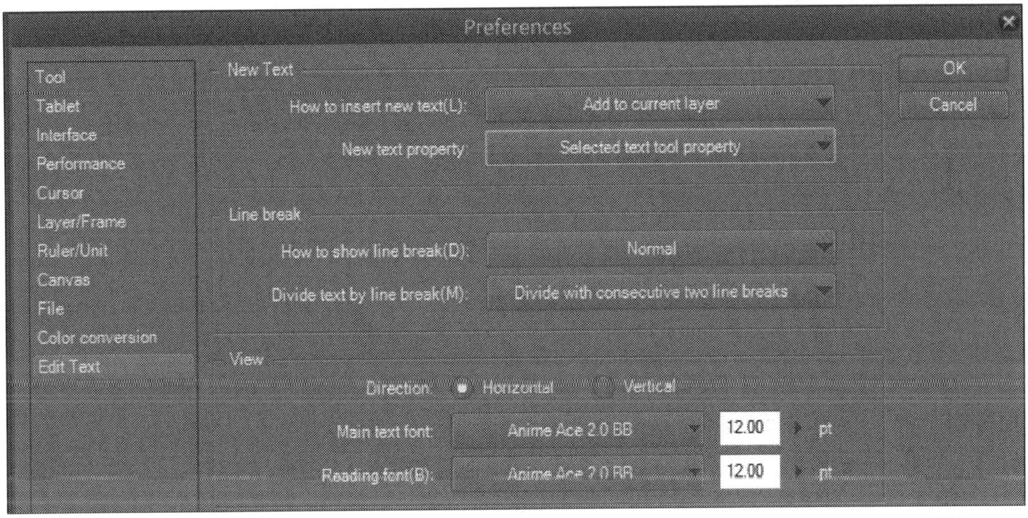

5. On the main Manga Studio EX 5 screen, select **Text tool**, and in **Tool Properties**, select the font to use for lettering in the comic project.
6. Go to **Story** | **Edit text**. If this is the first time you are using the **Story Editor** in this file but other changes have been made, you may be asked about the page histories. Click on **OK** to continue.

7. Now we are in **Story Editor**. Each page is listed and has a textbox. Enter some dialog or narration for the pages according to the script, as shown in this screenshot:

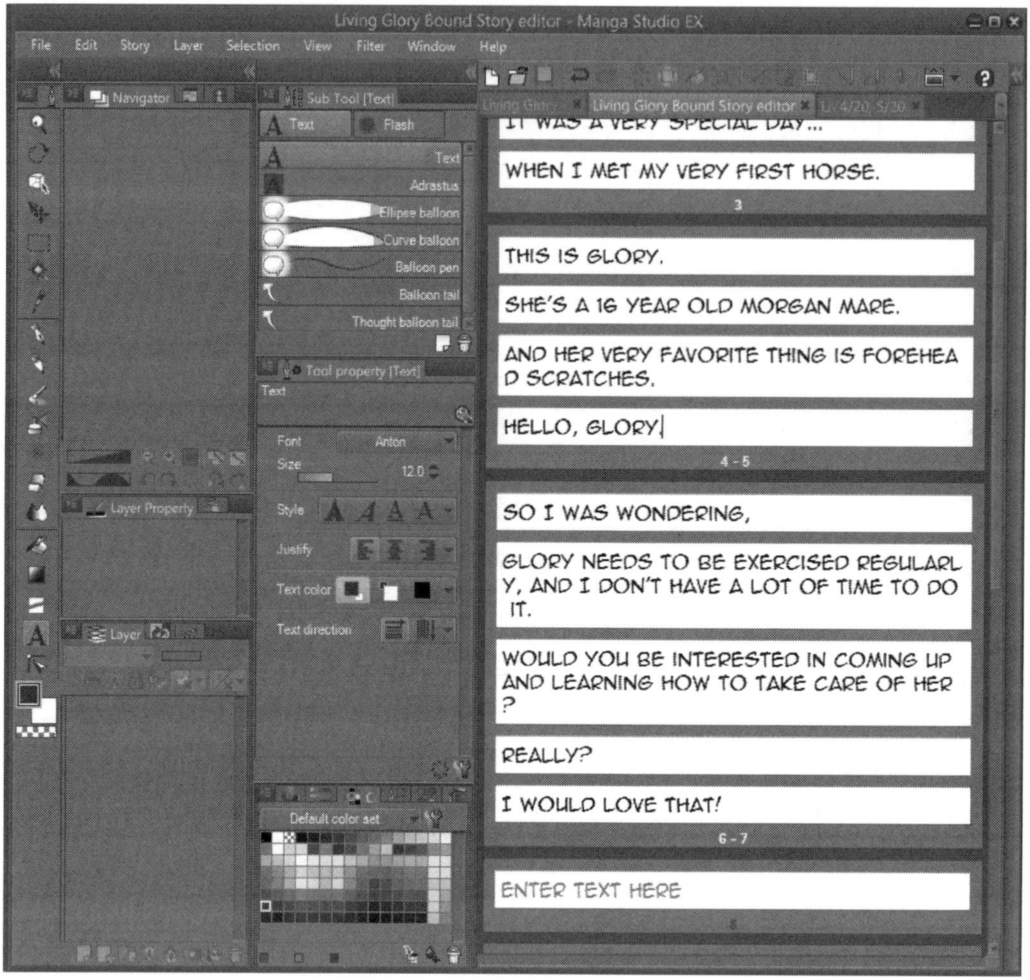

8. Once all of the text is entered, save the file.

9. Go to the Page Manager and open a page where some text has been entered.

10. Edit the text placement and layout as needed. As shown in the following screenshot, all of the text will be set in the corner after you've used the **Story Editor**:

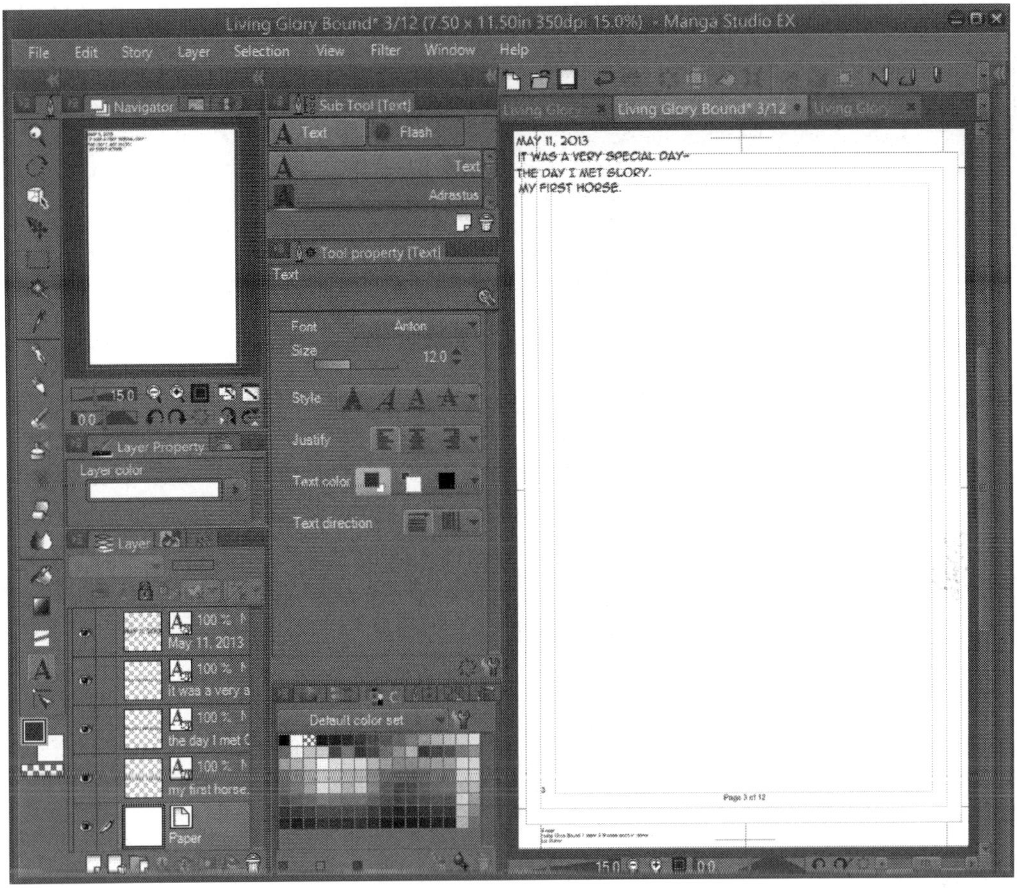

11. To continue editing or adding text, simply go back to the **Story Editor** tab and make any changes required.

How it works...

Before we use the **Story Editor**, we should check out the preferences and make sure that they will work the way we want them to. Changing the `New text` property ensures that the font and settings in the text tool that's active will be applied to all new text.

> Make a custom text tool with the settings for each comic's project that you letter! It will save time because you won't have to change the settings manually each time text needs to be written.

The **Story Editor** is where we can enter all of the text that we would like to apply to our comic pages. This is much faster than entering it page by page. Simply go through the script and enter all the dialog, narration, and sound effects.

Depending on how we have our preferences set, one press of the *Enter* key may create a new line of text on the same page. Personally, I like to set **Preferences** to hitting the *Enter* key twice for a new line of text. Do whatever is best for the way you work!

Once we've entered all our text, we can go to individual pages. Then we can edit the position of the text, add speech balloons, change the text size, and so on. To add more text to a page, either go back to the **Story Editor** and enter it there, or click on the page with the text tool and type directly on the page. Any text entered in this way will also show up in the **Story Editor**.

When closing the **Story Editor** tab, you may be asked whether you'd like to continue. We must be certain that we've saved after using the **Story Editor** and before closing out of it! Closing the **Story Editor** without saving will make us lose our changes!

See also

- *Creating a multi-page file*

Searching and replacing entered text

It happens... The script is perfect, the Manga Studio file is all set up, and the text is entered. We're all ready to get down to drawing. And then we realize that we have got a character's name wrong or have misspelled the name of the Elven city in all of the text! Rather than going through and fixing an error like this by hand, we can use the **Search and replacement** tool to edit at the push of a button. Let's give it a try!

Getting ready

We'll need a story file that has text in it. The more the text, the better!

How to do it...

To find and replace text in the story file, follow these steps:

1. Go to **Story(P)** | **Edit text(Z)** | **Search and replacement(F)**.
2. In the **Search string(F)** box, type the word or phrase to search for.
3. In the **Replacement string** box, type the word or phrase to insert as a replacement for the searched string.

4. To search and replace the terms without worrying about case sensitivity, check the box next to **Do not differentiate case**.
5. We then select a search direction: **Forward(P)** if we are at the beginning of the entered text, and **Backward(N)** if we are at the end.
6. Simply click on the **Search** button to go to the next occurrence of the search string.
7. Click on the **Replacement** button to replace one occurrence of the search string.
8. Also, you can click on **All replacement** to search for all occurrences and replace them with the replacement string.
9. Once you're done, click on **Close**.

How it works...

This feature is very much like the *Find and Replace* option in many popular word processing programs. It works in the same way, so if you're familiar with those, this should be a snap!

The **Search string** box is the text that we want to search for. Say, we typed a character's name as `Bryan` for an entire graphic novel and the name was supposed to be `Byron`. We have to type `Bryan` in to the **Search string** box.

Then, the **Replacement string** text box is where we type the text that we want to use to replace the search string. In the preceding example, we type `Byron` in the **Replacement string** box.

We can simply search for the next occurrence of the word or phrase that we're looking for by clicking on **Search**.

> Can't find the page where you mentioned the axionic microfilament shaft or some other specific name in your story? Enter the word or phrase and click on **Search** without entering a replacement string. Manga Studio EX 5 will take you directly to the page you're looking for.

Clicking on the **Replacement** button will replace the occurrence that we just searched for. Clicking on **All replacement** will automatically search for and replace every occurrence of the search string in the text.

See also

- *Using the Story Editor to enter text*

2

Customizing Brushes

In this chapter, you will learn the following recipes:

- Creating a gritty inking brush
- Breaking out with a broken glass brush
- Creating a cracked detail brush
- Foliage made simple
- Creating a cross-hatching brush
- Making a fabric trim brush
- Making a ruffle brush
- Making a brick brush
- Blowing up an explosion brush
- Creating a feathering texture brush

Introduction

Brushes in Manga Studio 5 can do a lot more than just making a pencil mark when you use your stylus to draw. By customizing your brushes, you can speed up your workflow and create special effects. Spend a little time now making a brush that imitates ruffled fabric, and save time later when you introduce a character with a penchant for wearing ruffles!

The brush settings can look a little intimidating at first, but once you know what everything does, you'll be flying through the brush creation process! This chapter is a good introduction to some brushes that you may need in your drawing process.

For all the recipes in this chapter, it is advised that you have a page open to make test marks on as you make your new brush. This is the best way to test what each option in the **Tool property** window does and how tweaking the options can make a difference in the look of our brush.

Let's make some drawing tools!

Creating a gritty inking brush

Some styles require a line that isn't smooth and even. We're going to make a gritty and uneven-textured inking brush to add some flair to our lines.

Getting ready

One of the materials used for this pen is from a free brush available from Smith Micro. At the time of writing this book, the brush is available at `http://my.smithmicro.com/manga-studio-ex-5-free-content.html`, as **Dry Bleeding Flat Watercolor**. This brush will need to be installed in order to get access to the material. Download the brush from the Smith Micro website. Then, click on the icon circled in the following screenshot (found in the **Sub Tool** palette) and click on **Import sub tool...**:

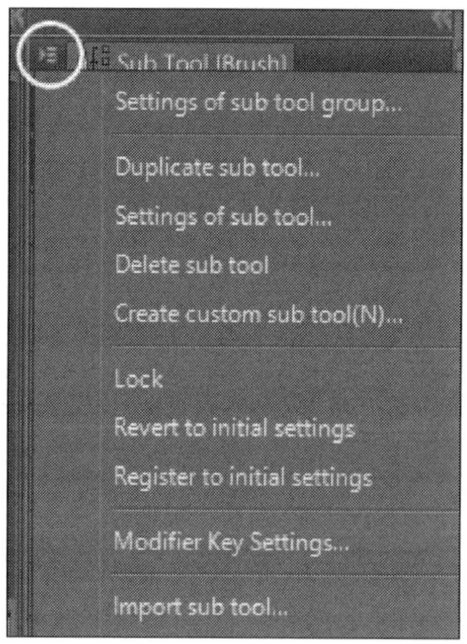

Navigate to the location of the downloaded brush file and click on **Open**. The **Dry Bleeding Flat Watercolor** brush will be installed and the material will be added to the **Material** library.

How to do it...

These steps will walk us through the process of creating a new inking brush with a gritty look:

1. Under the **Pen** tools, select **G-pen**.
2. In the bottom-right corner of the **Sub Tool** palette, click on the **Create copy** icon to create a copy of the selected sub tool. It is shown circled in this screenshot:

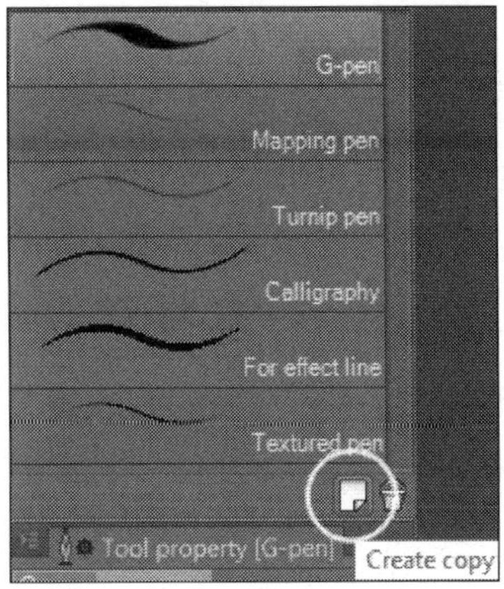

3. In the **Duplicate sub tool** screen, enter the name `Gritty Ink Pen`. Click on **OK**.
4. In the **Tool property** palette, click on the wrench icon in the bottom-right corner. It is marked in the following screenshot:

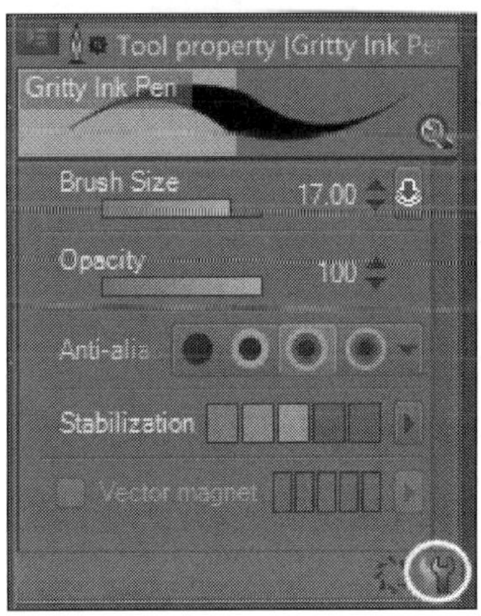

5. In the **Sub Tool Detail** screen, click on **Brush tip** on the left-hand side.
6. Next to **Tip shape**, click on the **Material** button. Then, click on the **Add brush tip shape** icon (it looks like the circled icon in the screenshot shown after step 2).
7. From the **Select brush tip shape** screen, select the material named **Droplet 1** and click on **OK**. Refer to the following screenshot for an example of what it looks like:

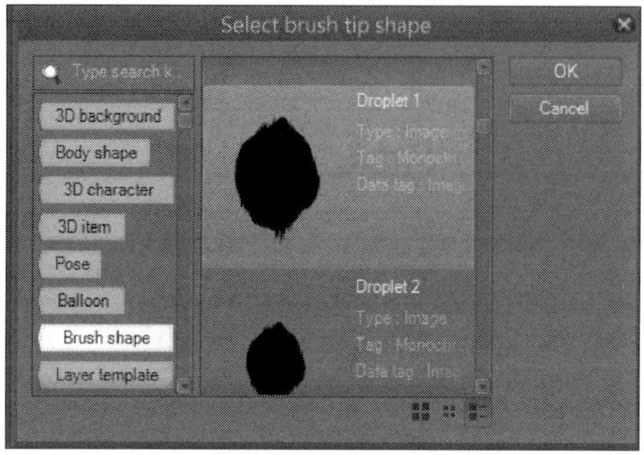

8. Click on the **Add brush tip shape** icon again.
9. From the **Select brush tip shape** screen, select the material named **Dry Bleeding Watercolor** and click on **OK**. Refer to this screenshot for an example of what it looks like:

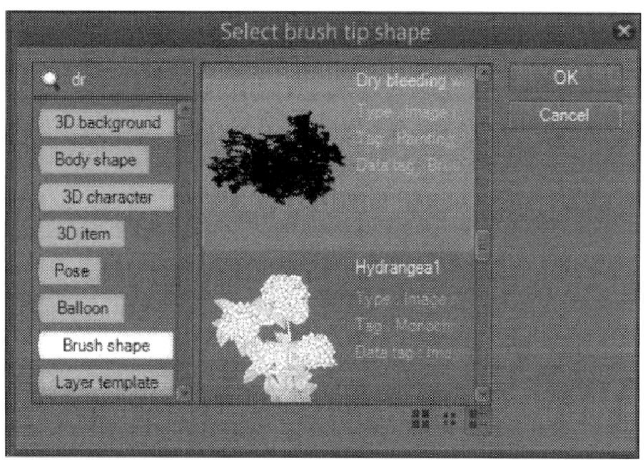

10. In the brush tip settings, set **Thickness** to `70`. Set **Direction of applying** to **Vertical**.

11. On the right-hand side of the **Thickness** settings, click on the button with the dark gray square in it to open up the **Set to change parameter by pen pressure or velocity of tablet** settings.
12. Check the box next to **Pen pressure**. In the graph at the bottom of the screen, pull the middle of the curve up. Check out to the following screenshot to understand this:

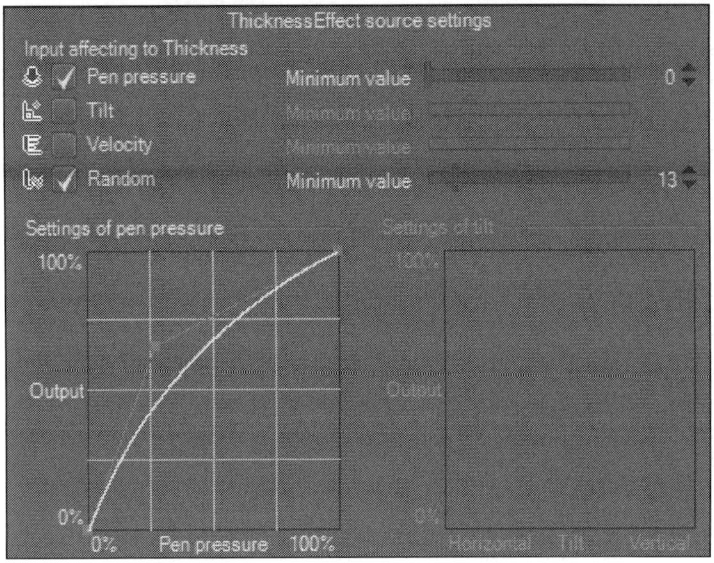

13. Check the box next to **Random** and set the minimum value to `13`.
14. Click on the gray box icon to the right of the **Direction** settings. Click on the radio button next to **Direction of pen**. Then, check the box next to **Random** and set the **Degree of effect** slider to `10`. Refer to this screenshot to double-check the settings:

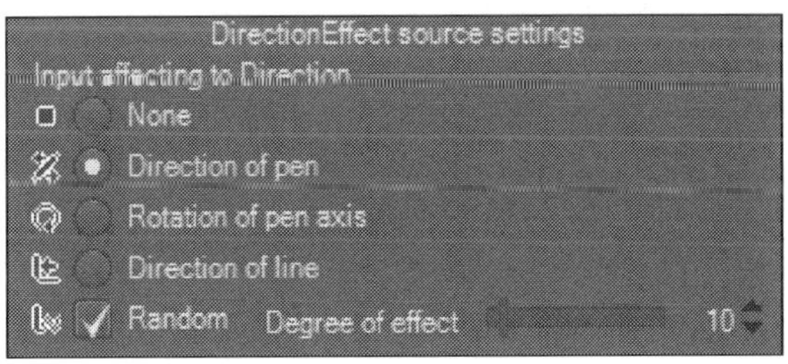

15. In the **Brush tip** settings, check the box next to **Adjust brush density by space**. The brush tip settings should now look like what is shown in the following screenshot:

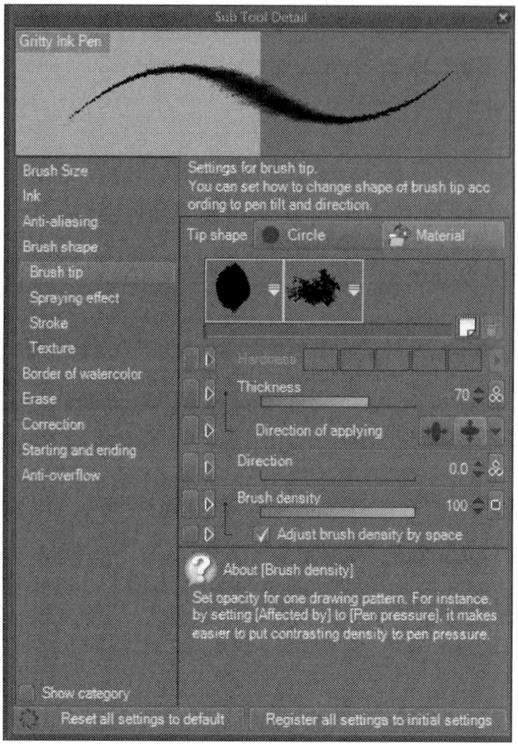

16. Make sure that **Anti-aliasing** is set to **None**.
17. Test the new brush and adjust the settings as needed for your personal preference.

How it works...

This is actually a fairly easy brush to create, because it just uses the brush tip settings.

First, we duplicate a pen tool. We're making a pen tool, so we start with the base of a pen tool to build on. I chose the G-pen for this recipe because I like its pressure sensitivity settings, but if there's another pen that you like more, then by all means duplicate it and build your gritty pen using it! The great thing about Manga Studio 5 is that you can customize it to fit the way you like to work.

Clicking on the wrenches in the **Tool property** palette shows us all the options for customizing our tool.

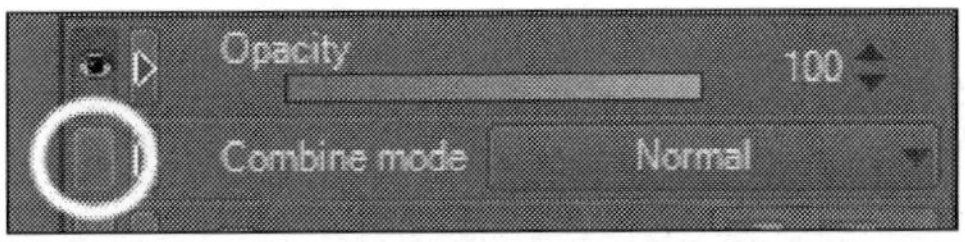

To add an option from the **Sub Tool Detail** window to the **Tool property** palette, click on the gray box to the left of the option's name, as marked by the circle in the preceding screenshot.

This box will change to get an eye icon inside it, like the box above the one circled in the preceding screenshot. This will make the option show up in the **Tool property** palette, giving easy access to the settings without having to open the **Sub Tool Detail** palette.

Next, we must tell Manga Studio what brush tip materials we want it to use. By using two materials, we can create a custom look. The two materials work together, layered on top of one another, to create a new brush tip shape.

The **Thickness** settings change the way the brush tip is shaped. Instead of a circular brush, we can make an oval brush by adjusting the thickness. In the case of this brush, because we're using brush tip materials instead of a circular tip, we control the squash or stretch of the shapes.

The **Set to change parameter by pen pressure or velocity of tablet** settings let us control the conditions under which variables change. This option can be adjusted for many of the options in the **Sub Tool Detail** screen. In this case, we set the thickness to both be affected by the pressure of the pen when we draw, and have a random adjustment as well. This helps achieve the "dry brush" effect of the pen.

Anti-aliasing tells the program how sharp or blurry the edges of the brush should be made. In this case, we don't want the edge to be soft. We want a nice, hard look for this tool—we're making something "gritty"! Setting **Anti-aliasing** to **None** gives us the look that we want.

The following is a set of focus lines inked with the tool we just made:

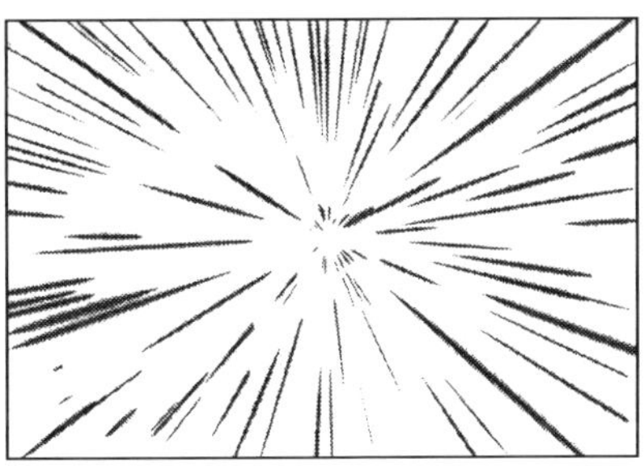

Breaking out with a broken glass brush

One of the great things about working digitally is that you can save time by utilizing the features of the software you use and making them work for you. In this case, we're going to add some broken glass around the falling figure in this drawing:

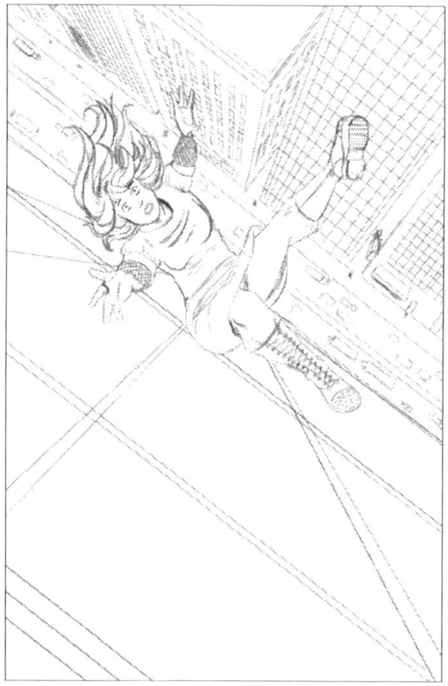

How to do it...

This recipe will walk us through creating a custom material and then using it to make our brush:

1. Open a blank canvas, preferably of 300 to 600 dpi resolution.
2. Using your preferred drawing tools on an empty layer, draw the outlines of several jagged shapes. These will be our shards of broken glass.
3. Create a new layer beneath the outline layer. Select the glass shapes and fill them with solid white.
4. Lower the opacity of the white layer to 50 percent.
5. Merge the outline layer with the 50 percent transparent white layer.

6. Make sure that the background of your image is transparent. Your image should look something like this:

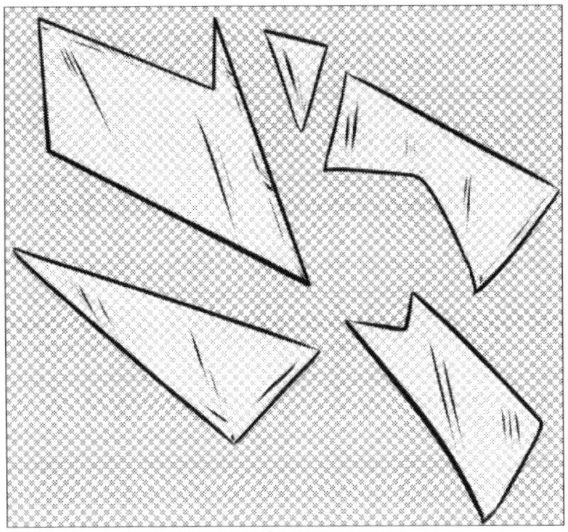

7. Go to **Edit** | **Register Image as Material**.
8. In the **Material property** window, name your new material. Select the **Brush** folder (which is under **Image material**) to store it in.
9. Check the box under the **Material image** preview that says **Use for brush tip shape**.
10. Add tags by clicking on the tag and the **+** sign icon in the bottom-right corner of the **Search tag** box. Check out the following screenshot to understand what your **Material property** screen should look like:

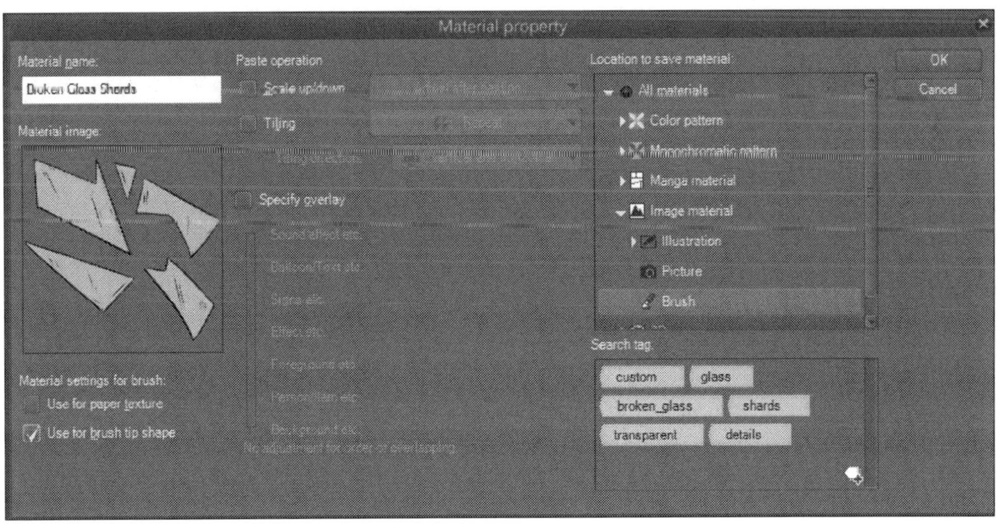

11. Click on **OK**.
12. Select **G-pen** from the **Pen** subtool. In the bottom-right corner of the **Sub Tool** palette, click on the icon to create a copy of the selected subtool.
13. In the **Duplicate sub tool** screen, enter the name `Broken Glass`. Click on **OK**.
14. In the **Tool property** palette, click on the wrench icon in the bottom-right corner to open the **Sub Tool Detail** palette.
15. Click on **Brush Size** on the left-hand side of the **Sub Tool Detail** palette. Then, click on the icon next to the slider on the **Brush Size** screen to choose **Set to change parameter by pen pressure or velocity of tablet**. Make sure that the **Pen pressure** box is checked, and set the value to `15`. Change the curve on the graph so that it is concave.
16. In the **Anti-aliasing** options, set the anti-aliasing to **Middle**.
17. Click on **Brush tip** on the left-hand side of the **Sub Tool Detail** palette.
18. Click on the **Material** button next to **Tip shape**. Then click on the **Add brush tip shape** icon below the **Material** button.
19. Select the glass shard shapes that you created in steps 1 to 11, and highlight them in the **Select brush tip shape** window. Refer to the following screenshot to understand this:

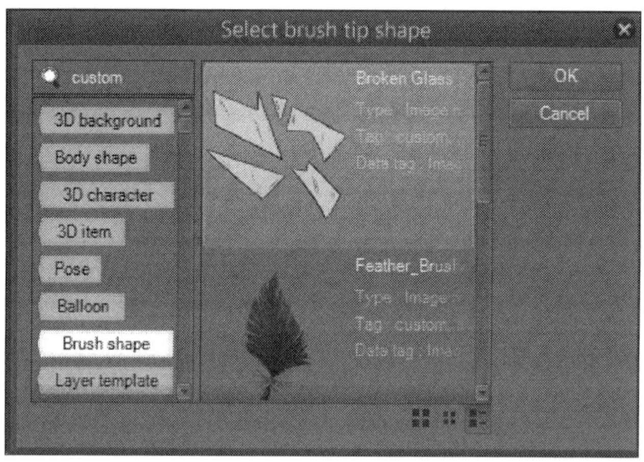

> Use one of the search tags added in step 10 to find the brush tip shape easily!

20. Click on **OK** to select the glass shards as the material to use.
21. In the **Brush tip** settings—back in the **Sub Tool Detail** palette—click on the box to the right of the slider for the **Thickness** settings to open **Set to change parameter by pen pressure or velocity of tablet**. Check the box next to the **Random** option and set the minimum value to `65`.
22. Click on the box to the right of the **Direction** slider. Check the box next to the **Random** option and set **Degree of effect** to `100`.
23. On the left-hand side of the **Sub Tool Detail** palette, click on the **Stroke** option.
24. Set the **Gap** option to **Fixed** by clicking on the button with one full circle in the center.
25. Use the slider under the **Gap** option to set the value to `150`.
26. Set **Repeat method** to **Random**.
27. Test your new brush.

How it works...

In order to get the look that we want, we need to first create a material to use for the brush tip. Filling the glass shards with a 50 percent opaque white color will give a translucent look to the finished product.

> If we want our glass shards to be completely transparent (crystal-clear glass), then we have two options. The first is not to fill the glass shard material with 50 percent opaque white. The second is to use the completely broken glass brush on a new layer and set that layer to **Multiply**. For more information on layer modes, refer to *Chapter 4, Using Layer Modes*.

Once we've made the shapes we like, we have to set them as a new material, and tell Manga Studio that we want to use this material as a brush tip in the future. This, as well as saving it in the **Brush** folder under **Image material**, will make it show up when we load the brush tip shape in step 19.

We want our glass shards to look random. This is what we set when we change the **Thickness**, **Direction**, and **Gap** options to **Random**. As we use the brush, the shapes will rotate randomly and their distance from one another change.

Here is the sketch from the beginning of the recipe, now with the broken glass added:

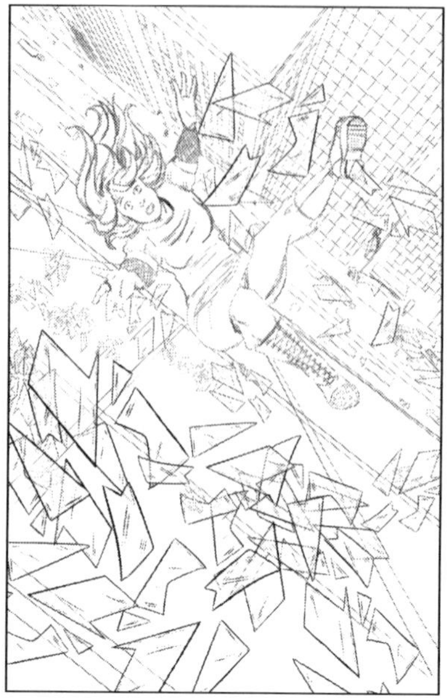

There's more...

By making each of our glass shards a different material, we can increase the amount and randomness in the brush and make the glass effect look even better:

1. Open a new file of at least 300 dpi.
2. Draw the outline of a glass shard shape on an empty layer using your preferred drawing tool.
3. Create a new layer below the glass shard's outline and fill the inside of the glass shard shape with white.
4. Set the opacity of the white fill layer to 50 percent.
5. Select the outline layer and go to **Layer** | **Merge with layer below** to merge the outline and the fill into one layer.

6. Repeat steps 2 to 5 until you have as many glass shards as you want to include in your brush. Each shard shape should be on its own layer! Check out the following screenshot, and note that each glass shard has a layer of its own in the **Layer** palette on the left-hand side of the screen:

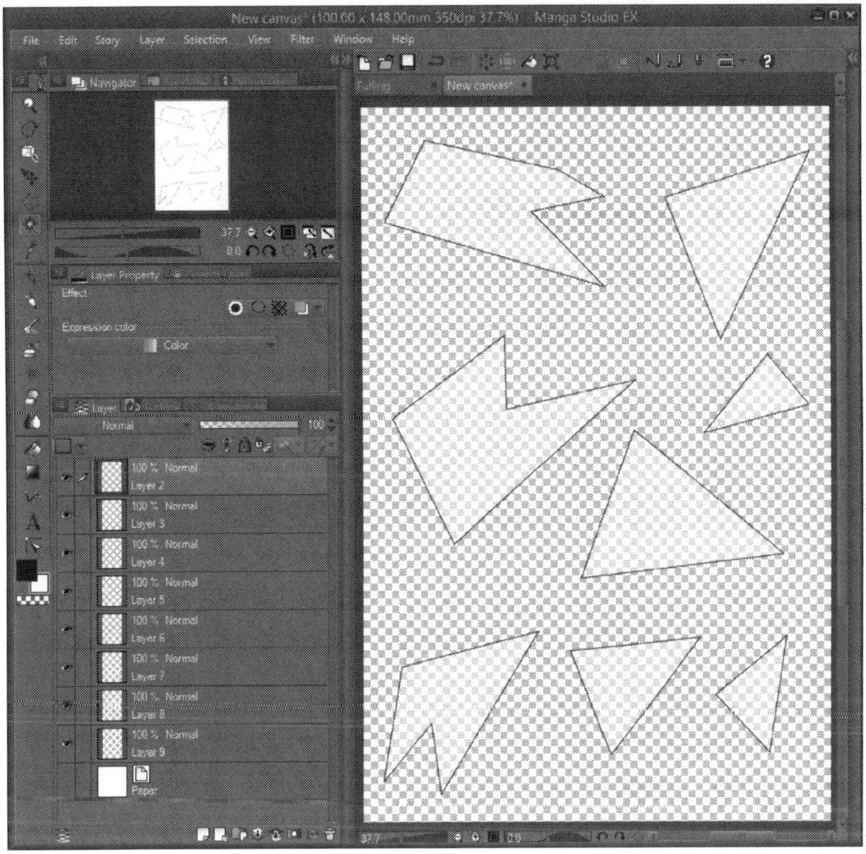

7. Turn off all but one layer. You should now have only one glass shard shape visible in the file.
8. Go to **Edit** | **Register Image as Material**.
9. In the **Material property** window, name your new material. Select the **Brush** folder under **Image material** to store it in.

10. Check the box under the **Material image** preview that says **Use for brush tip shape**.
11. Add tags by clicking on the tag and the **+** sign icon in the bottom-right corner of the **Search tag** box. Check out this screenshot to understand what your **Material property** screen should look like:

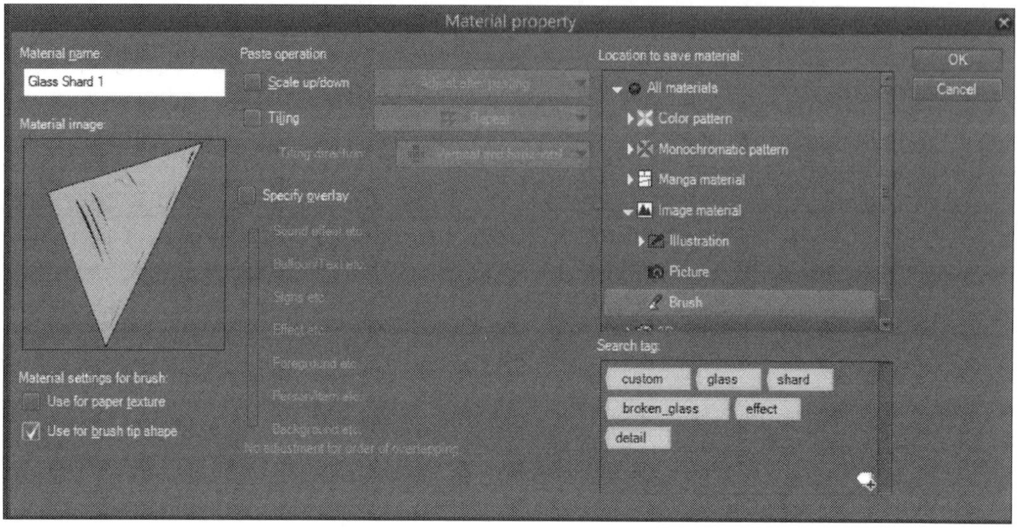

12. Complete steps 7 to 11 for the rest of the layers.
13. Select **G-pen** from the **Pen** subtool. In the bottom-right corner of the **Sub Tool** palette, click on the icon to create a copy of the selected subtool.
14. In the **Duplicate sub tool** screen, enter the name `Broken Glass`. Click on **OK**.
15. In the **Tool property** palette, click on the wrench icon in the bottom-right corner to open the **Sub Tool Detail** palette.
16. Click on **Brush size** on the left-hand side of the **Sub Tool Detail** palette. Then click on the icon next to the slider on the brush size screen to use **Set to change parameter by pen pressure or velocity of tablet**. Make sure that the **Pen pressure** box is checked and set the value to `15`. Change the curve on the graph so that it is concave.
17. In the **Anti-aliasing** options, set the anti-aliasing to **Middle**.
18. Click on **Brush tip** on the left-hand side of the **Sub Tool Detail** palette.
19. Click on the **Material** button next to **Tip shape**. Then click on the **Add brush tip shape** icon below the **Material** button.
20. Select each of the individual glass shard shapes that you made in steps 2-12. This can be done by holding down *Shift* or *Ctrl* on the keyboard and clicking on each shape individually.

21. Click on **OK** to load the brush tip materials.
22. In the **Brush tip** settings, back in the **Sub Tool Detail** palette, click on the box to the right of the slider for the **Thickness** settings to open **Set to change parameter by pen pressure or velocity of tablet**. Check the box next to the **Random** option and set the minimum value to `65`.
23. Click on the box to the right of the **Direction** slider. Check the box next to the **Random** option and set **Degree of effect** to `100`.
24. On the left-hand side of the **Sub Tool Detail** palette, click on the **Stroke** option.
25. Set the **Gap** option to **Fixed** by clicking on the button with one full circle in the center.
26. Use the slider under the **Gap** option to set the value to `150`.
27. Set **Repeat method** to **Random**.
28. Test out your new brush.

The following is what this glass brush looks like when used on an image:

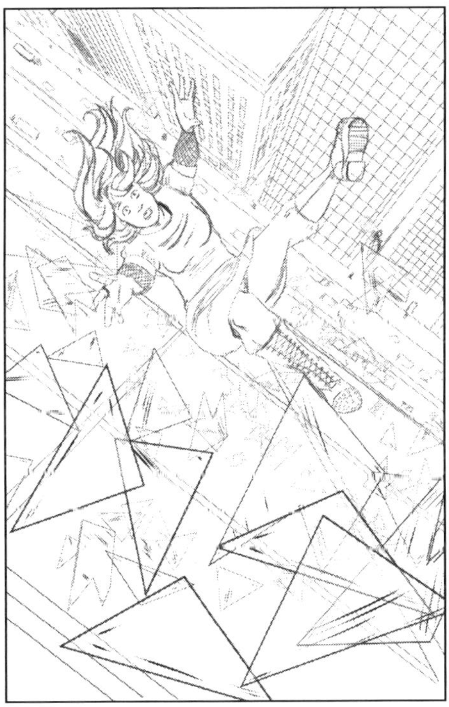

Creating a cracked detail brush

Our next brush will make drawing ruins, rubble, and general scenes of devastation easier.

Getting ready

To start off, open a new blank canvas of at least 300 dpi resolution. We will use this canvas to draw our new brush tip shape in order to make our cracks. Make sure that **Basic expression color** is set to **Gray** and not **Color**. Refer to the screenshot given here to know where to change this option while creating your new canvas:

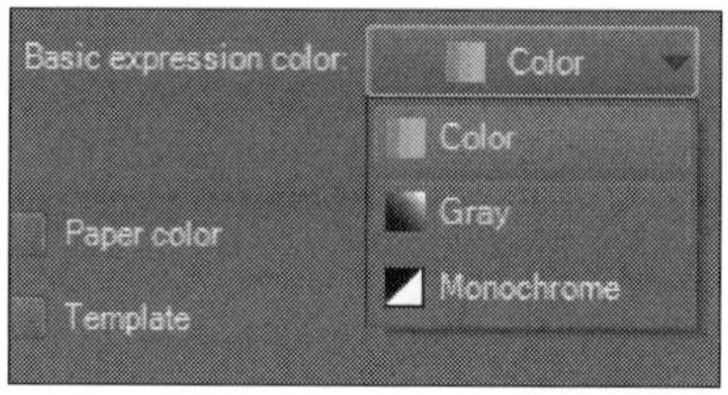

How to do it...

These steps will walk you through the rest of the brush creation process:

1. With your new canvas open, navigate to **View** | **Grid** to turn on the grid lines.
2. Find the grid line that runs down the center of the canvas vertically.
3. Use this center line as a guide for the cracks, but do not follow it exactly! Make the cracks branch off and go away from the center. This creates a more convincing effect. Check out the following screenshot, and note that the crack pattern touches the center line at the top and bottom of the canvas:

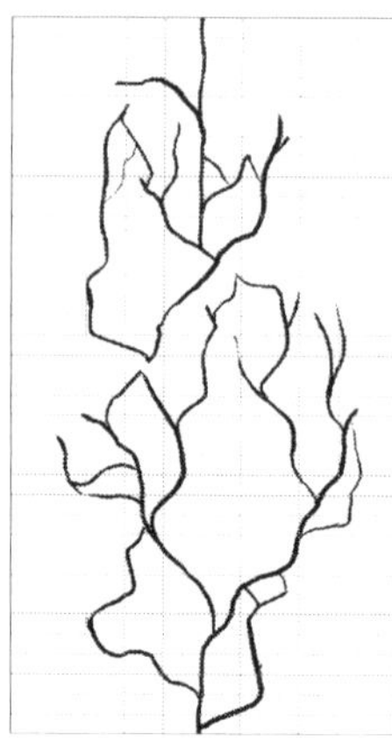

4. Once you are satisfied with the crack pattern, discard any background or **Paper** layers so that the only visible layer is the drawing. The background should be transparent.
5. Go to **Edit** | **Register Image as Material**.
6. Name the material with a descriptive title.
7. Double-check the **Material image** preview to make sure that the space around the leaves is transparent (it will show as the same gray color as the rest of the **Material property** window).
8. Beneath **Material image**, check the box marked **Use for brush tip shape**.
9. Choose the **Brush** folder, which is under **Image material**, to save the new material in.
10. Add tags to the **Search tag** box. Refer to the screenshot shown here for suggestions:

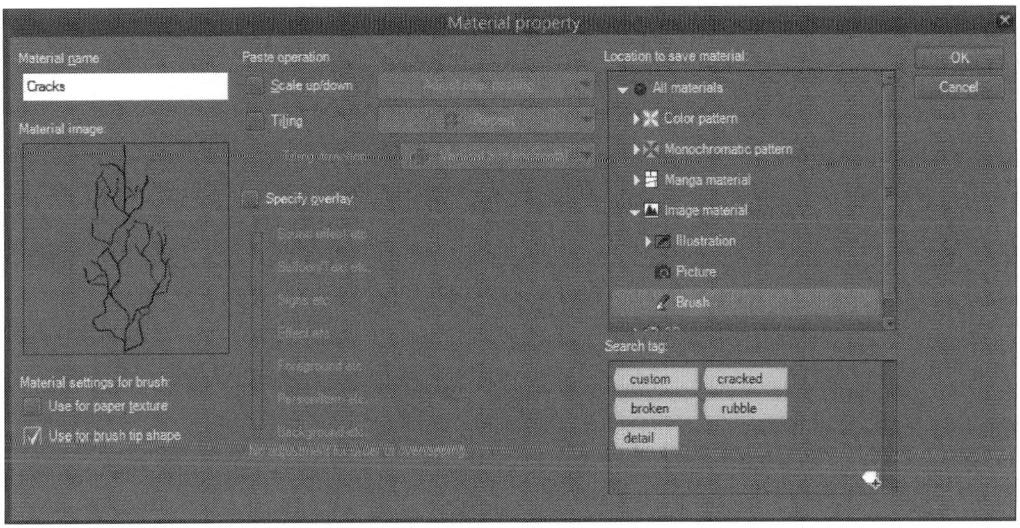

11. Click on **OK** in the **Material property** window.
12. Select the **Decoration** tool from the Manga Studio 5 toolbox.
13. Choose the **Artificial** category of decoration tools. Then select the **Barbed wire** tool.
14. Click on the **Create copy of currently selected sub tool** icon in the bottom-right part of the **Sub Tool [Decoration]** palette.
15. Name the new brush tool using a descriptive title. For this recipe, I have chosen `Cracks` as the brush name.
16. In the **Tool property** palette, click on the wrench icon in the bottom-right corner to open the **Sub Tool Detail** palette.

17. Using the slider or the text entry box, change **Brush Size** to `50`.
18. Click on the **Brush tip** option.
19. Delete the existing brush tip material by selecting it and then clicking on the delete icon under the **Material** box. It looks like a trash can!
20. Click on the **Add brush tip shape** icon directly to the left of the delete icon.
21. Search for and select the material created in steps 1-11 of this recipe. Then click on **OK**.
22. Set the rest of the **Brush tip** options to match what is shown in this screenshot:

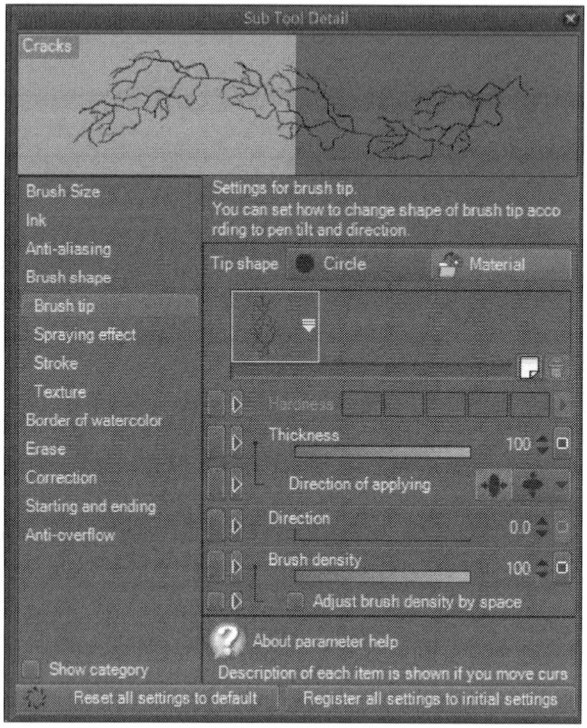

23. Test your new brush!

How it works...

By drawing the cracked pattern of this brush on a gray layer, we make it such that we can tint the cracks on the fly by choosing a foreground color. I've used this new cracked brush on the rubble in the background of the following drawing:

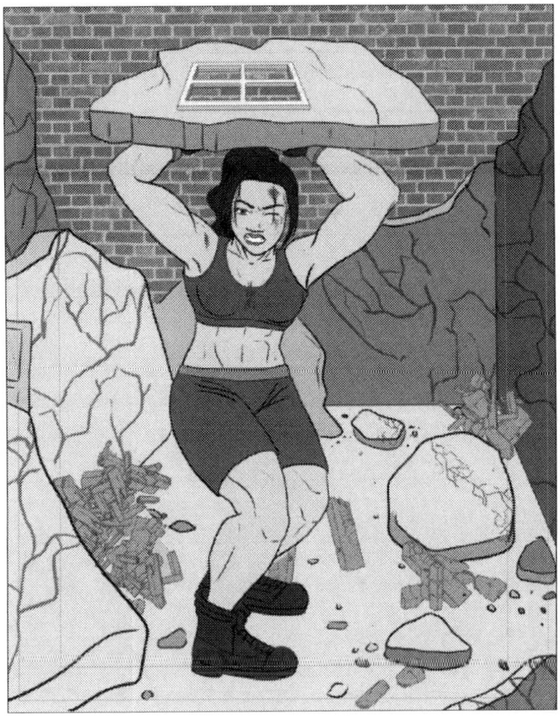

Note that the cracks in the background, while dark, are not black. Setting the brush in this manner allows more versatility later. We could use this same brush later for other special effects, such as distant lightning or the hanging roots of a tree, simply by changing the color of the brush!

Aligning parts of the brush tip material to the center line of the canvas allows us to keep the crack pattern repeating without an obvious interruption. Whenever we create a brush tip that repeats like this, we want to ensure that the center line is matched so that it continues seamlessly.

The decoration tools have already been created similarly to the effect we wanted to achieve with this brush, which is why we chose to duplicate one of them instead of an inking brush. This means fewer individual settings to tweak, which saves time and headaches! I am all about saving time!

Making a foliage brush

A foliage brush is an adaptation of a free brush that is available from Smith Micro. At the time of writing this book, the brush is available at `http://my.smithmicro.com/manga-studio-ex-5-free-content.html` as **Leaf in middle distance**.

How to do it...

For this brush, we'll need to make a material and then use it to make a brush that "rolls out" like a ribbon:

1. Open a new canvas with at least 300 dpi resolution.
2. Draw a row of leaves, similar to the top of a tree or a bush.
3. Fill the leaves with white color. Use the following screenshot as a guide to create the leaves' shapes:

> The dark fill around the leaves is simply for showing the shape of the white fill.

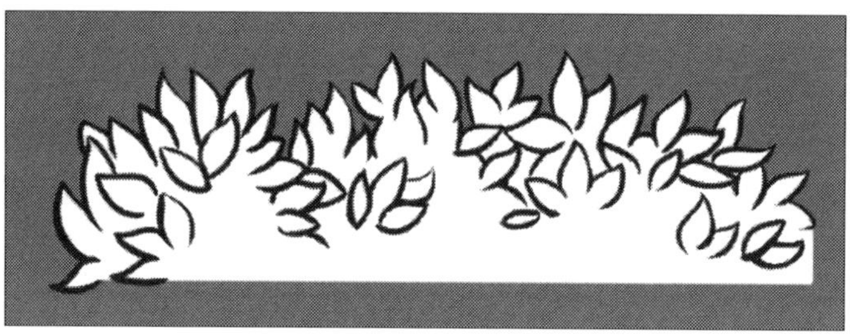

4. Turn off any visible **Paper** layers or other fills.
5. If needed, combine the leaf outline layer and the fill layer. There should now be only the leaf outlines and the white fill visible on the canvas. The background should be *transparent*.
6. Go to **Edit** | **Register Image as Material**.
7. Name the material using a descriptive title.
8. Double-check the **Material image** preview to make sure that the space around the leaves is transparent (it will have the same gray color as the rest of the **Material property** window).

9. Beneath **Material image**, check the box marked **Use for brush tip shape**.
10. Choose the **Brush** folder, which is under **Image material**, to save the new material in.
11. Add some tags to the **Search tag** box. Refer to the following screenshot for suggestions:

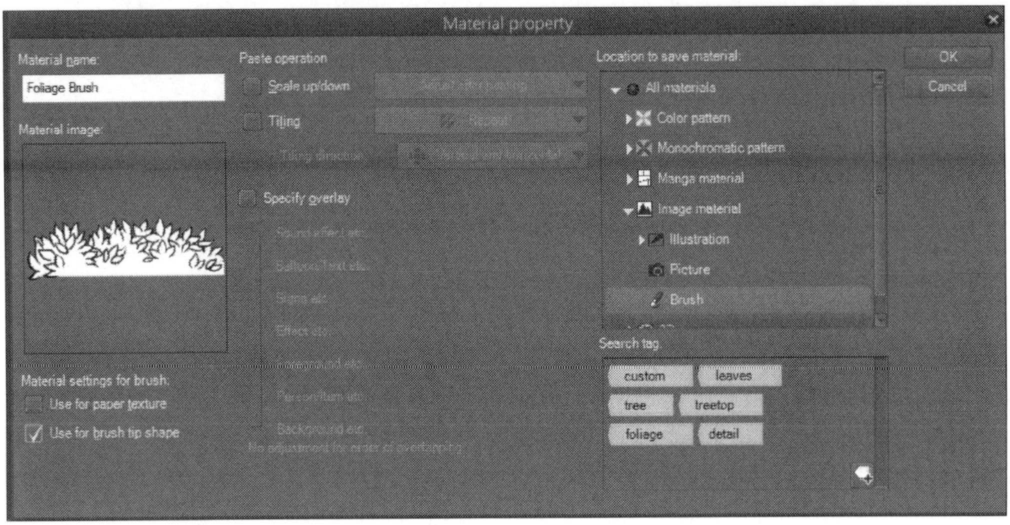

12. Click on **OK**.
13. Select the **Decoration** tool from the Manga Studio toolbox.
14. Under the **Vegetation** category, select the **Grass A** tool. Click on the **Create copy of currently selected sub tool** icon in the bottom-right portion of the **Sub Tool [Decoration]** palette.
15. Name the new subtool with something descriptive.
16. In the **Tool property** palette, click on the wrench icon in the bottom-right corner to open the **Sub Tool Detail** palette.
17. Click on **Ink** on the left-hand side of the palette. Ensure that **Opacity** is set to `100` and **Combine mode** is **Normal**.
18. Click on **Anti-aliasing** on the left-hand side of the palette. The anti-aliasing should be set to **None**.
19. Select **Brush tip** from the left-hand side of the **Sub Tool Detail** palette. If the brush has a material currently loaded under **Tip shape**, select that material and click on the delete icon.

20. Once any existing material has been deleted from the brush, click on the **Add brush tip shape** icon directly to the left of the delete icon.
21. Search for and select the material created in steps 1-12 of this recipe. Then click on **OK**.
22. Set **Thickness** to `100`.
23. If the brush tip shape appears vertical instead of horizontal, set the **Direction** value to `100`. Note that the following screenshot shows the direction set to `0.0`, and the brush tip shape is loading vertically in the preview at the top of the screen:

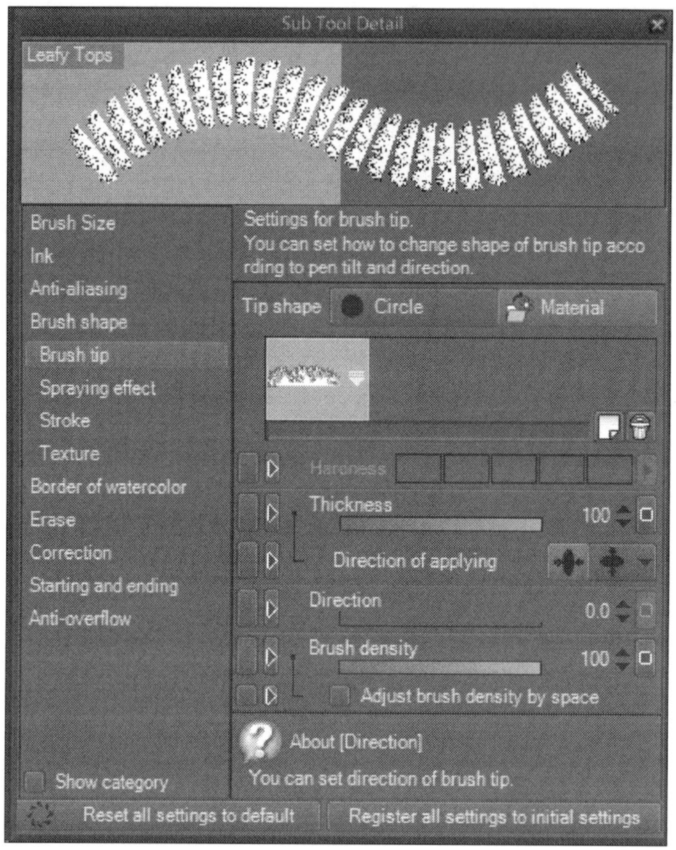

This screenshot, on the other hand, shows **Direction** set to `100`:

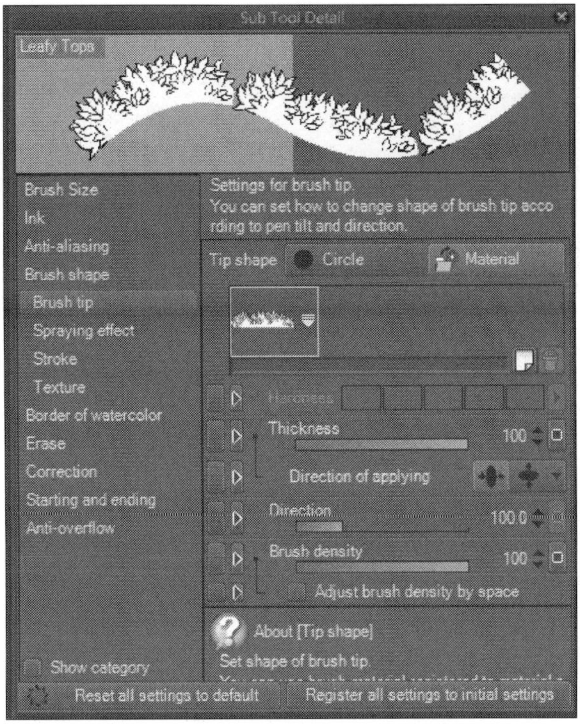

24. Click on the box to the right of the slider for the **Direction** settings to open **Set to change parameter by pen pressure or velocity of tablet**. Deselect the checkbox next to the **Random** option.

25. Click on **Stroke** on the left-hand side of the **Sub Tool Detail** screen. Click on the checkbox next to **Ribbon** to activate this option. Refer to the following screenshot:

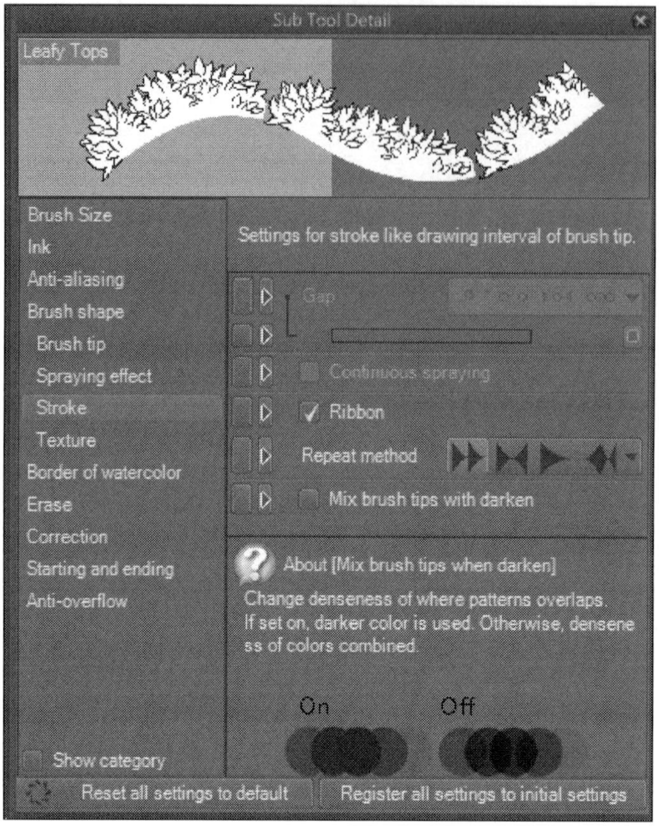

26. Test out your new brush!

How it works...

This brush works best when it's used in layers. To understand what I mean, look at the process of creating the top of a tree.

After sketching the trunk of the tree and the general shape of the leaves, use the brush to go around the outline of the top. Work in a clockwise direction to ensure that the bottom leaves are in the correct orientation. Look at the following figure and note the direction of the arrows. This is the direction to work in:

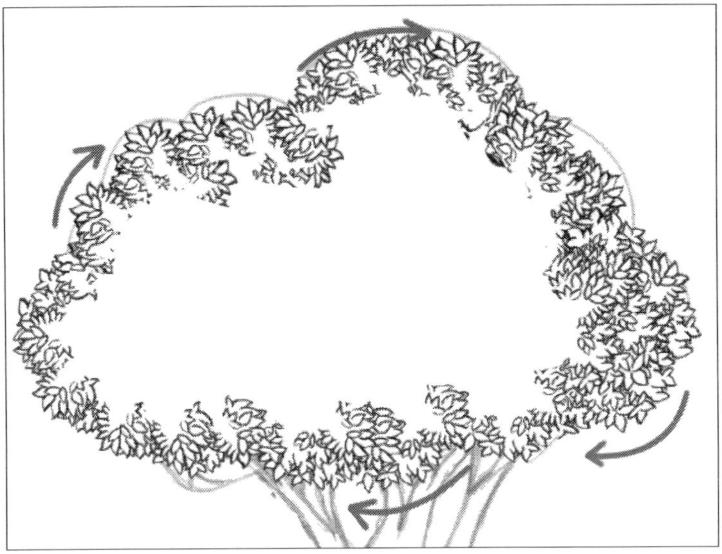

This doesn't look bad, but it could look better. Continue working in a clockwise direction, but now inside the first layer of leaves, as shown in this screenshot:

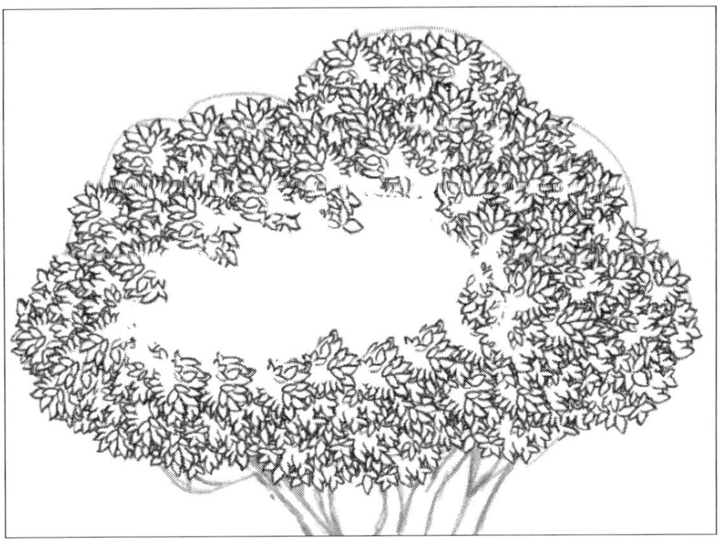

Finally, fill the empty space to smooth it all out. The following screenshot shows the tree all filled, using nothing but our foliage brush!

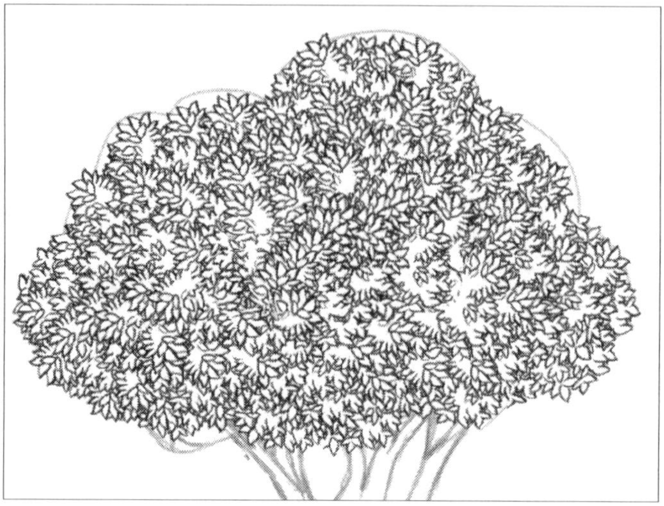

By using the **Ribbon** setting, we get a brush tip that repeats in a line, like the pattern printed on a spool of a ribbon. It will "unroll" as we use the brush. Layering the leaves then gives a lively finished product with lots of details!

Creating a cross-hatching brush

Hatching is the term used to describe the shading of a drawing achieved using groups of parallel lines. Cross-hatching is a group of parallel lines crossed by another group of parallel lines moving in another direction. Hatching and cross-hatching can give a lovely look of depth and texture to monochromatic illustrations. Let's explore how to create a brush to make our hatching and cross-hatching go a little faster than doing it completely by hand!

Getting ready

To start off, open a new blank canvas of at least 300 dpi resolution. We will use this canvas to draw our new brush tip shape in order to make our cracks. Make sure that **Basic expression color** is set to **Gray** and not **Color**.

Refer to the screenshot given here to understand where to change this option while creating your new canvas:

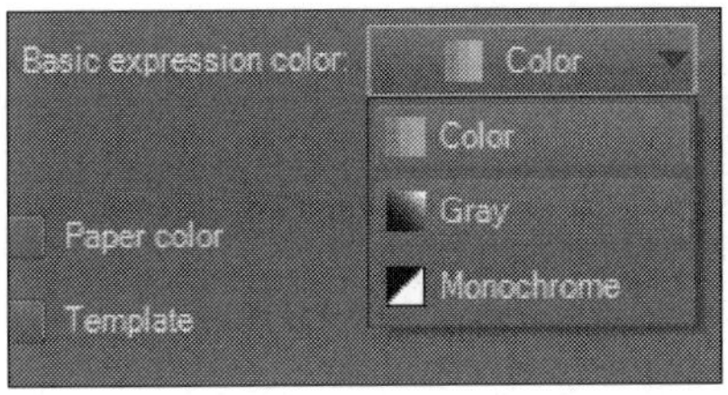

How to do it...

These steps will walk you through the rest of the brush creation process:

1. Select the **Figure** tool and then the **Ruler** subtool.
2. Next, select **Special ruler** from the **Sub Tool [Figure]** palette.
3. In the **Tool property** palette, choose **Parallel line** from the **Specify ruler** drop-down menu. This is shown here:

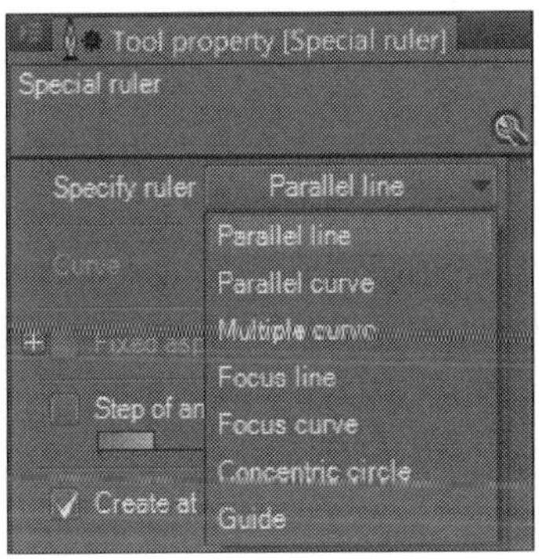

4. Click inside the canvas and hold with the left mouse button. While still holding, drag the mouse cursor across the canvas at an angle. Release the mouse button to set the ruler.
5. Select your preferred pen tool.

6. Ensure that the **Snap to Special Ruler** option in the toolbar above the canvas is active. This will make the selected pen follow the parallel line ruler. Refer to the following screenshot for the location of this option:

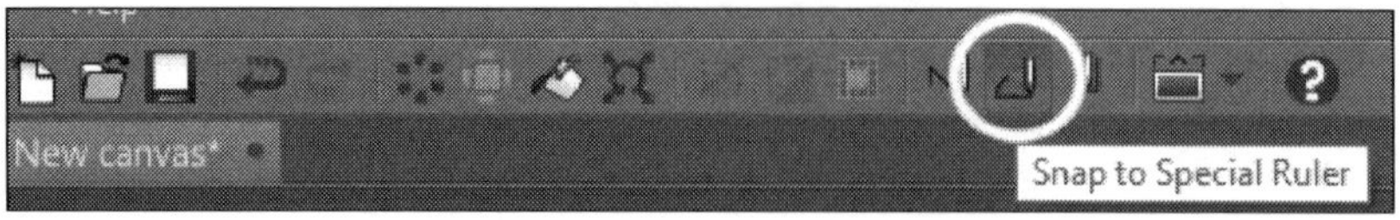

7. Using your preferred pen tool, draw a group of parallel lines, as shown in this screenshot (note that the very thin lines are the ruler lines):

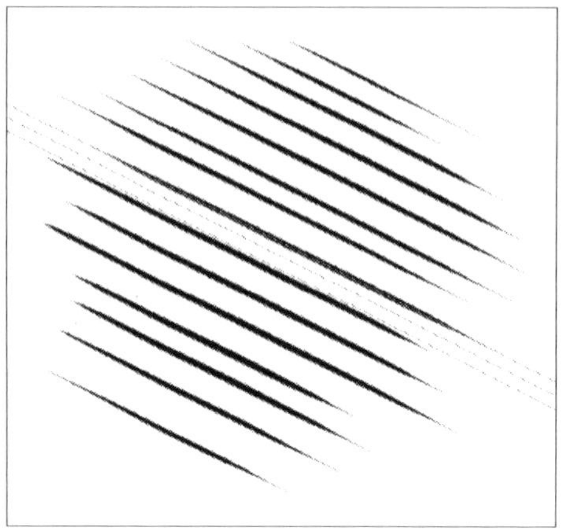

8. Turn off or discard any **Paper** color layers or any fill layers behind the parallel lines, leaving only the lines and a transparent background.
9. Select the **Operation** tool and then the **Object** subtool.
10. Click on the ruler that was created in step 4. Once it is selected, go to **Edit** | **Clear** (on the PC, right-click and select **Clear** from the window that appears) to get rid of the ruler.

> If the ruler is not cleared, the image cannot be used as a brush tip shape in step 14.

11. Go to **Edit** | **Register Image as Material**.
12. Name the material using a descriptive title.

13. Double-check the **Material image** preview to make sure that the space around the lines is transparent (it will have the same gray color as the rest of the **Material property** window).
14. Beneath the **Material image**, check the box marked **Use for brush tip shape**.
15. Choose the **Brush** folder under **Image material** to save the new material in.
16. Add some tags to the **Search tag** box. Check out the following screenshot for suggestions:

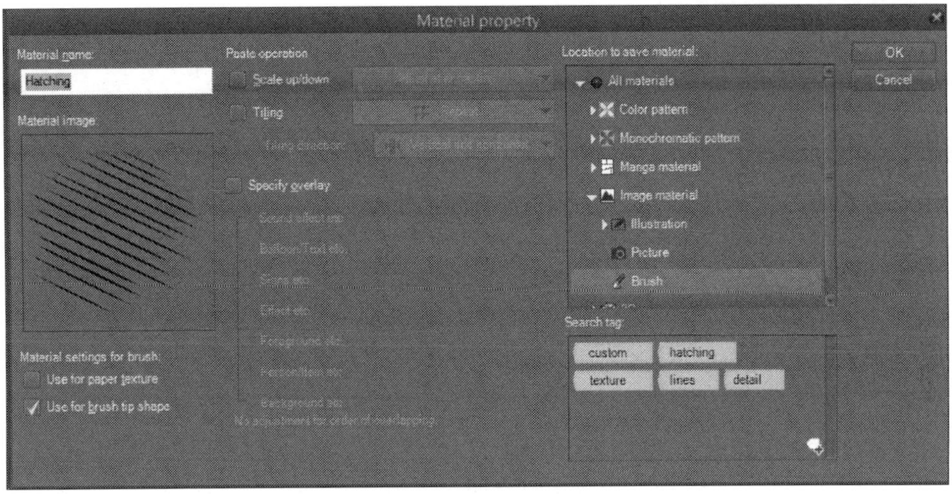

17. Click on **OK** in the **Material property** window.
18. Select the **Decoration** tool from the Manga Studio 5 toolbox.
19. Choose the **Hatching** category of decoration tools. Then select the **Cross-hatching x1** tool.
20. Click on the **Create copy of currently selected sub tool** icon in the bottom-right portion of the **Sub Tool [Decoration]** palette.
21. Give the new brush tool a descriptive title.
22. In the **Tool property** palette, click on the wrench icon in the bottom-right corner to open the **Sub Tool Detail** palette.
23. Click on the **Brush tip** option.
24. Delete the existing brush tip material by selecting it and then clicking on the delete icon under the **Material** box. The icon looks like a trash can.
25. Click on the **Add brush tip shape** icon directly to the left of the delete icon.

26. Search for and select the material created in steps 1-15 of this recipe. Click on **OK**.
27. Click on the icon next to the slider to the right of the **Direction** settings to open **Set to change parameter by pen pressure or velocity of tablet**. Deselect the checkbox next to **Random**, and click on the radio button next to **Direction of line** to activate this option.
28. Test out your new brush!

How it works...

This brush is pretty simple, especially since we can build it on an existing cross-hatching brush that comes with Manga Studio 5.

Of course, we have to make the art for our brush tip and save it as a material. After that, it's simply a matter of duplicating the prepackaged brush and customizing the duplicate. In the case of this tool, we want a look more like hand-done hatching, with the lines all going in the same direction as we use the brush, instead of the random direction that the default brush gives. Turning off the **Random** option under **Direction** gives us that look, and making the direction follow our line makes the brush easier to use in an illustration.

The following drawing was shaded using a combination of gray fill (the skin), screentones (the bulk of the hair), and the brush we just created:

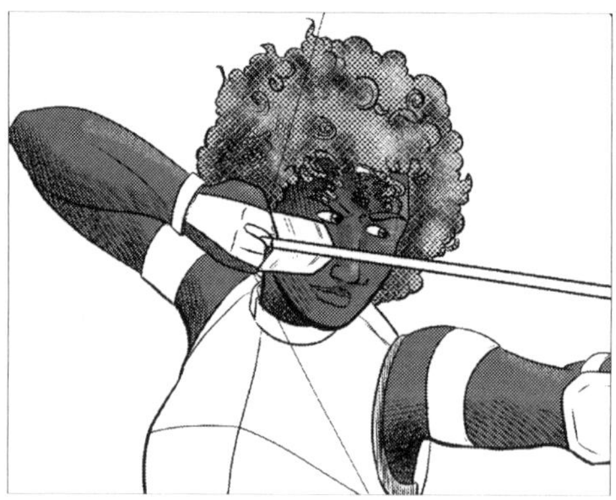

New layers were created over the gray fill and the screentone layers. On the new layers, the cross-hatching brush was then used in the direction of the shaded surface to add the shading. Change the brush tip size to larger or smaller depending on the area that you are shading.

Since we created the brush tip on a gray image, the brush is capable of being tinted too. Simply select the desired color and get to work!

Making a fabric trim brush

Let's face it. Most of us don't fancy spending our drawing time rendering patterns on cloth by hand, especially for panel after panel of a comic story! That's where Manga Studio's brushes and materials come in handy.

The brush settings from this recipe can be used for many other applications. Simply change the material and the brush will be changed! Try drawing a long, thin strip of wood grain instead of a fabric pattern, for example. The possibilities are endless.

Getting ready

The most important part of making one of these brushes is planning. Search for reference photos and decide what look you want to achieve. Look at decorative fashion trims and fabrics, and study how the pattern is put together before sitting down to make the brush. This will make it much easier to put together!

For this recipe, we'll be making a trim with a southwestern motif.

How to do it...

This recipe will walk us through the creation of a pattern brush for use for a decorative trim on a character's outfit:

> A brush like this is best for use in small areas, such as a trim on the edge of a character's coat or sleeve. For larger areas, such as plaid skirts or houndstooth coats, check out the recipes in *Chapter 7, Adding and Creating Tones and Materials*.

1. Open a new canvas with **Basic expression color** set to **Color** and at least 300 dpi resolution.
2. With your new canvas open, navigate to **View** | **Grid** to turn on the grid lines.

3. Use the grid lines as guides to assist you in drawing your chosen pattern. Almost all of the following patterns were drawn using the **Polygon** tool, which can be found by going to **Figure** | **Direct draw**. (The pattern looks complex, but in reality, it's mainly triangles! This is where the planning portion of the process helps. Without planning, the patterns look very complex to reproduce.)

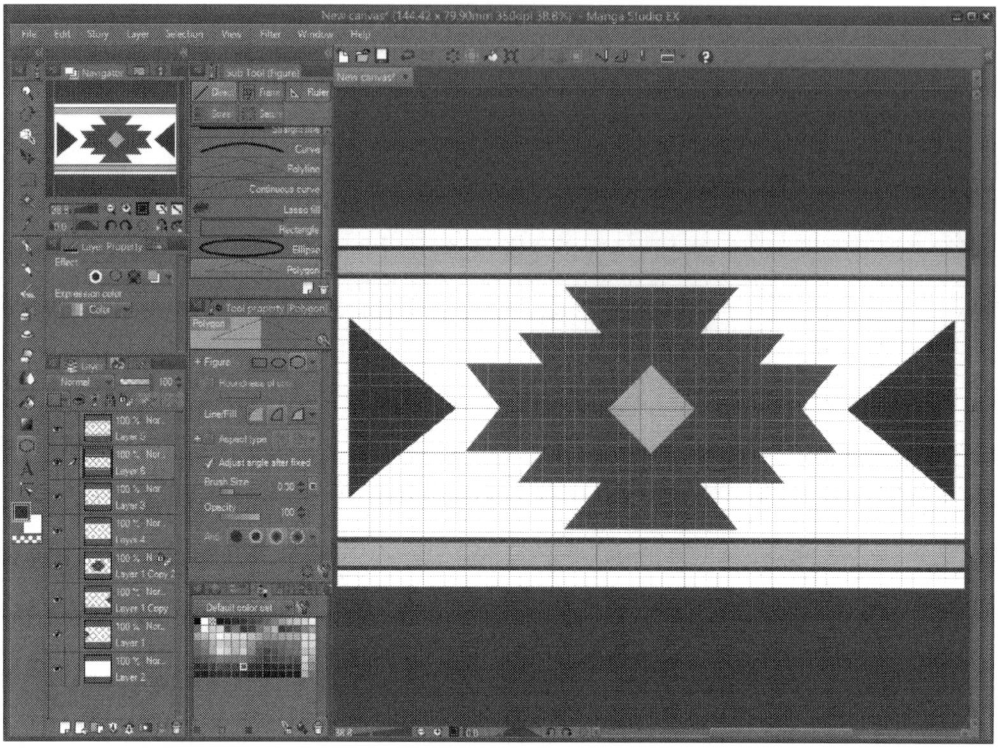

4. Combine all the layers when the pattern is completed.
5. Go to **Edit** | **Register Image as Material**.
6. Give the material a descriptive title.
7. Double-check the **Material image** preview to make sure that the space around the leaves is transparent (it will have the same gray color as the rest of the **Material property** window).
8. Beneath **Material image**, check the box marked **Use for brush tip shape**.
9. Choose the **Brush** folder, which is under **Image material**, to save the new material in.

10. Add some tags to the **Search tag** box. Refer to the following screenshot for suggestions:

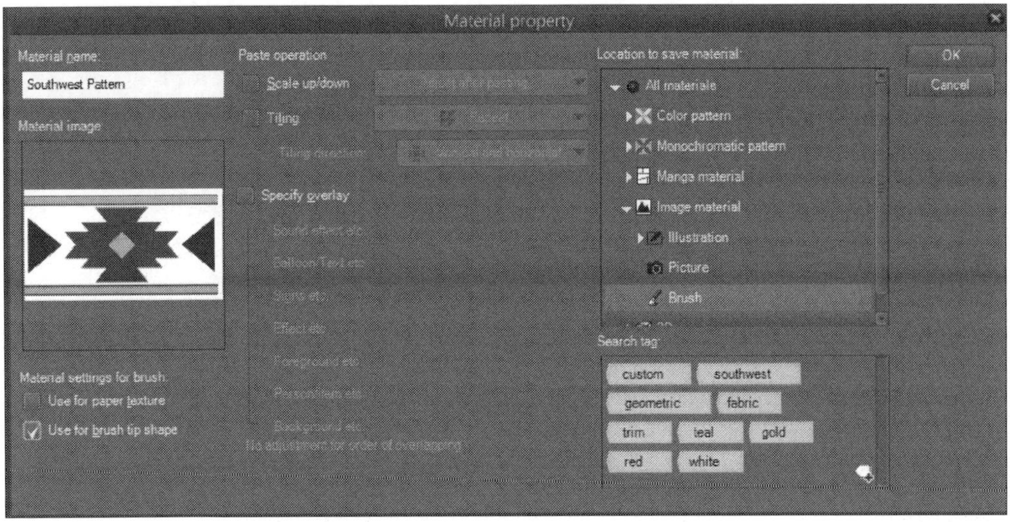

11. Click on **OK** in the **Material Property** window.
12. Select the **Decoration** tool from the Manga Studio 5 toolbox.
13. Choose the **Clothing** category of decoration tools. Then select the **Tirolean Tape** tool.
14. Click on the **Create copy of currently selected sub tool** icon in the bottom-right part of the **Sub Tool [Decoration]** Palette.
15. Name the new brush tool using a descriptive title.
16. In the **Tool property** palette, click on the wrench icon in the bottom-right corner to open the **Sub Tool Detail** palette.
17. Click on the **Brush tip** option.

18. Delete the existing brush tip materials by selecting them one at a time and then clicking on the **Delete selected brush tip shape** icon under the **Material** box. The delete icon is circled here:

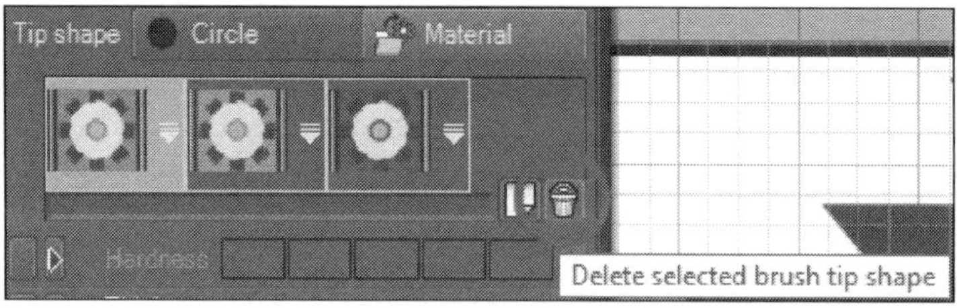

19. Click on the **Add brush tip shape** icon directly to the left of the delete icon.
20. Search for and select the material created in steps 1-11 of this recipe. Click on **OK**.
21. If your brush tip material is not oriented correctly, change the **Direction** settings under **Brush tip**. In the example shown here, the **Direction** value was set to `90` to make the material appear horizontal:

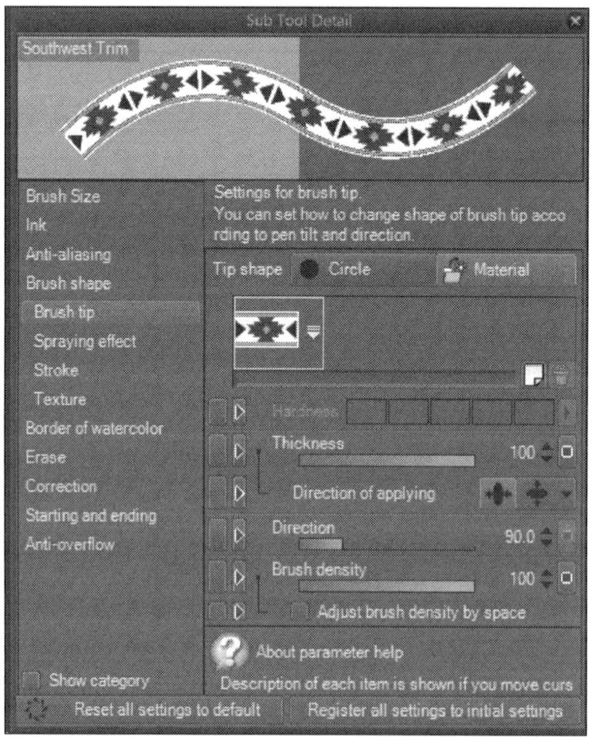

22. Click on the **Stroke** option on the left-hand side of the window. Make sure that the **Ribbon** checkbox is ticked. The following screenshot shows this setting:

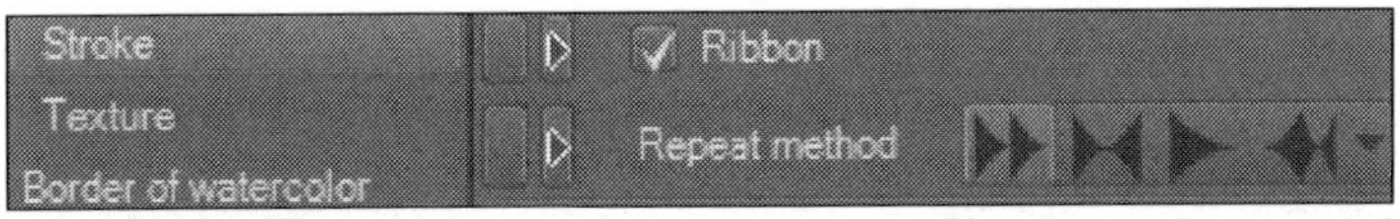

23. Test your new brush!

How it works...

By making this brush from a brush that is already set up as **Ribbon**, we save time setting it up. Less time messing around with the brush options means more time to work on art!

This screenshot shows the brush made in this recipe at work, as the band of this explorer's hat:

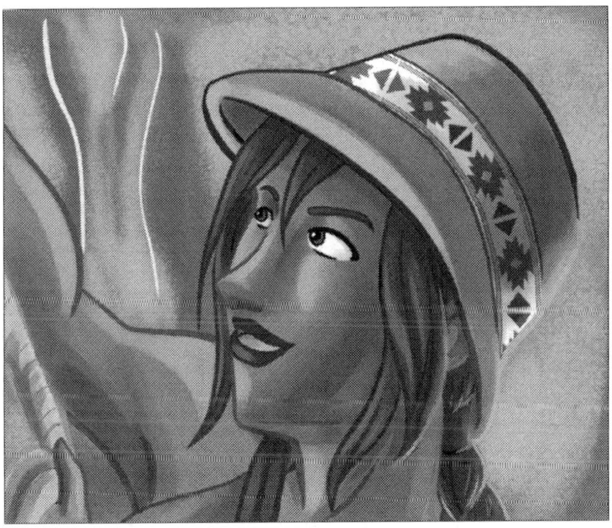

The shading on the brush details was achieved by making a layer above the trim, setting it to the **Multiply** layer mode, and shading with a desaturated brown. The highlights for the preceding drawing were done on a **Screen** layer mode with a bluish-white color. Both the shading and the highlight layers were set to about 50 percent opacity.

> With brushes such as these, practicing using them makes you perfect. It takes several passes to get the brush stroke right. Don't be afraid to undo and start over again! Layers of shading also help make the details look less "pasted on" and more as if they were drawn on by hand.

See also

- The *Creating and saving custom materials* recipe in *Chapter 7, Adding and Creating Tones and Materials*
- The *Drawing a custom fabric pattern* recipe in *Chapter 7, Adding and Creating Tones and Materials*
- The *Using Mesh Transformation to apply more realistic fabric patterns* recipe in *Chapter 7, Adding and Creating Tones and Materials*

Making a ruffle brush

By building on the **Simple frill** tool (found under the **Clothing** subtool in the **Decoration**) as a guide, we'll create a ruffled brush suitable for a magical girl or a sweet Lolita outfit!

Getting ready

To start off, we'll need a blank canvas of at least 300 dpi. This screenshot shows the height, width, and dpi settings for the canvas used in this recipe:

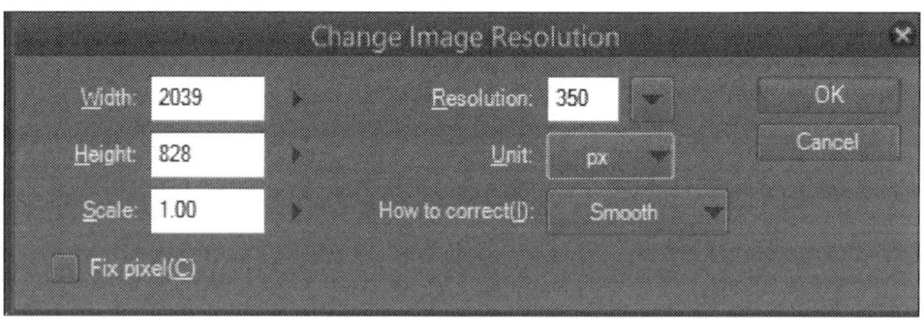

How to do it...

Here are the steps to be performed to make a frilly, fluffy brush for use in your art:

1. First, we need to draw our ruffle for the brush tip. Start by going to **View** | **Grid** to make grid lines visible on the canvas.
2. On a new raster layer, draw a wavy, uneven line near the bottom of the canvas. This line should touch the sides of the canvas on the same grid line on both the left and the right sides. Refer to the following screenshot for an example:

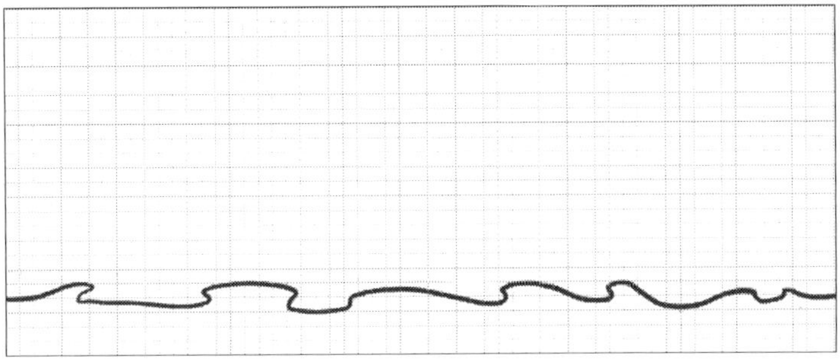

3. Draw lines up from the curves on this line to make gathers in the fabric. Refer to this screenshot to understand how to do it:

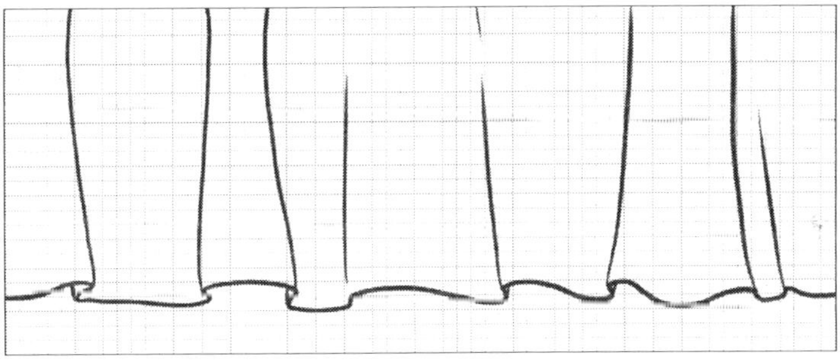

4. Any parts of the main line where it curves under itself should have a short line drawn upward from the tip of the curve to the main line. This is where the fabric curls up under itself as it gathers in the ruffles. Check out the following screenshot to understand this better:

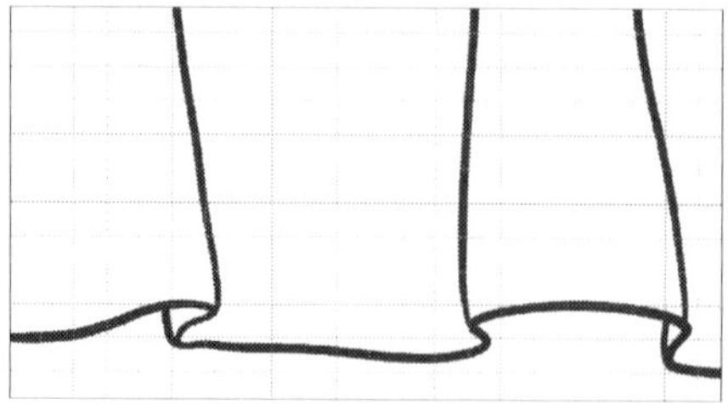

5. Delete the **Paper** color layer, if applicable. The canvas should now have the outlines of the ruffles and a transparent background.
6. Create a new layer beneath the ruffle outlines. Fill the ruffle outlines with white. Now the image should have a white ruffle with black outlines and a transparent background, as shown in this screenshot:

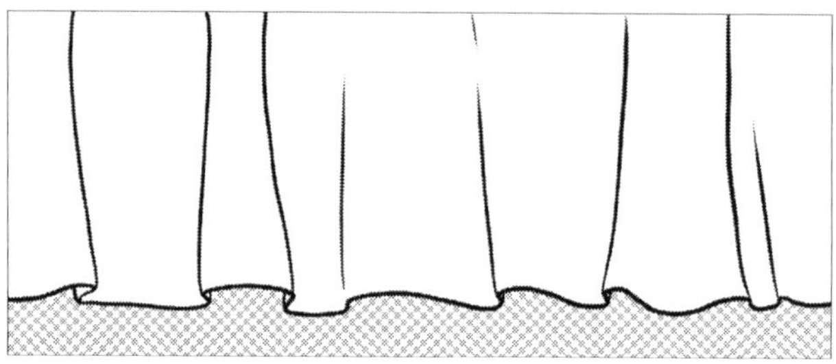

> At this point, we may want to check whether our ruffle pattern is going to repeat seamlessly when we make it into a brush. One way of doing this is by exporting the current image as an image file. Open the exported image and then navigate to **Edit | Change Canvas Size**. Multiply the width by 2 and enter the new width. Select either the left or the right edge of the canvas to scale from by clicking on the appropriate box on the grid. Then, duplicate the image and drag it with the **Move Layer** tool so that the left edge of one copy is up against the right edge of another. By doing this, we can catch any spots where the pattern does not match up. While performing this recipe, I discovered that I needed to thicken the line on the left-hand side of my ruffles. This was because the lines did not match up perfectly, as shown here:
>
> 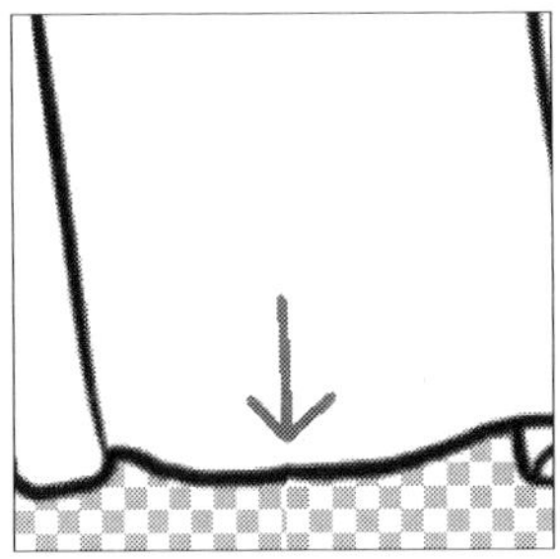

7. Create a new raster layer above the white fill layer. Select a light gray color.
8. Shade the ruffles using your preferred method, making sure that you pay attention to where the fabric bends back on itself, as these areas would be in shadows. The following screenshot shows how to make a selection with the **Lasso Marquee** tool and fill it with light gray:

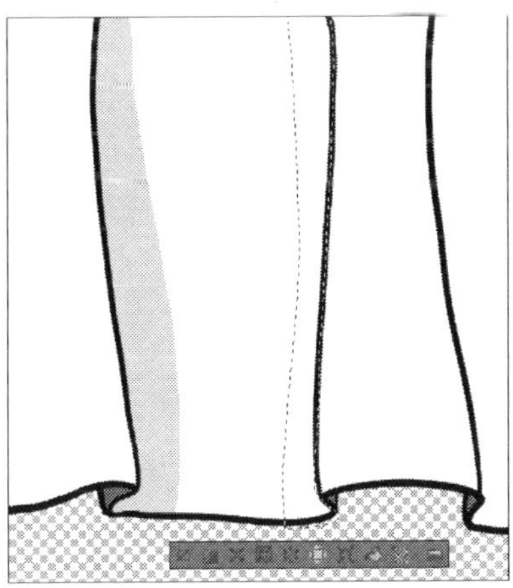

9. Continue adding details until you are satisfied. In the next screenshot, shading has been added to the top edge of the ruffles to complete the "gathered fabric" look:

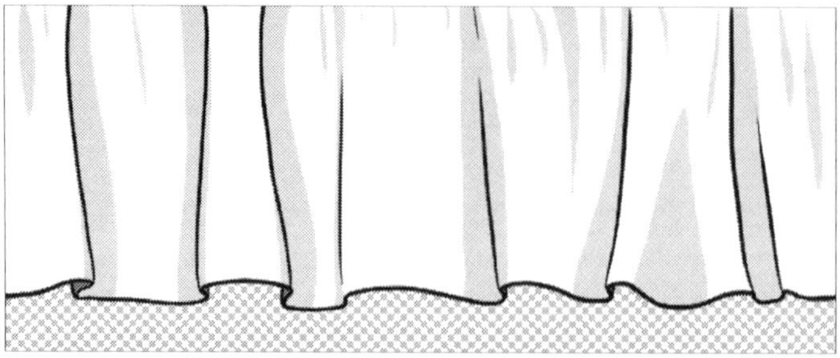

10. Once the ruffle artwork has been completed, navigate to **Layer** | **Merge Layers** to combine the art into a single layer. The background should still be transparent!
11. Go to **Edit** | **Register Image as Material**.
12. Give the material a descriptive title.
13. Double-check the **Material image** preview to make sure that the space around the leaves is transparent (it will have the same gray color as the rest of the **Material property** window).
14. Beneath **Material image**, check the box marked **Use for brush tip shape**.
15. Choose the **Brush** folder, which is under **Image material**, to save the new material in.
16. Add a few tags to the **Search tag** box. Refer to the following screenshot for suggestions:

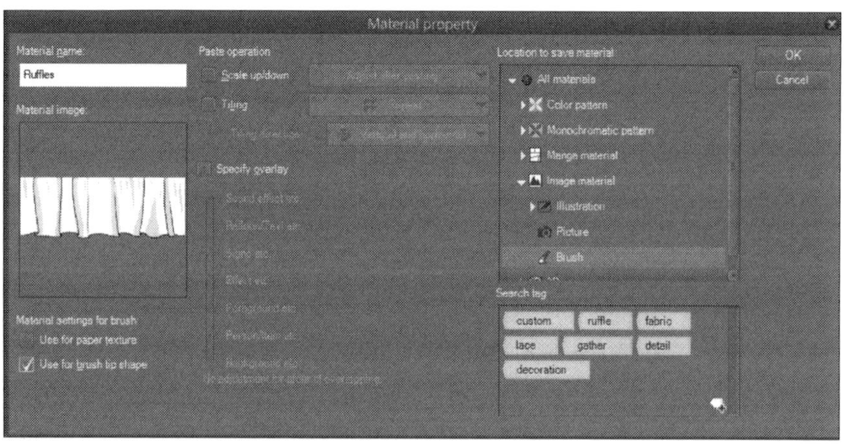

17. Click on **OK** in the **Material property** window.
18. Select the **Decoration** tool from the Manga Studio 5 toolbox.
19. Choose the **Clothing** category of **Decoration** tools. Then select the **Simple frill** tool.
20. Click on the **Create copy of currently selected sub tool** icon in the bottom-right part of the **Sub Tool [Decoration]** palette.
21. Name the new brush tool using a descriptive title.
22. In the **Tool property** palette, click on the wrench icon in the bottom-right corner to open the **Sub Tool Detail** palette.
23. Click on the **Brush tip** option.
24. Delete the existing brush tip materials by selecting them one at a time and then clicking on the **Delete selected brush tip shape** icon under the **Material** box.
25. Click on the **Add brush tip shape** icon directly to the left of the delete icon.
26. Search for and select the material created in steps 1-18 of this recipe. Click on **OK**.
27. There should not be any other settings to change, because the **Simple frill** brush is already set to the **Ribbon** stroke option. Test out your new brush! Shown here is a screenshot from a test to see whether the brush settings are correct:

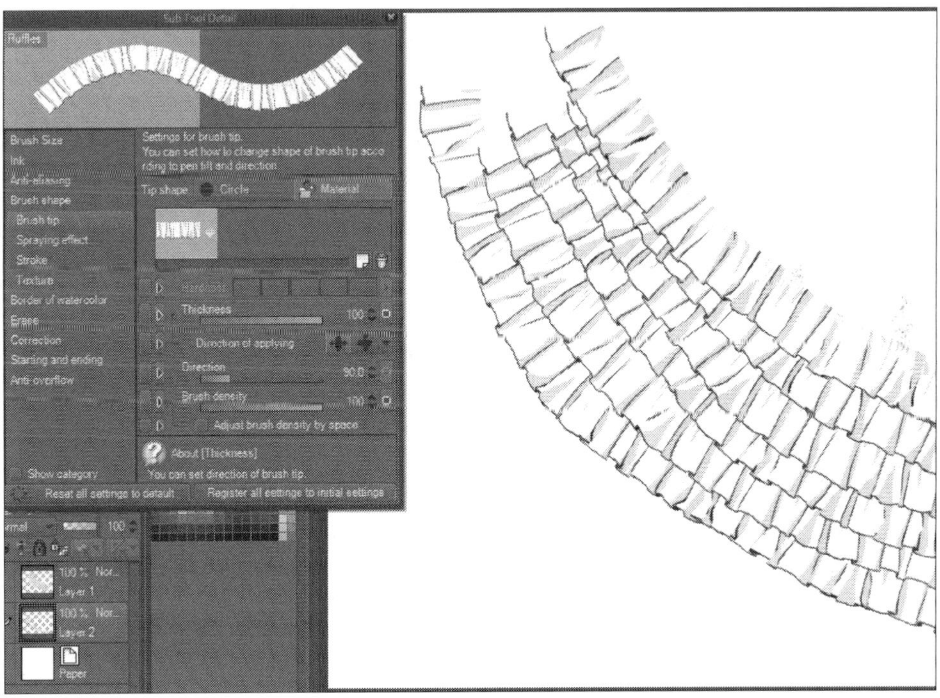

How it works...

Using the grid lines, we ensure that the sides of the ruffle pattern will line up and repeat seamlessly. After all, we don't want a bumpy, lumpy seam in our cute ruffles! This is the same concept as the one when we used the grid to draw our custom material in the *Creating a cracked detail brush* and *Making a fabric trim brush* recipes.

As an illustration of a potential application of this brush, here is a screenshot of a three-tiered, Lolita-style skirt that uses our ruffle brush between each tier:

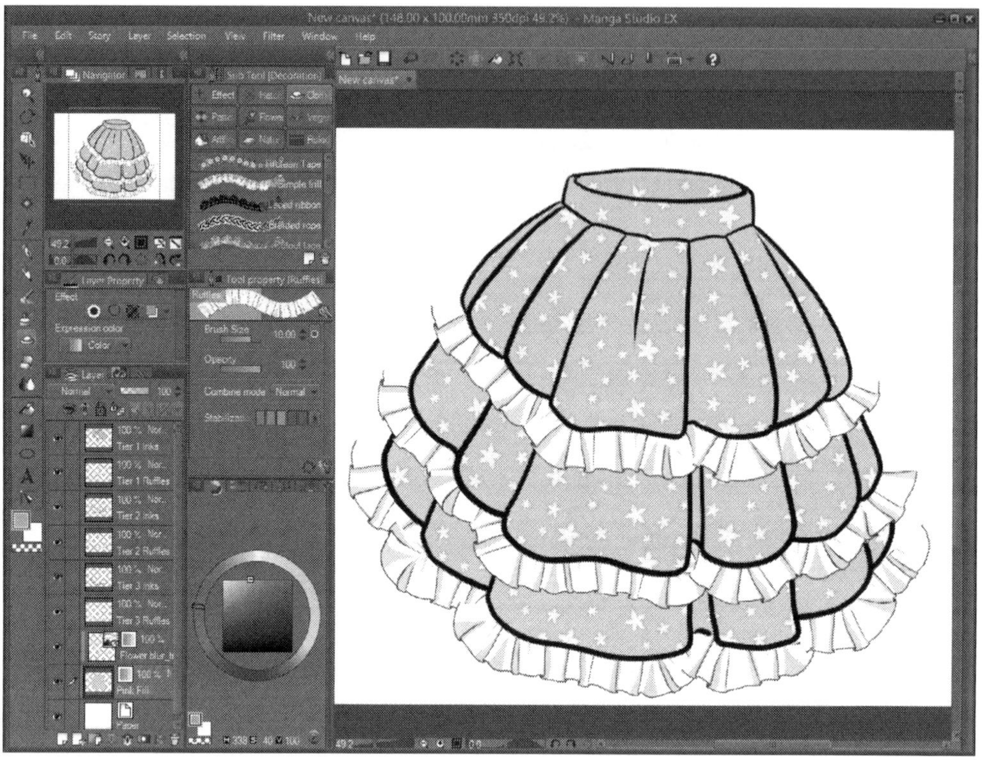

The individual tiers are each inked on their own layers. Then, between each layer of outlining, the ruffle brush has been used to add a single layer of detail. The pink fill color and the cherry blossom pattern are their own layers each, underneath the outlines of the tiers and the layers with the ruffle brush application on them.

Complete the image with finishing touches and the illustration is ready to go!

Making a brick brush

In this recipe, we're going to create a brush that we can use to obtain the look of a brick wall.

Getting ready

To start with, we'll need to create a blank canvas. For this recipe, I've used the postcard horizontal (350 dpi) default template. Set **Basic expression color** to **Color**.

How to do it...

You may find that this brush requires some additional experimentation before you get the look that you want. I hope this recipe will give you at least a starting point to take off from:

1. With the blank canvas open, go to **Figure** | **Direct draw** | **Rectangle** from the toolbox.
2. In the **Tool property** palette, check the box next to **Roundness of corner** and set the value to `2.0` using the slider. The location of the **Roundness of corner** option is shown in this screenshot:

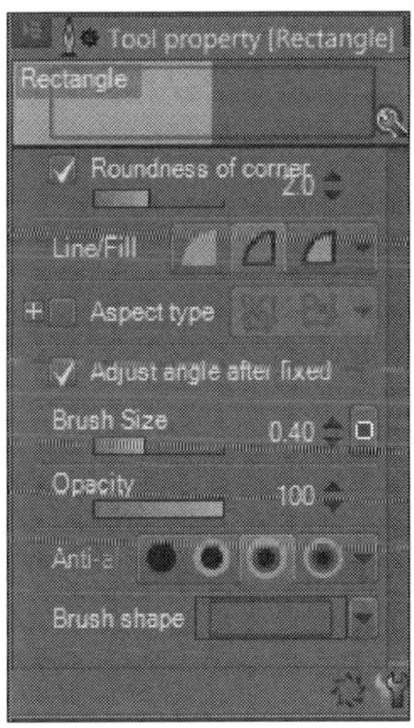

3. Set a value of `4.0` for **Brush Size**.
4. Draw a rectangle by clicking inside of the canvas area and dragging while holding down the mouse button. Release the mouse button when the desired rectangle size is reached.

> If the **Adjust angle after fixed** box is checked in the **Tool property** palette, you will have to click once more to confirm. Not doing so will adjust the rotation of the rectangle:

5. Select the **Rectangle Marquee** tool. Drag a selection around the rectangle you just created.
6. In the **Selection** toolbar, directly beneath the "marching ants" of the marquee selection, click on the **Scale Up/Scale Down/Rotate** icon (seventh from the left).
7. A set of handles and a bounding box will appear around the rectangle marquee selection. With this active, check the box next to **Keep the original image** in the **Tool property** palette. The following screenshot shows the handles and the bounding box on the right, and the location of the **Keep the original image** checkbox on the left:

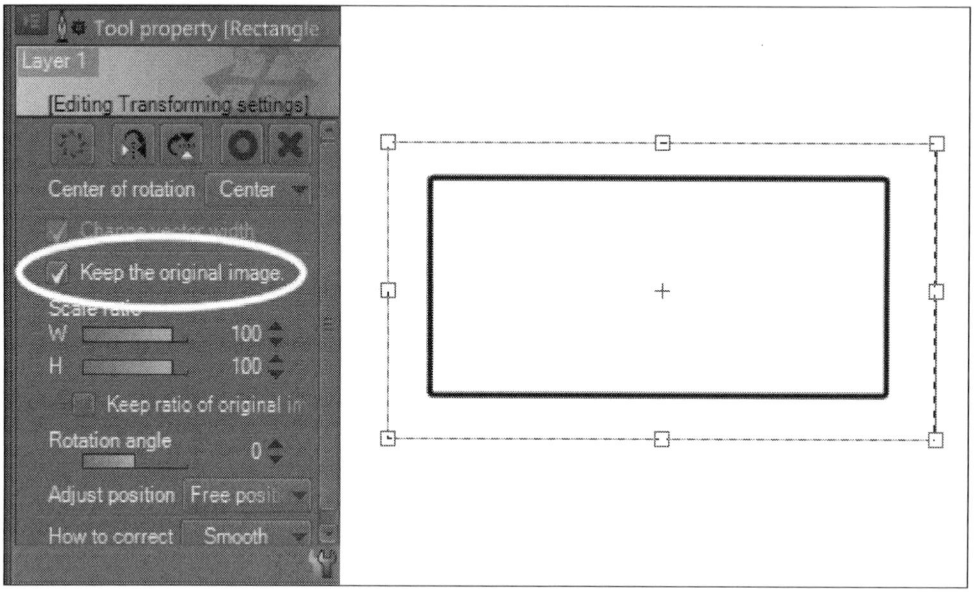

8. Click inside the bounding box and drag to the right while still holding down the mouse button. A second rectangle will appear next to the first.

9. Continue selecting and duplicating rectangles to make brick patterns. These will become our brush tip materials. Check out the screenshot given here to see the brick patterns made for this recipe:

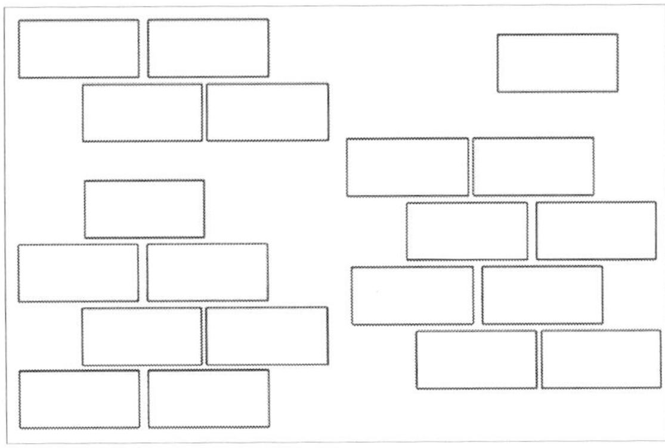

10. Now we will start making our rectangles look more like bricks. Create a new layer above the layer with the brick patterns. Select one of the brick patterns to focus on. Use the rectangles as a "sketch" and ink over the brick shape, making the outline uneven. Add a texture with the **Charcoal** subtool (this is found by going to **Pencil | Pastel**), if desired. The following screenshot shows one of the completed brick patterns created for this recipe:

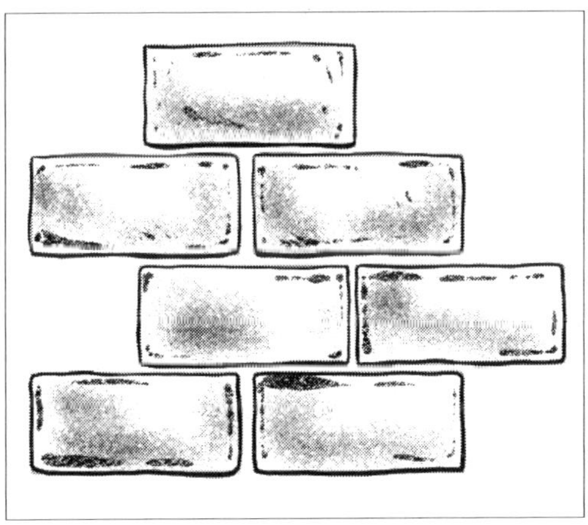

11. Continue step 6 for each brick pattern, drawing each on its own separate layer.
12. Turn off any **Paper** layers by clicking on the eye icon to the left of the layer name in the **Layer** palette.

13. Follow step 8 for all but one layer of the brick patterns.
14. Go to **Edit** | **Register Image as Material**.
15. In the **Material property** window, name your new material. Select the **Brush** folder under **Image material** to store it in.
16. Check the box under the **Material image** preview that says **Use for brush tip shape**.
17. Add tags by clicking on the tag and the **+** sign icon in the bottom-right corner of the **Search tag** box. Check out this screenshot to understand what your **Material property** screen should look like:

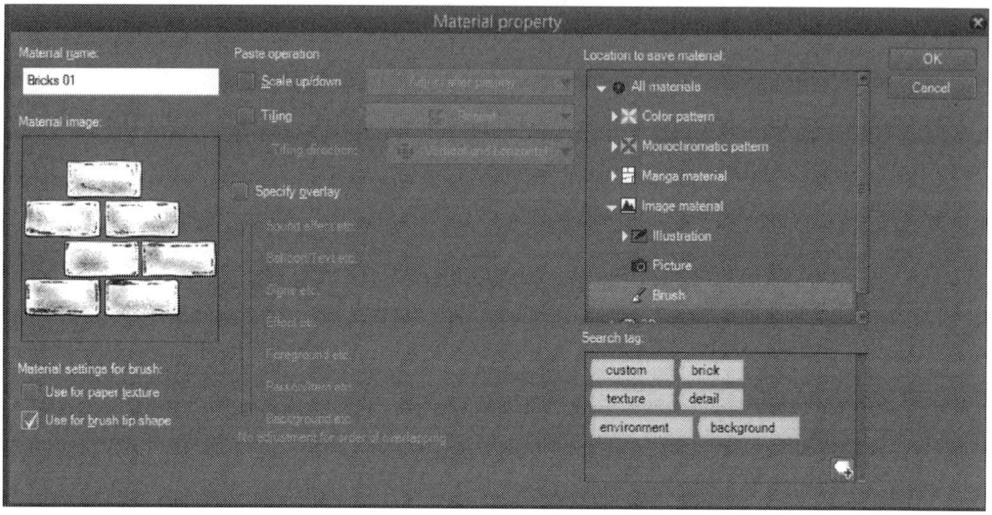

18. Turn off the currently active layer. Make the next layer visible and active in the **Layers** palette.
19. Repeat steps 10-14 for every remaining layer of the brick pattern.
20. Select the **Decoration** tool from the Manga Studio 5 toolbox.
21. Choose the **Artificial** category of decoration tools. Then select the **Rubble** tool.
22. Click on the **Create copy of currently selected sub tool** icon in the bottom-right portion of the **Sub Tool [Decoration]** palette.

23. Name the new brush tool using a descriptive title. Refer to the following screenshot for a suggestion:

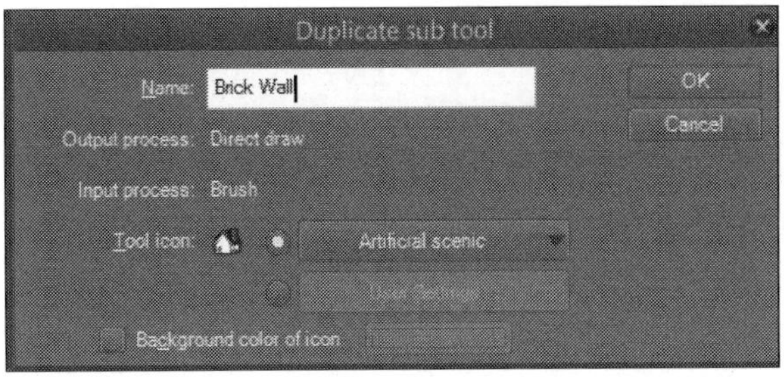

24. In the **Tool property** palette, click on the wrench icon in the bottom-right corner to open the **Sub Tool Detail** palette.
25. Click on the **Brush tip** option.
26. Delete the existing brush tip materials by selecting them one at a time and then clicking on the **Delete selected brush tip shape** icon under the **Material** box.
27. Click on the **Add brush tip shape** icon directly to the left of the delete icon.
28. Search for and select a material created in steps 1-19 of this recipe. When selected, the material will be highlighted, as shown in the following screenshot:

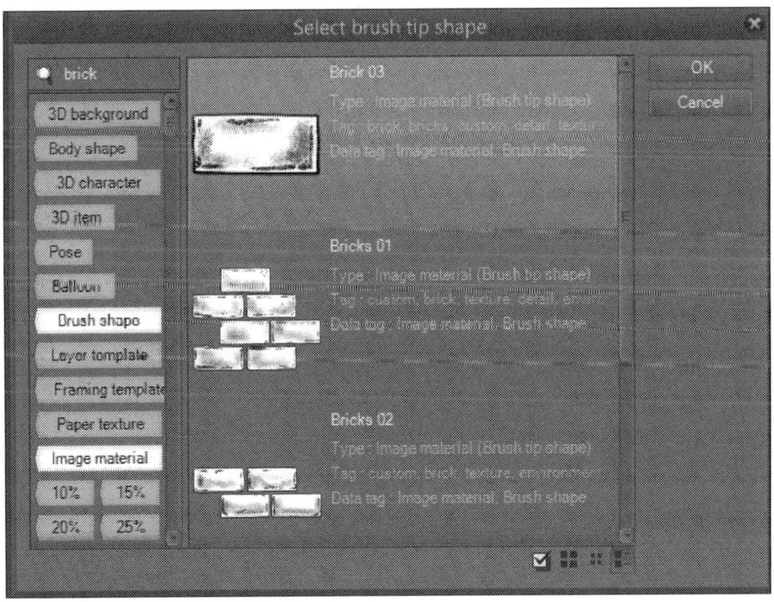

29. Click on **OK**.
30. Repeat steps 23-25 as needed to add all the brick patterns to the brush tip materials.
31. Click on the dark gray box to the far right of the **Direction** option under **Brush tip**. Click on the radio button next to **None** to select it. If the checkbox next to the **Random** option is selected, click on it to deselect it. Here is a screenshot that shows the location of this menu:

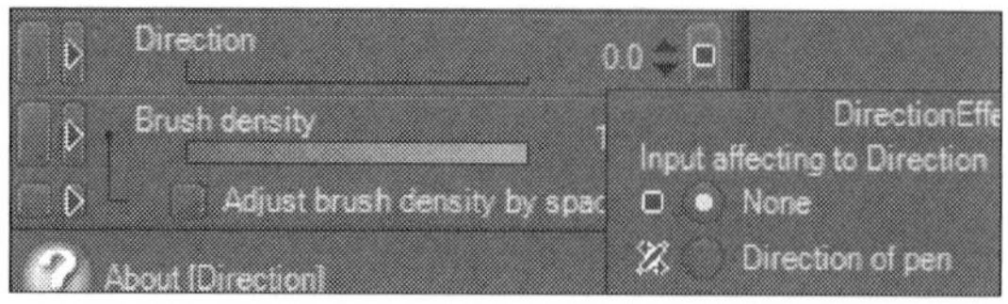

32. The **Brush tip** options should now be the same as what is shown in the following screenshot:

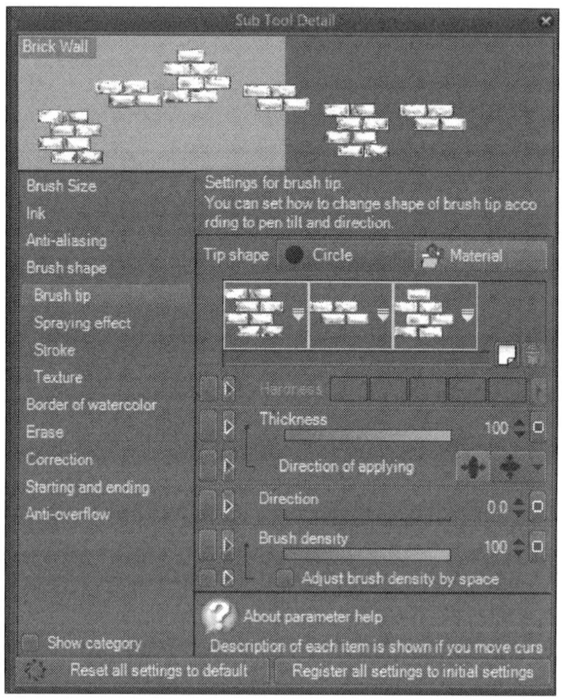

33. Click on the **Stroke** option in the left-hand side menu of the **Sub Tool Detail** screen.
34. Set the **Gap** slider to a value that leaves some space between each occurrence of **Brush tip**. This will vary depending on the size that the brush tip materials were drawn in at the beginning of this recipe. The **Gap** value used in this recipe is `136`.
35. Click on the dark gray box to the far right of the **Gap** option. Then click on the checkbox next to **Pen pressure**. Set the minimum value to `100`. On the same screen, click on the checkbox next to the **Random** option. Set the minimum value to `60`. Refer to this screenshot:

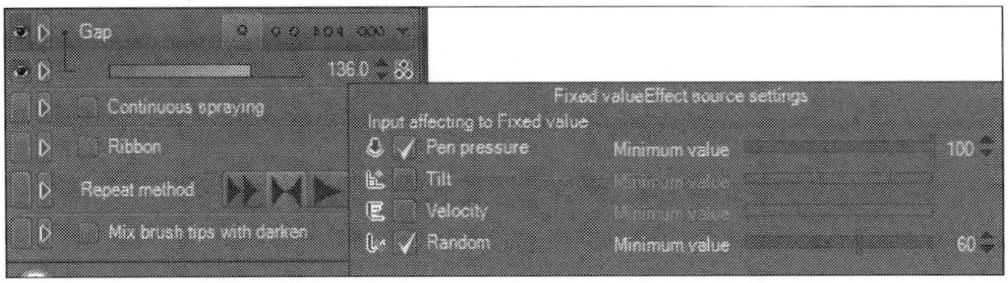

36. Set **Repeat method** to **Reverse** by clicking on the second icon next to the option. It is highlighted in the following screenshot:

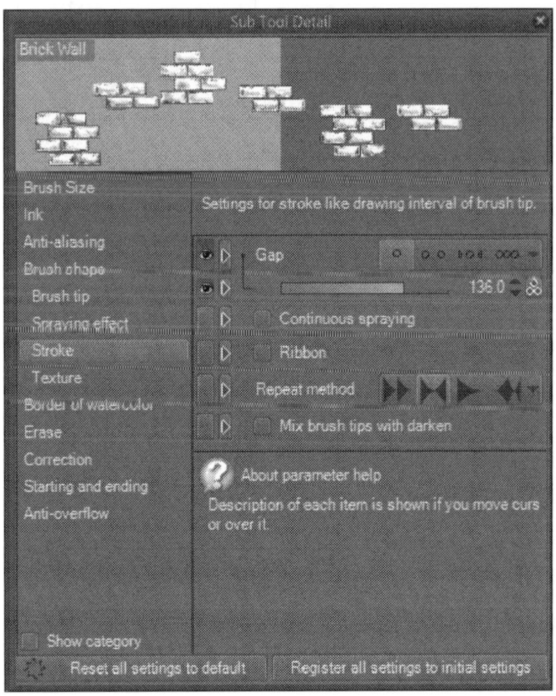

37. Test your brush and make adjustments as needed to fit your personal tastes!

How it works...

This brush works best in small doses, as a little detail on a background drawing perhaps. Distant buildings that need just a bit of brick detailing will benefit from this brush. Be patient while using it, and don't be afraid to experiment with the brush settings or add or take away some brush tip materials!

The following is an illustration made with this brush used in the background. I went for straight lines back and forth over the entire background. Then, an orange-to-rust-colored gradient was added. The brick outlines were lowered to about 60 percent opacity to fade them more into the background and make them less obtrusive.

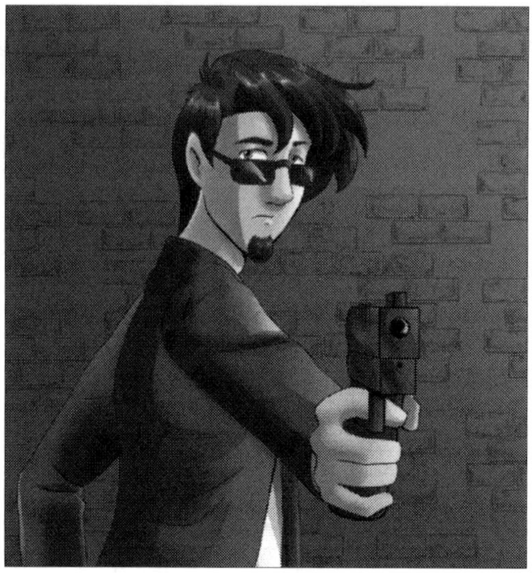

Blowing up an explosion brush

Sometimes, in comics and illustrations, you may just find that something you're drawing needs to be blown up. This brush can also be used for a billowing smoke effect!

Getting ready

Create a new canvas of at least 300 dpi resolution. Make sure that **Basic expression color** is set to **Gray**.

How to do it...

The following steps will walk us through the use of the spraying effect options to create a brush that looks like an explosion:

1. On the blank canvas, mark the general shape of the smoke cloud for the explosion. The following screenshot shows this, done by going to **Brush** | **India ink** | **Darker bleed** and using a pure black color:

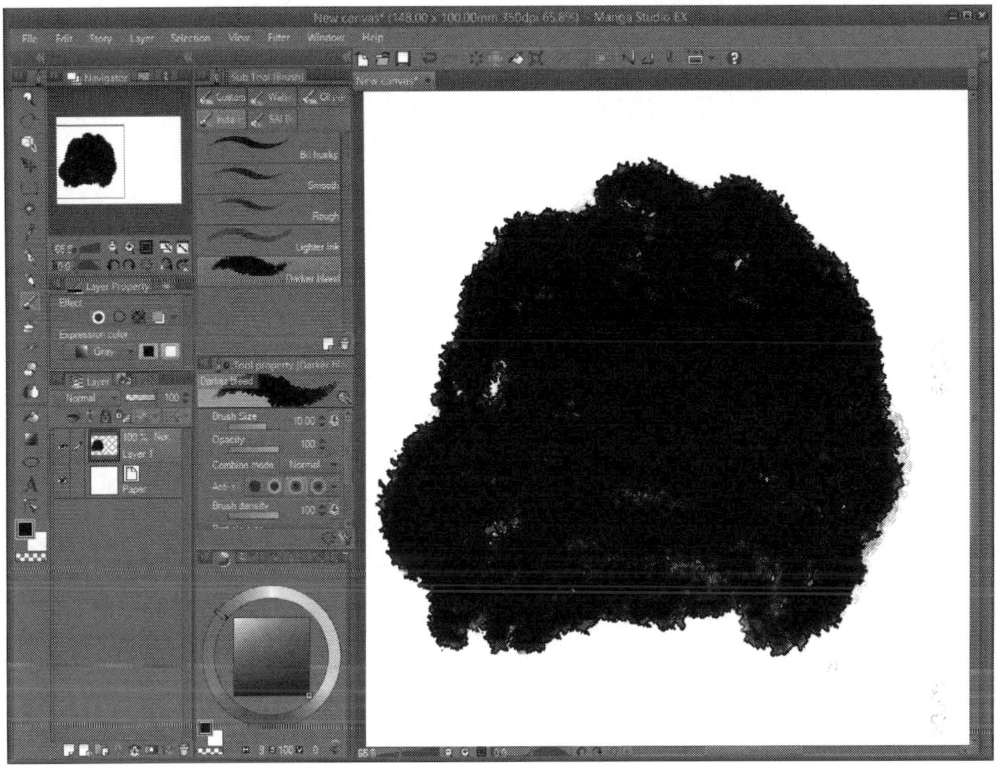

2. Using the **India ink** or pen tools, continue adding details until you are satisfied with the look of the explosion cloud. As shown in the following screenshot, the **Lighter ink** tool (which can be found under **India ink**) with black was used to obtain the gray shading. Then, **G-pen** was used in both black and white to add more details:

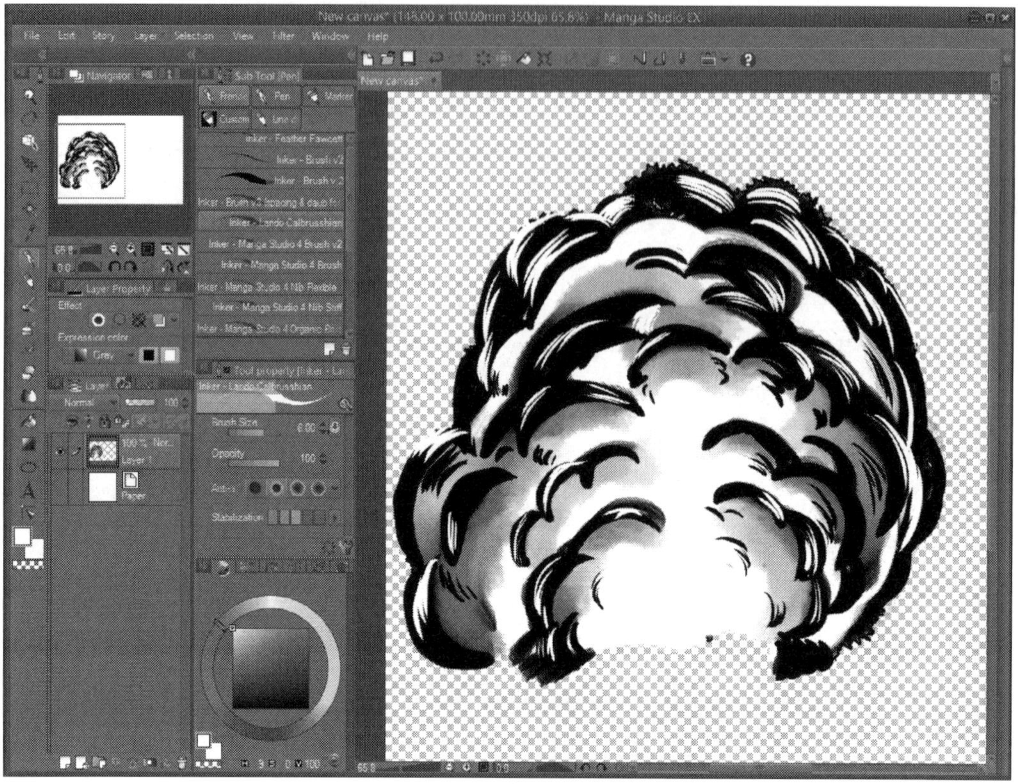

3. On a new layer, create a second explosion shape, using the same techniques and tools as before. Here is a screenshot that shows both the shapes created for this recipe:

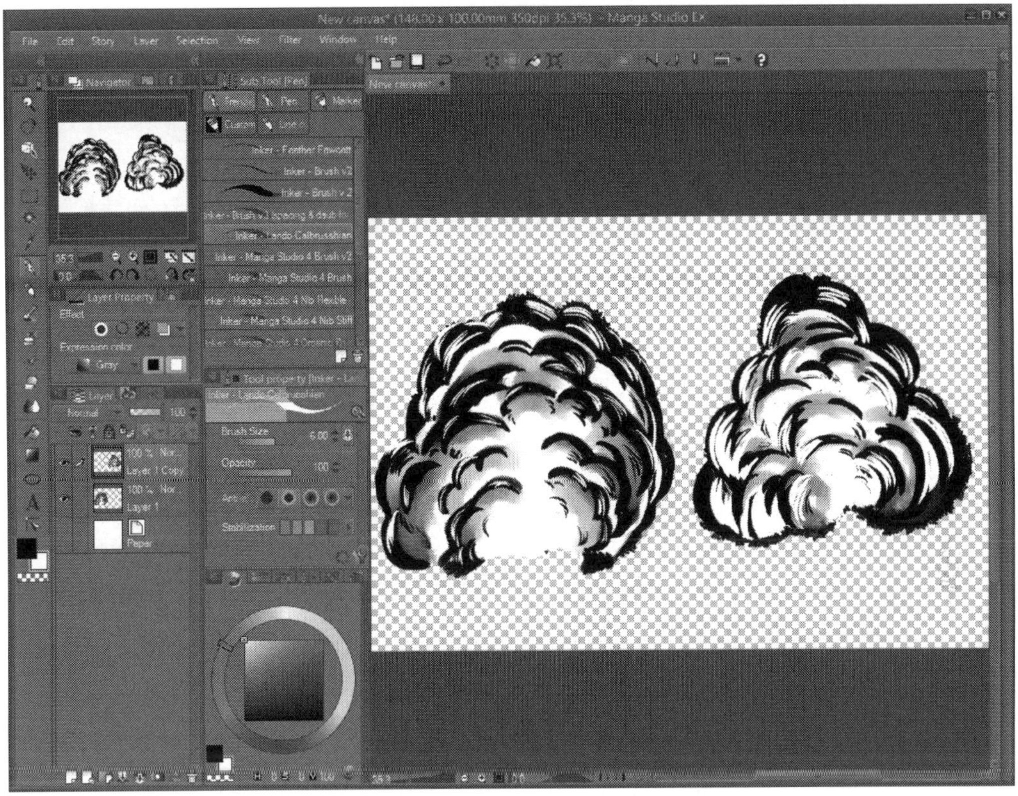

4. Turn off one layer so that only one of the explosion shapes is shown. Remember that they should both be on separate layers! Click on the visible layer to select it (highlight it in blue), if it is not already the active layer.
5. Go to **Edit** | **Register Image as Material**.
6. In the **Material property** window, name your new material. Select the **Brush** folder under **Image material** to store it in.
7. Check the box under the **Material image** preview that says **Use for brush tip shape**.

8. Add tags by clicking on the tag and the **+** sign icon in the bottom-right corner of the **Search tag** box. Check out the following screenshot to see what your **Material property** screen should look like:

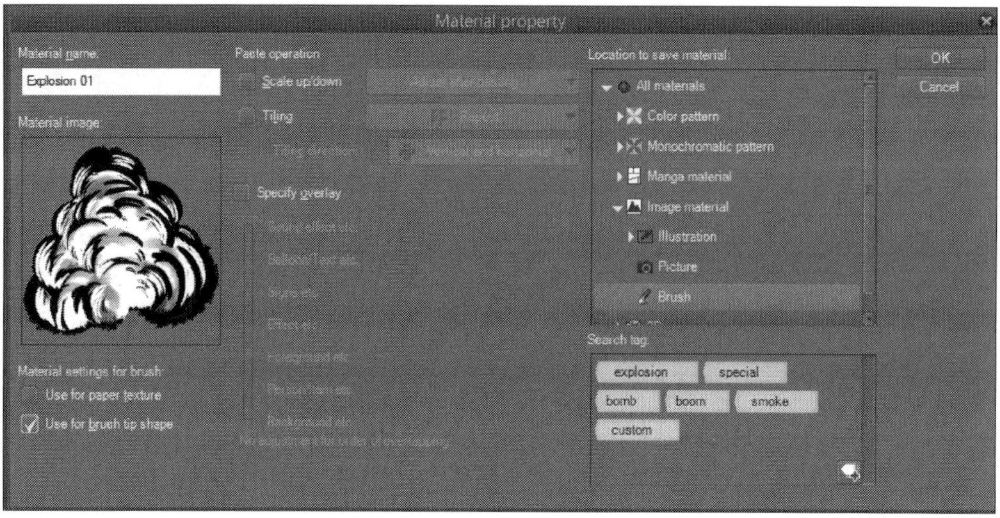

9. Turn off the currently active layer. Make the next layer visible and active in the **Layers** palette.
10. Repeat steps 5-7 for every remaining layer.
11. Select the **Decoration** tool from the Manga Studio 5 toolbox.
12. Choose the **Effect** category of decoration tools. Then select the **Heart color** tool.
13. Click on the **Create copy of currently selected sub tool** icon in the bottom-right portion of the **Sub Tool [Decoration]** palette.
14. Name the new brush tool using a descriptive title.
15. In the **Tool property** palette, click on the wrench icon in the bottom-right corner to open the **Sub Tool Detail** palette.
16. Click on the **Brush tip** option.
17. Delete the existing brush tip materials by selecting them one at a time and then clicking on the **Delete selected brush tip shape** icon under the **Material** box.
18. Click on the **Add brush tip shape** icon directly to the left of the delete icon.
19. Search for and select the materials created in steps 1-10 of this recipe. Click on **OK**.

20. Click on the gray box to the far right of the **Brush density** settings and uncheck the box marked **Random**.
21. Ensure that the **Brush tip** settings are the same as what is shown in this screenshot:

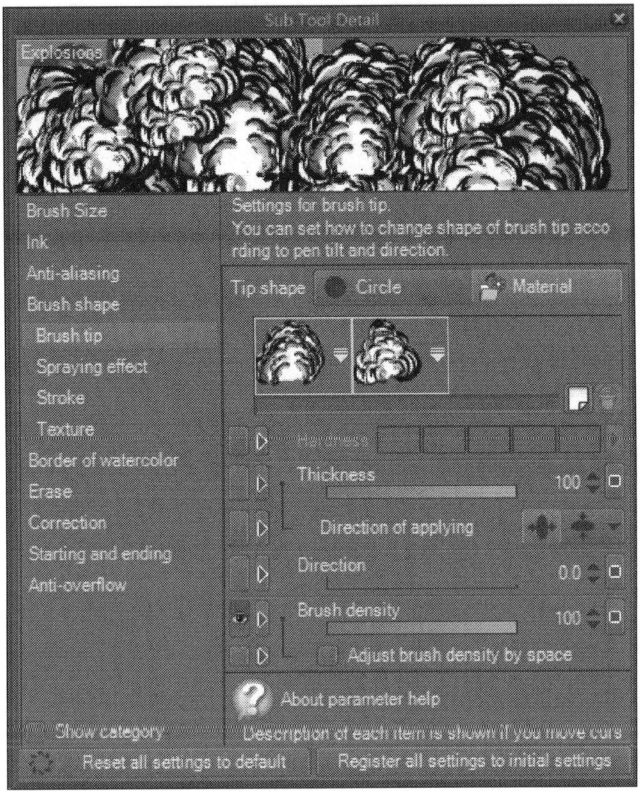

22. Click on the **Spraying effect** settings on the left-hand side of the **Sub Tool Detail** screen.
23. Set **Particle size** to `85` (this number may vary, depending on the size of your brush tip material).
24. Click on the right-facing arrow next to **Particle density** to open the text entry box, shown in the following screenshot. Enter a value of `16`, like this:

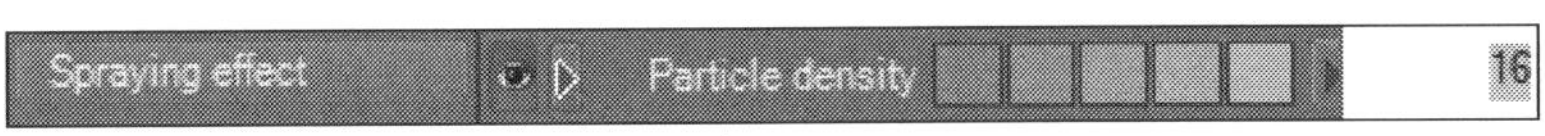

25. Then click on the right-facing arrow next to **Spray deviation** to open the text entry box. Enter a value of `100`, as shown here:

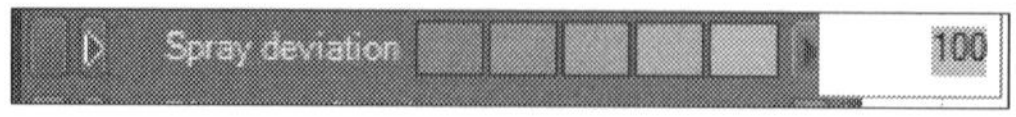

26. The **Spraying effect** window should now look like what is shown in the following screenshot:

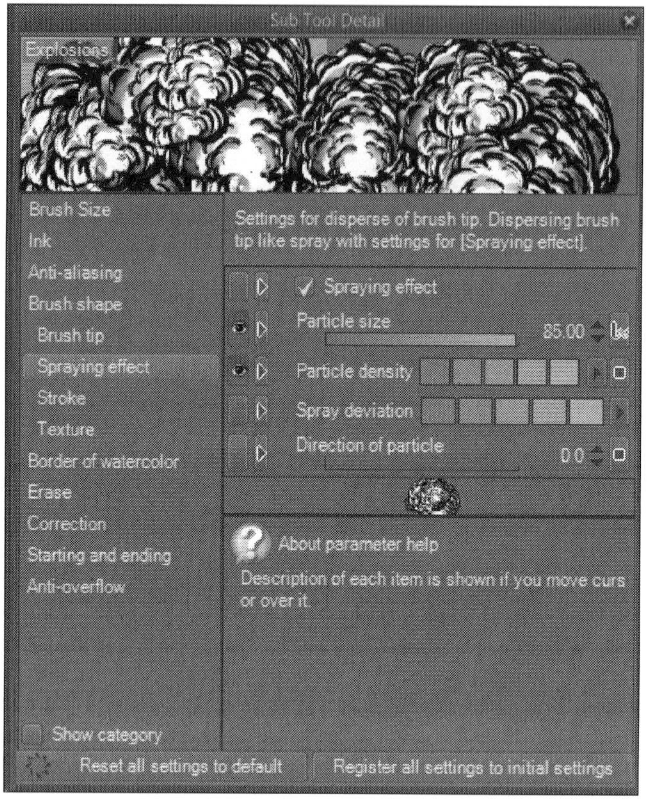

27. Click on the **Stroke** option in the left-hand side menu in the **Sub Tool Detail** window.

28. Set the **Gap** option to **Fixed** by clicking on the first circle icon. Then set the slider below it to `95.0`, as shown in this screenshot:

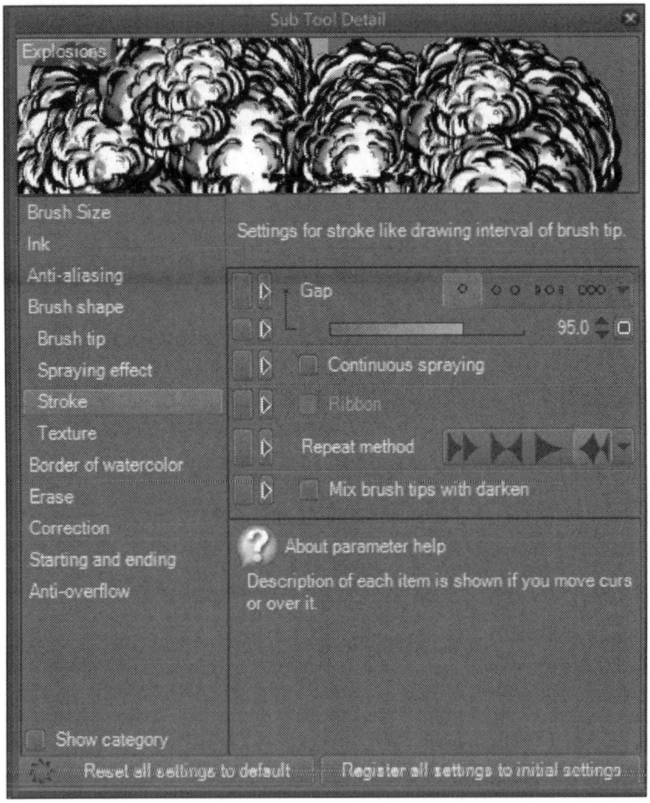

29. Test your new brush!

How it works...

By using the **Spraying effect** options, we get a more random look for the brush. The "particles" (the brush tip materials) get sprayed over the canvas instead of following the line of the brush tightly and making a stroke. This allows us to get a chaotic, random look.

With a little creativity, the possibilities for this brush are pretty much limitless. The following drawing was made by layering a red-yellow gradient in a layer over the brush. The gradient layer was set to **Color burn**. Then, focus lines were added in white on the top and set to 50 percent opacity to complete the exploding fireball look!

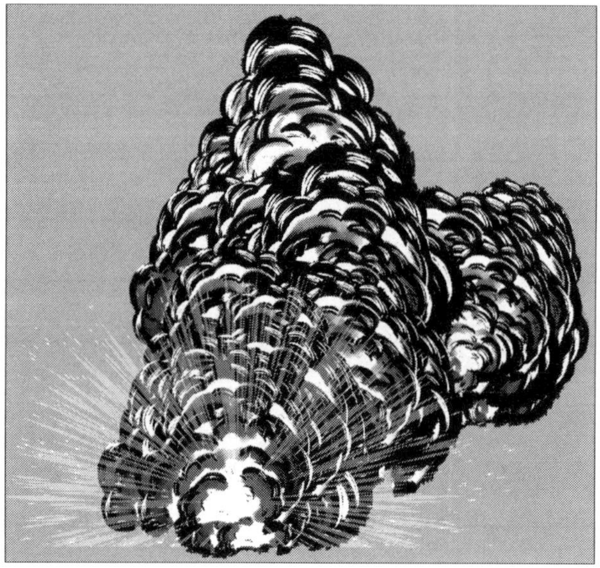

See also

- The *Using the Color burn mode* recipe in *Chapter 4, Using the Layer Modes*
- *Chapter 6, Using New Rulers and Line Tools*, in the *Making focus lines with the Dense saturated line tool* recipe

Creating a feathering texture brush

This simple brush is great for adding some inked texture to a piece, whether it's deep shading or some furry tiger stripes!

Getting ready

Create a new canvas of at least 300 dpi resolution. Make sure that **Basic expression color** is set to **Gray**.

How to do it...

Creating this brush is quick and easy! Let's get started:

1. Using your favorite pen tool, create on your new canvas a mark like the one pictured in the next screenshot. Note that both its ends taper and it is quite thick in the center, as follows:

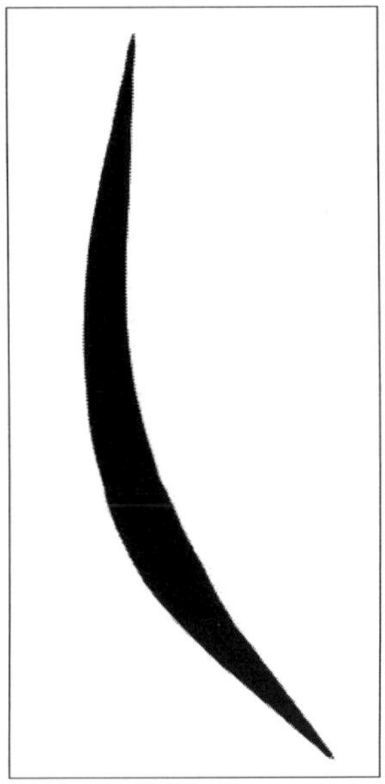

2. Delete any **Paper** color or fill layers behind the new brush tip so that only the mark made in step 1 and a transparent background remain on the canvas.
3. Go to **Edit** | **Register Image as Material**.
4. In the **Material property** window, name your new material. Select the **Brush** folder under **Image material** to store it in.
5. Check the box under the **Material image** preview that says **Use for brush tip shape**.

6. Add tags by clicking on the tag and the **+** sign icon in the bottom-right corner of the **Search tag** box. Refer to the following screenshot to see what your **Material property** screen should look like:

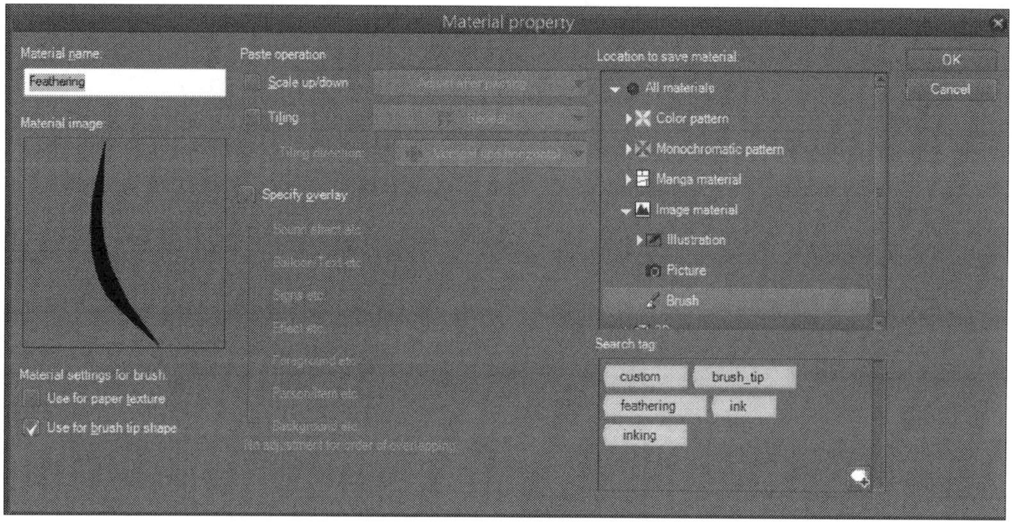

7. Click on **OK** in the **Material property** box.
8. Under the **Pen** tools, select **G-pen**.
9. In the bottom-right corner of the **Sub Tool** palette, click on the icon to use **Create copy of selected subtool**.
10. On the **Duplicate sub tool** screen, enter the name `Feathering`. Click on **OK**.
11. In the **Tool property** palette, click on the wrench icon in the bottom-right corner. It is marked in this screenshot:

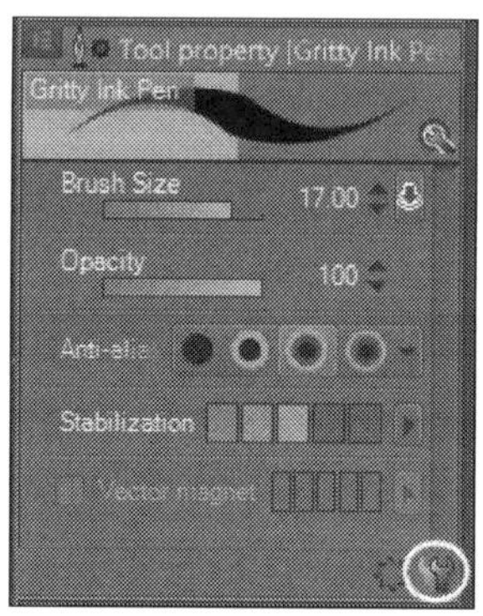

12. On the **Sub Tool Detail** screen, click on **Brush tip** on the left-hand side.
13. Next to **Tip shape**, click on the **Material** button. Then click on the **Add brush tip shape** icon under the **Material** box.
14. Search for and select the **Feathering** material created in Steps 1-7.
15. Click on the gray box to the far right of the **Direction** settings, and then click on the radio button next to **Direction of line**. The following screenshot shows the location of this option:

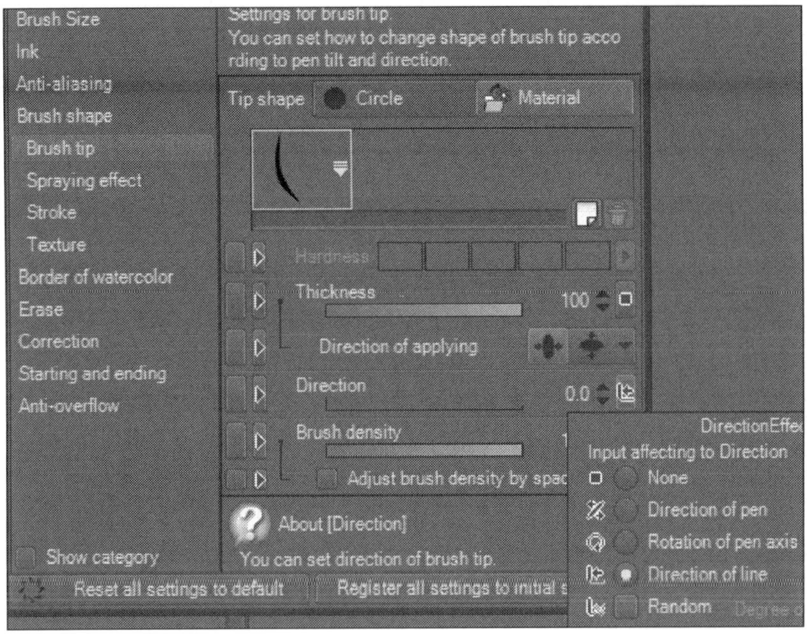

16. You're done! Test your brush and make any adjustments needed to suit your personal preferences.

How it works...

By changing the **Direction** options to use **Direction of line**, we create a brush that is feathered on the left and the right sides. As we made it by duplicating the **G-pen**, it is also pressure-sensitive, allowing tapered lines of feathering. The stripes in the following tiger face drawing were made using this feathering pen:

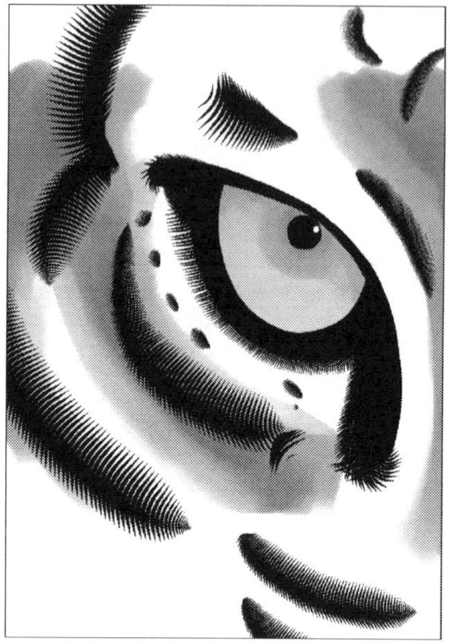

3

Getting a Handle on Vectors

In this chapter, you will learn the following recipes:

- Creating a vector layer
- Making marks on a vector layer
- Adjusting vector lines
- Adding control points to the vector line
- Deleting control points from the vector line
- Scaling and rotating the vector line

Introduction

Manga Studio has the capability to create both raster and vector graphics. What are the differences between these two?

Raster images are images based on pixels—dots of light and color information interpreted by the computer to create a picture. A raster is a grid of *x* and *y* coordinates of a display space. Raster images are used on the Internet and for most digital art. If we zoom too close into a raster image, we'll see the squares of color used to make up the picture.

With a raster image, we can lose quality if we try too much resizing. Say we create a postcard-size image, but then decide to have it made into a huge billboard, logo, or banner for behind a convention table. If the raster image doesn't have enough resolution, we could end up with a pixelated, low-quality print.

Vector images, however, are made from points, lines, and curves that are based on mathematical expressions. Because these images are made from mathematical expressions instead of dots on a grid, they can be scaled up or down infinitely without losing the quality or becoming pixelated. Look at the three lines in the following screenshot:

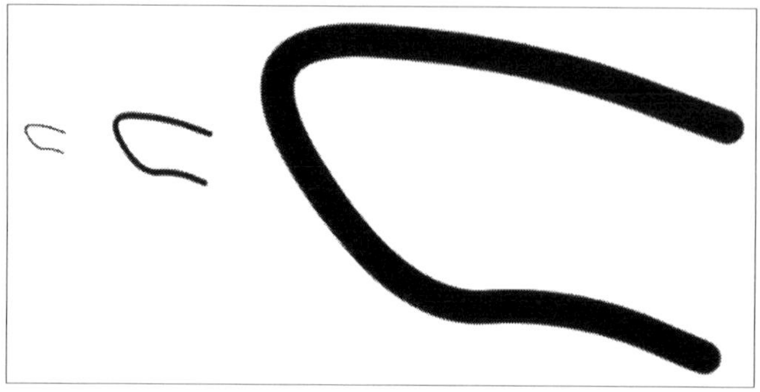

These are all copies of the same vector line that have been resized. Note how crisp each resized line is, including the largest one. A raster line drawn in the smallest size and resized to the largest would become blurry and pixelated—not smooth, as the vector line is.

Vectors are most often used for logos, but they can be useful for creating comics or illustrations as well. The lines can be adjusted without being redrawn, so if you have trouble drawing confident lines for inking, then working in vectors may be the solution for you.

Some pieces of graphics software will only work with either vector or raster information. Manga Studio can work with both, even within the same image file. We can have one layer of the image filled with vector information while all the others are raster, if that's the way we want to do our work!

Let's explore the wonderful world of vector graphics in the next few recipes.

Creating a vector layer

There are a few ways to create a vector layer, and all of them are very easy. Follow this recipe to make your first vector layer.

Getting ready

You will need a file open to complete the following recipe. Any file will do. Also, you will need the **Layer** palette visible. If it is not already visible, go to **Window** | **Layer** to open it.

How to do it...

This recipe will show you one method of creating a new vector layer:

1. Navigate to **Layer | New Layer | Vector layer**.
2. Enter a name for the layer in the **New vector layer** box.
3. Choose a color for **Expression color** (**Monochrome**, **Gray**, or **Color**) from the drop-down menu in the **New vector layer** dialog box.
4. If applicable, choose a **Blending Mode** from the drop-down menu in the **New vector layer** dialog box.
5. Click on **OK** to create the new layer.

There's more...

You can also use the following method to create a new vector layer:

1. Locate the **Layer** palette.
2. Click on the **New vector layer** icon in the bottom-right section of the palette. It is marked with a white box in this screenshot:

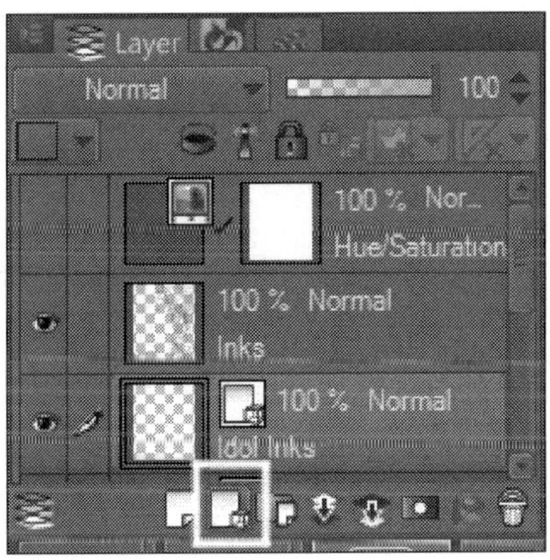

3. A new layer will be generated. To rename the layer, double-click on it with the mouse in the **Layer** palette.

Making marks on a vector layer

Now that we have a layer to put our vectors on, it's time to draw on it! Just about any drawing tool can be used on a vector layer, but of course, each produces different results.

Getting ready

Again, you will need a file open to complete the following recipe. Any file will do. Also, you will need the **Layer** palette visible. If it is not already visible, go to **Window** | **Layer** to open it. Follow the instructions from the *Creating a vector layer* recipe to add a vector layer to the file, and make sure that it is the active (selected) layer.

How to do it...

The following steps will walk us through drawing on a vector layer with an inking pen tool:

1. Select your favorite inking pen. The examples in this recipe use the G-pen.
2. Be sure that the vector layer is selected in the **Layer** palette. A vector layer will have the vector layer icon above the layer name. This icon is circled in the following screenshot:

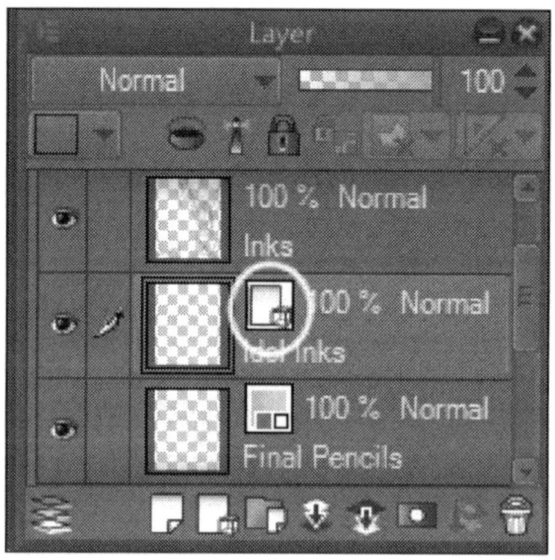

3. Draw a line with the chosen pen tool.
4. To verify that the line is a vector line, go to **Operation** | **Object** and click on the line. When clicked on, the line should show a thin red line down the center, and small boxes along the length of the line (called control points). Once you have finished inking, refine your lines, if needed, by following the instructions in the *Adjusting vector lines* recipe.

How it works...

Manga Studio 5's vector layers will make any mark on them on a vector line. This allows us to get any kind of look that we want for our artwork. By using the pen tools, we can use line thicknesses to make our inking more dynamic. Alternatively, using the direct drawing tools, we can get sharp, crisp, and neat lines. No matter what we choose to make a mark with, we still get the flexibility of a vector.

> Need to connect two vector lines and turn them into one line? Click on the **Correct line** tool in the toolbox, and then select the **Connect vector line** subtool. Use this tool to select the intersection of the two vector lines and they will be connected automatically. This set of subtools also has other useful tools for making vector lines with brush tools!

There's more...

We can also use the direct drawing tools to make marks on vector layers. Let's ink the following sketch of a monkey statue using two **Direct draw** tools, **Line** and **Curve**:

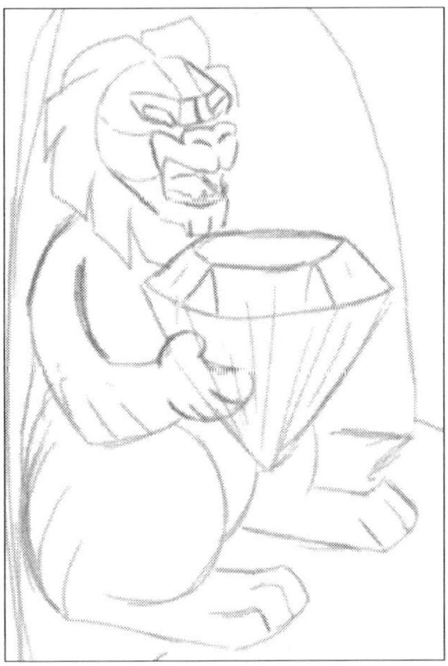

1. Be sure that the vector layer is selected in the **Layer** palette. A vector layer will have the vector layer icon above the layer name.
2. Go to **Figure** | **Direct draw** | **Straight line** in the Manga Studio 5 toolbox.

3. Click with the cursor and hold at one end of the straight line. Drag to the other end of the line and release the mouse button.
4. To ink curved lines, select the **Curve** tool. Click at one end of the curve and hold down the mouse button. Drag to the other end of the curve and release the mouse button. Then, drag the mouse back along the line to curve the line.
5. Continue using the tools until you're done.

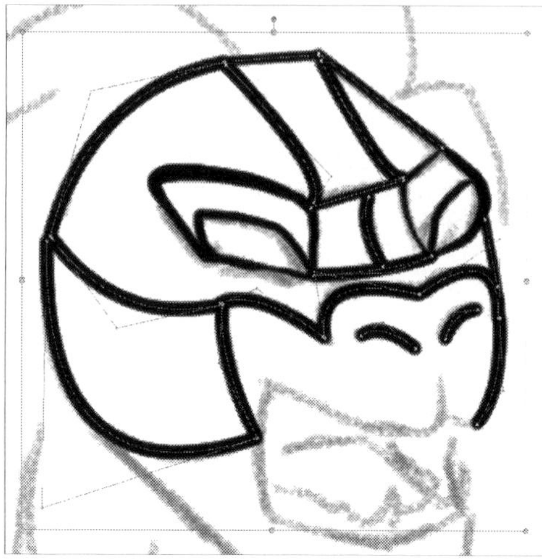

See also

- *Adjusting vector lines*
- *Adding control points to the vector line*
- *Deleting control points from the vector line*
- *Scaling and rotating the vector line*

Adjusting vector lines

Now you'll learn how to modify and adjust vector lines. Using control points, we can refine the vector to achieve the exact shape we want.

Getting ready

You will need a file open, with at least one vector layer and one line created on that vector layer. It can be created using a brush tool or one of the **Direct draw** tools.

How to do it...

The following steps will walk us through adjusting lines made with vectors:

1. Select the **Operation** tool, circled in the following screenshot, and make sure that the **Object** subtool is selected. In the **Tool property** palette, make sure that the **Operation** option is set to **Control point** and **Scale/Rotate**.

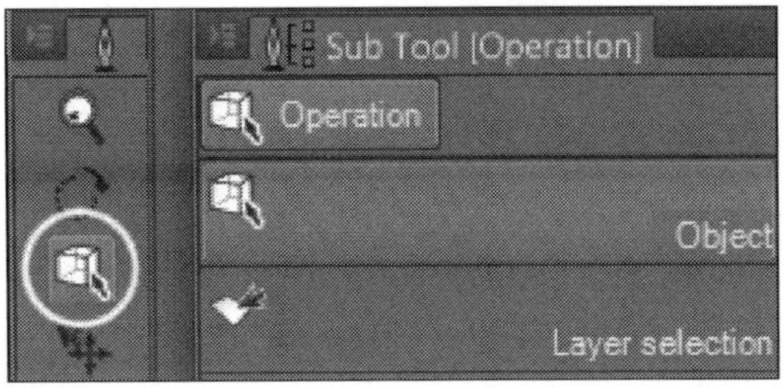

2. Click on the vector line that needs to be adjusted. You will see a red line down the center, yellow boxes at each control point, and a bounding box surrounding the line, as shown in this screenshot:

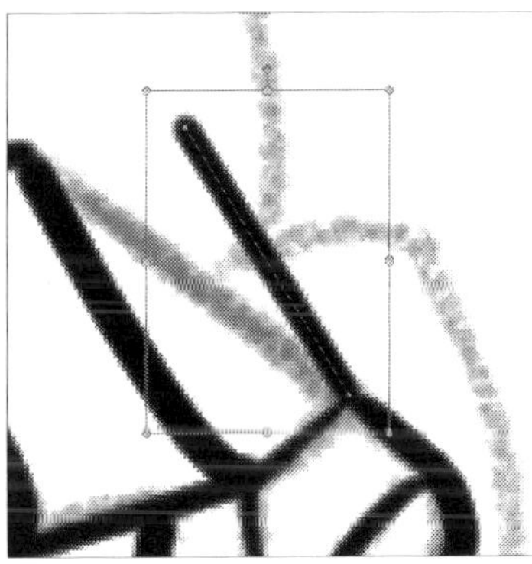

3. Determine what adjustment needs to be made. In this example, the top control point (the yellow box) needs to be moved to the left to match the sketch lines more closely. Click on the yellow control point to select it. The selected control point will turn red.

4. Click and hold with the left mouse button on the selected control point. While still holding down the mouse button, drag the control point to the new location. Then release the mouse button. The following screenshot shows the vector line in its new position:

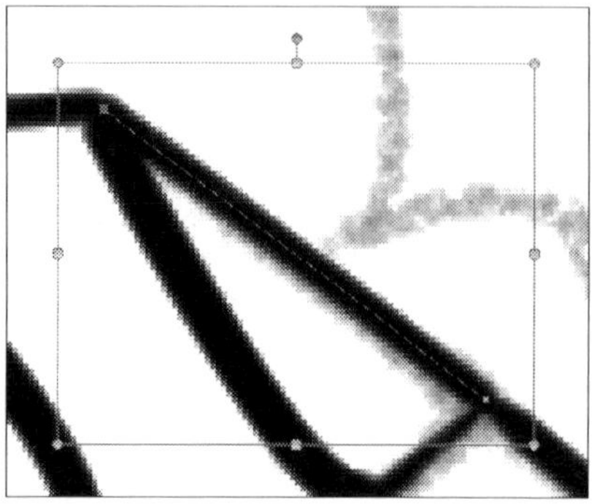

How it works...

Control points are the anchors of the vector line. By adjusting the anchors, we can change the look of the line or the entire flow of the drawing without having to redraw the line. Any control point can be moved and manipulated, including the control points that make up curves.

There's more...

Let's discover how to adjust vector curves in this next set of instructions:

1. Using the **Object** selection tool, select a curved vector line.
2. On curve vectors, there will be control points that have handles coming off them. The look of the handle depends on the setting used while drawing with the curve tool. To change the setting of **Curve**, open the **Sub Tool Detail** panel by clicking on the wrench icon at the bottom of the **Tool property** palette. This screenshot shows the location of this setting:

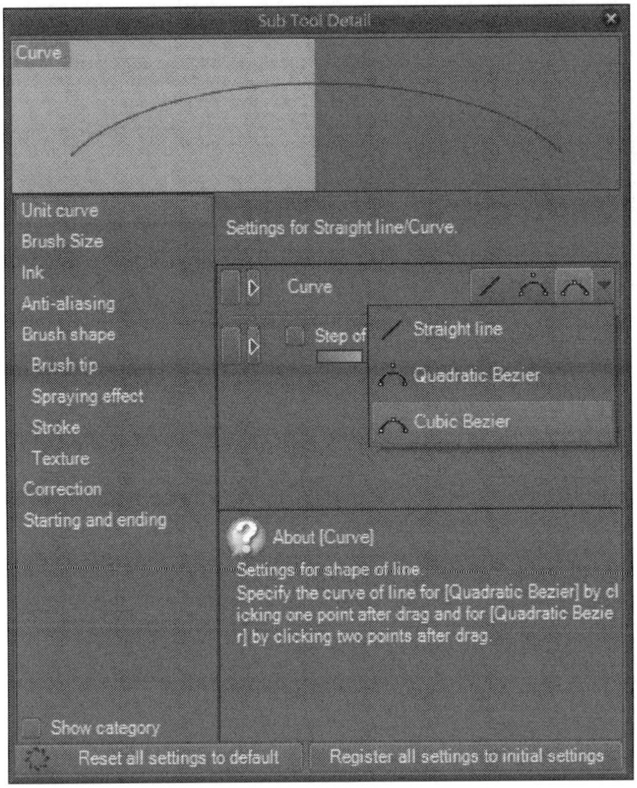

3. To adjust the start and end points of the curve, follow the preceding instructions.
4. To adjust the curvature of the line, select the handle coming off the control point by clicking on it. Then hold down the left mouse button and drag to adjust the curve. In the following screenshot, the handle for adjusting the curve is the intersection of the two lines above the curve. They form a 90-degree angle with one another.

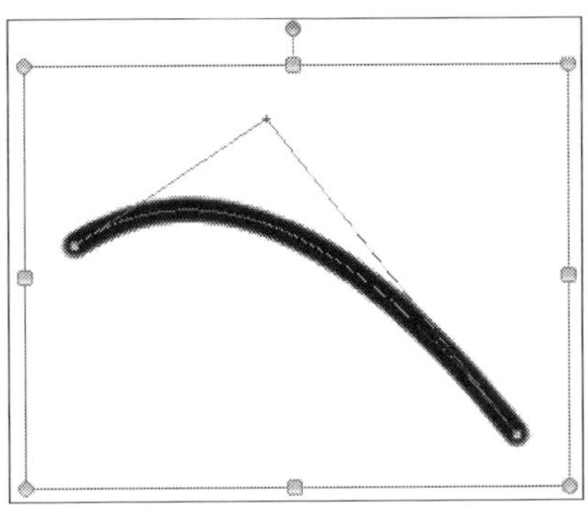

5. Once the curve is adjusted to the new position, release the mouse button.

The type of preceding curve shown is called a **Quadratic Bézier**. The other option for curves in Manga Studio 5 is the **Cubic Bézier**.

A Quadratic Bézier is created by clicking and dragging a straight line. Then, after releasing the mouse button, we drag out in one direction or the other to create a single curve between the start and end of the line. Quadratic Bézier curves will create one curve no matter what the distance between the two anchor points of the line is.

A Cubic Bézier is created by dragging out a straight line between the start and end. After releasing the mouse button, one curve can be dragged out. After the mouse button is pressed again, a second curve can be added for further refinement.

The line shown in the next screenshot is a Cubic Bézier. Note how it has two separate handles emanating from the control points, instead of just one as in the Quadratic Bézier. One handle goes toward the right, creating the start of the curve. The other handle goes toward the left, making the line slightly curve back again.

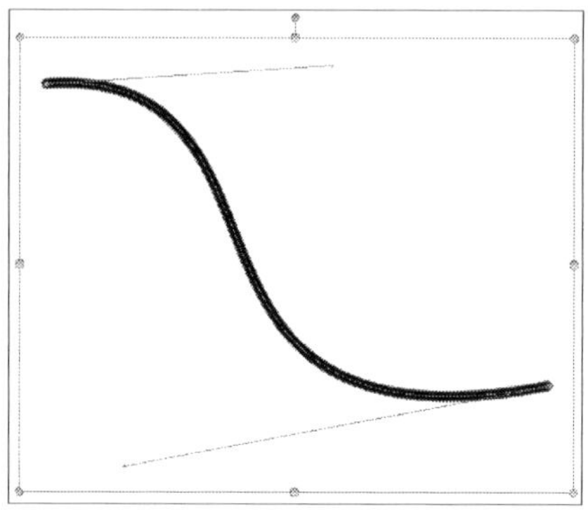

To adjust a Quadratic Bézier curve, select one of the two handles and drag it with the mouse as needed.

See also

- *Adding control points to the vector line*
- *Deleting control points from the vector line*
- *Scaling and rotating the vector line*

Adding control points to the vector line

By adding points to vectors, we can further refine our line.

Getting ready

You will need a file open, with at least one vector layer and one line created on that vector layer. It can be created with a brush tool or one of the **Direct draw** tools. In the following example, we will be using a line created with the **Curve** tool, set for a Cubic Bézier curve.

How to do it...

The following steps will teach you how to add more control points to a vector:

1. Select the **Operation** tool, if it is not the active tool already. Ensure that the **Object** subtool is selected.
2. Click on the line that needs to be modified.
3. On the PC, right-click with the mouse where the control point needs to be added. The following menu will appear.
4. Click on **Add control point**.
5. A control point will be added to the line. Refer to the following screenshot and note the third control point, with handles, between the start and end points:

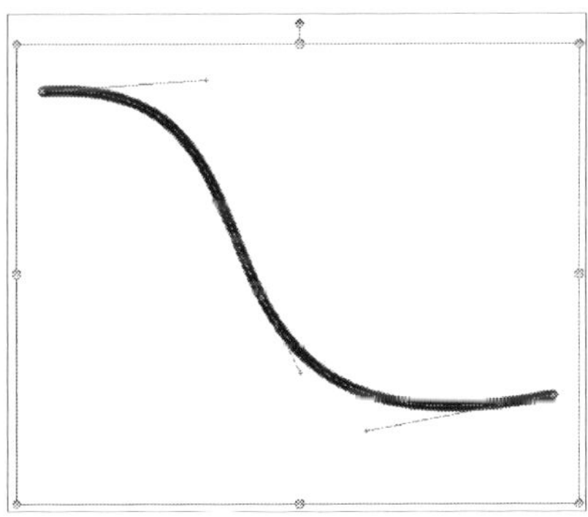

6. Use the instructions in the *Adjusting vector lines* recipe to make changes to the control points.

How it works...

By adding more control points to the line, we have a lot more control over the shape of our vector. The line shown in this screenshot is the same Cubic Bézier line, but with the third control point in the middle, because of which we can make a completely different shape:

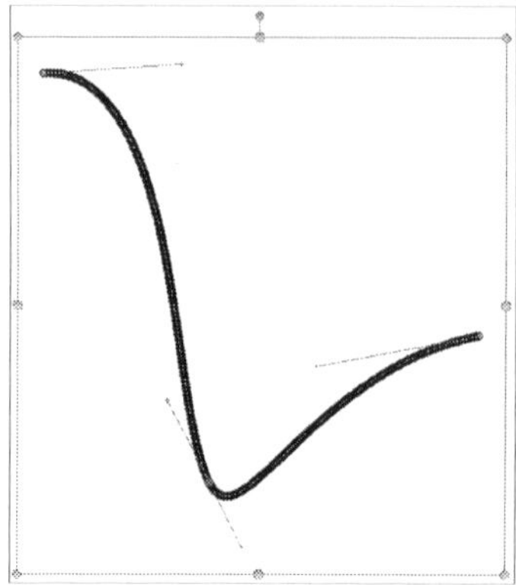

See also

- *Deleting control points from the vector line*

Deleting control points from the vector line

Besides adding points to a vector line, control points can also be deleted from it to further refine its look.

Getting ready

Again, you will need a file open, with at least one vector layer and one line created on that layer. It can be created with a brush tool or one of the **Direct draw** tools. In the following example, we will be using a line created with the **G-pen** tool.

How to do it...

The following steps will teach you how to delete control points from a vector line:

1. Select the **Operation** tool, if it is not the active tool already. Ensure that the **Object** subtool is selected.
2. Click on the line that needs to be modified. Then click on the control point to be removed to select it.

3. On the PC, right-click on the selected control point.
4. Click on **Delete control point(V)**.
5. The control point will be deleted.

How it works...

Deleting control points is especially useful for refining the look of a vector drawn with a brush or pen tool. The following screenshot shows a vector drawn with the **G-pen** tool:

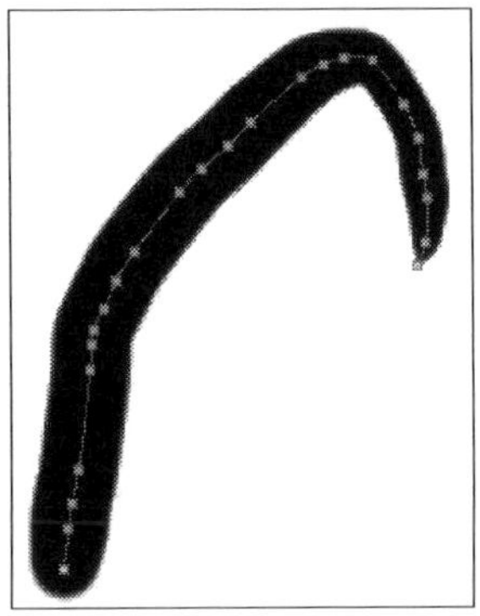

Note the abundance of control points—too many control points and the line looks wiggly! This is exactly what is happening in the case of this line. It's not smooth the way we want it to be because there's too many points, all causing their own little variations in the line.

If we get rid of all the points that we don't need, we get a line that looks like what is shown in this screenshot:

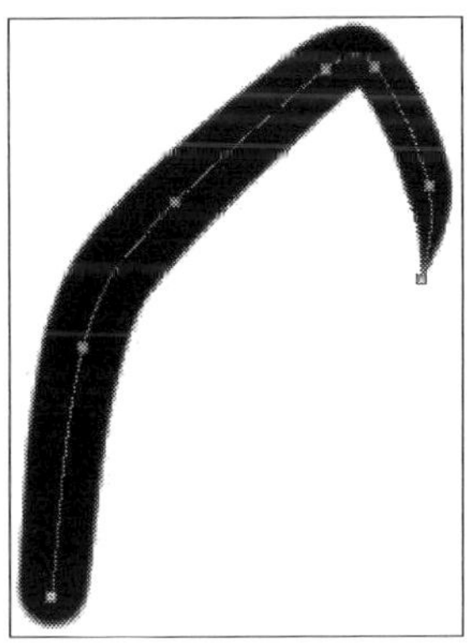

See how much smoother it is! The original line had 24 control points in it. The modified line has just seven!

> A less precise but faster way of simplifying the drawn vector line is by using the **Simplify vector** line subtool under the **Correct line** tool. Click and drag with this tool over the line you wish to simplify, and it will erase the control points along the selection automatically.

There's more...

In addition to deleting points from the vector line, you can also use the **Vector eraser** tool to erase vectors. We'll now explore the three modes of the **Vector eraser** tool:

1. Select the **Eraser** tool and then the **Vector** subtool.
2. Look at the **Tool property** palette. It will look like what is shown in the following screenshot:

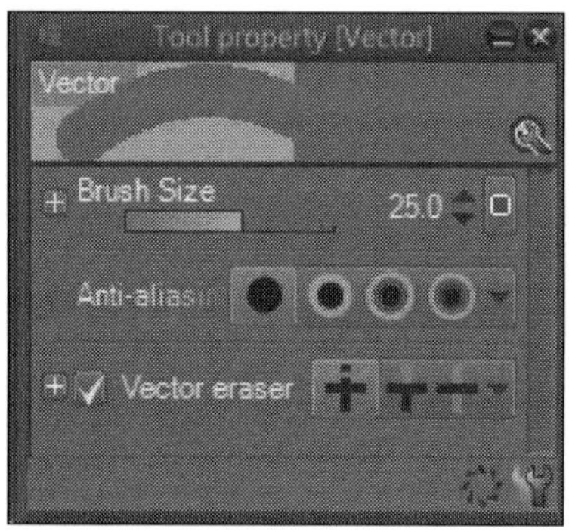

3. Selecting the first option under **Vector eraser** in the **Tool property** palette will activate the **Erase touching part** options. Using the **Vector eraser** in this mode will make it act as a normal raster eraser; only those sections of the line that have the eraser tool used on them will be erased.
4. To the right of the **Erase touching part** icon is the **Erase up to intersection** option. Click on it to activate it. This option erases a vector line up to its intersection with another vector line. Click on a line that intersects with another vector somewhere along its length and the entire section up to the intersection will be erased, even if you click only on a small section of the line.
5. The far right icon under the **Vector eraser** option is the **Overall line** option. Click on this icon to select it. One click anywhere on a vector line will erase the entire line when this option is active.

See also

- *Adjusting vector lines*
- *Adding control points to the vector line*

Scaling and rotating the vector line

Now that you know a bit about creating vector lines and adjusting their shape, let's learn how to scale and rotate them as well.

Getting started

You will need a file open, with at least one vector layer and one line created on that vector layer. It can be created with a brush tool or one of the **Direct draw** tools.

How to do it...

Let's follow these steps to rotate and scale a line:

1. Select the **Operation** tool, if it is not the active tool already. Ensure that the **Object** subtool is selected.
2. Click on the line to be modified. When it is selected successfully, a red line will appear, running through the center. Also, the control points will become visible in yellow, and a bounding box will appear around the line. Here is a screenshot that shows this bounding box:

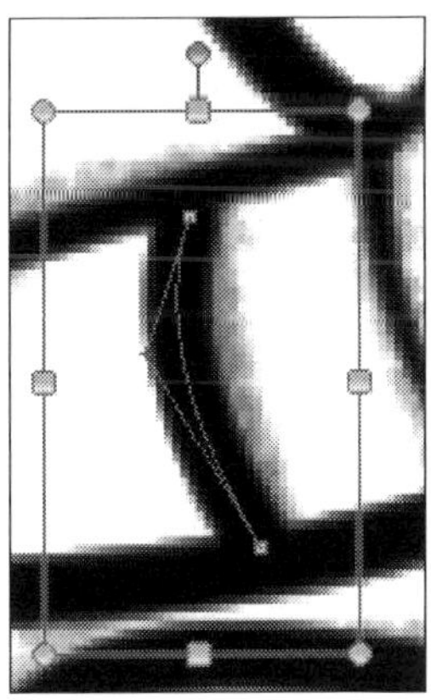

3. To rotate the line, move the mouse cursor onto the blue circle above the top center of the bounding box. The cursor will become a curved arrow that points to the left and right.

4. Click and hold the left mouse button. Then drag to the left or right to rotate the line. The following screenshot shows the same line from the preceding screenshot rotated to the left:

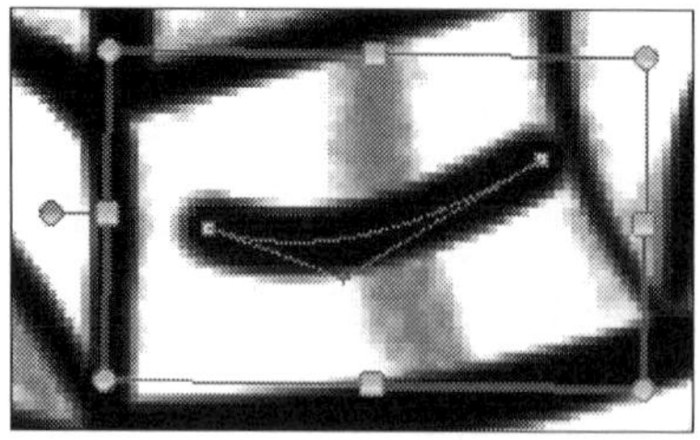

> To rotate an object in 45-degree increments, hold down the *Shift* key while dragging with the mouse.

5. To scale the line, move the cursor onto one of the handles around the perimeter of the bounding box. It will become a double-headed arrow, pointing up and down, left and right, or diagonally. This depends on the handle that is being "moused over."
6. Adjust the bounding box handles until the line achieves the desired size. This screenshot shows the line scaled up to fit its new position:

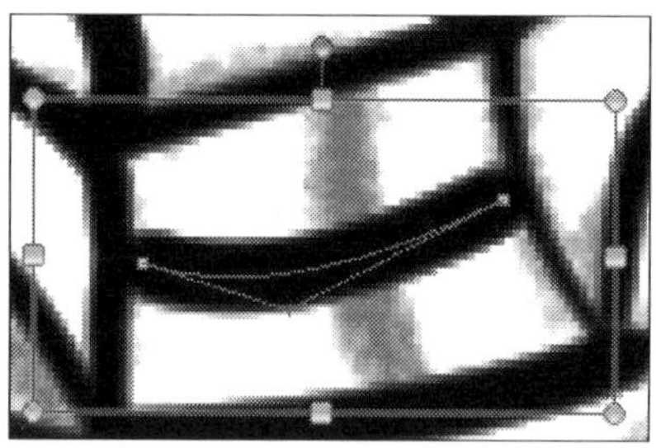

> To scale a line but constrain its proportions, hold down the *Shift* key while dragging with the mouse.

How it works...

The bounding box is how we modify the entire line at once. Use the nine handles around the perimeter to scale or rotate the vector line. Just remember that the ninth handle—the one at the top of the bounding box, shown in a color different from the others—is the rotation handle, and the others are for scaling!

There's more...

Follow these steps to scale or rotate more than one vector line at a time:

1. Select the **Operation** subtool, if it is not already selected.
2. Click to select a line.
3. Hold down *Shift* and continue selecting the lines to be altered.
4. Once all the desired lines have been selected, follow the preceding directions to scale or rotate them.

See also

- *Adjusting vector lines*

4

Using the Layer Modes

In this chapter, you will learn the following recipes:

- Using the Darken mode
- Using the Multiply mode
- Using the Color burn mode
- Using the Linear burn mode
- Using the Subtract mode
- Using the Lighten mode
- Using the Screen mode
- Using the Color dodge mode
- Using the Add mode
- Using the Overlay mode
- Using the Soft light mode
- Using the Hard light mode
- Using the Difference mode

Introduction

So, what exactly are layer modes? Layer modes are different ways in which we can have a layer interact with the layers underneath it. They can be used to adjust colors or to create special effects in our artwork. It's very simple to change a layer mode, but the changes they make can be invaluable to the process of creating art digitally! Now, let's explore layer modes.

The following screenshot shows the file we'll be using for the demonstrations in this chapter:

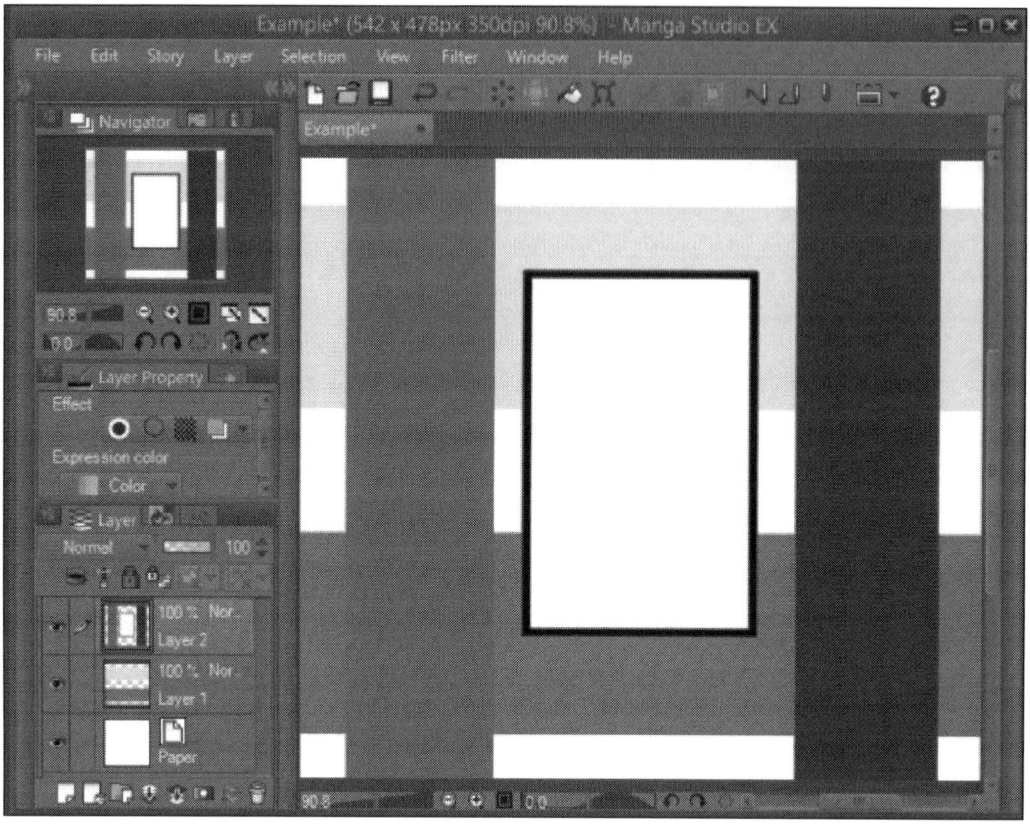

As we can see in the **Layer** palette in the bottom-left corner, there are two layers in this image (and a **Paper** color layer). The bottom layer contains two horizontal stripes of solid color—the top one is yellow and the bottom one is a light purple. The upper layer contains two vertical stripes—the one on the left is a medium blue and the one on the right is a deep red. In the center of this layer is a rectangle with a black outline and a white fill. We will be changing the layer mode on this top layer. The layer needs something to interact with below it to reflect the changes that each mode makes.

Using the Darken mode

The following pages will walk us through all the different layer modes available in Manga Studio 5.

How to do it...

This simple recipe will show you how to change a layer mode to the **Darken** mode:

1. In the **Layer** palette, click on the layer to edit (if the **Layer** palette is not visible, go to **Window** | **Layer** to open it).
2. From the top-left corner of the **Layer** palette, click on the drop-down menu. The **Normal** option will be visible, unless the mode has already been changed.
3. Click on the **Darken** mode.

How it works...

Changing the combine mode of the layer changes how it interacts with the layers below it. Each mode has its own different look. Let's explore each of these now.

The following screenshot shows an example of the **Darken** mode:

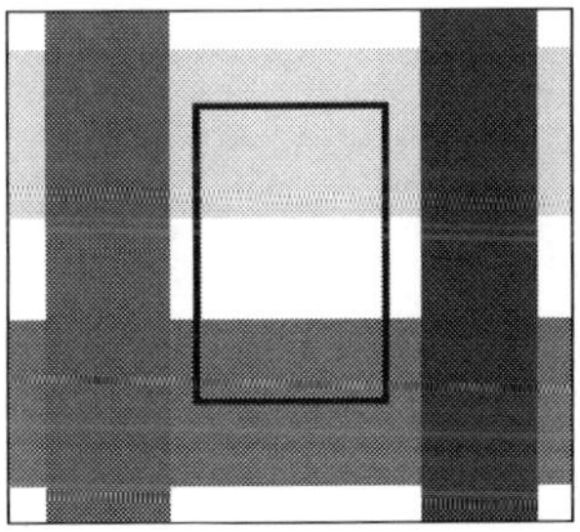

In the **Darken** mode, the white fill of the central box becomes transparent, allowing us to see the yellow and purple colors behind it. The area where the blue and yellow stripes overlap turns to a green color. The program compares the colors on each layer and combines the color in the bottom layer with the darker color in the top layer.

Using the Multiply mode

How to do it...

This simple recipe will show you how to change a layer mode to the **Multiply** mode:

1. In the **Layer** palette, click on the layer to edit (if the **Layer** palette is not visible, go to **Window** | **Layer** to open it).
2. From the top-left corner of the **Layer** palette, click on the drop-down menu. Next, click on the **Multiply** mode.

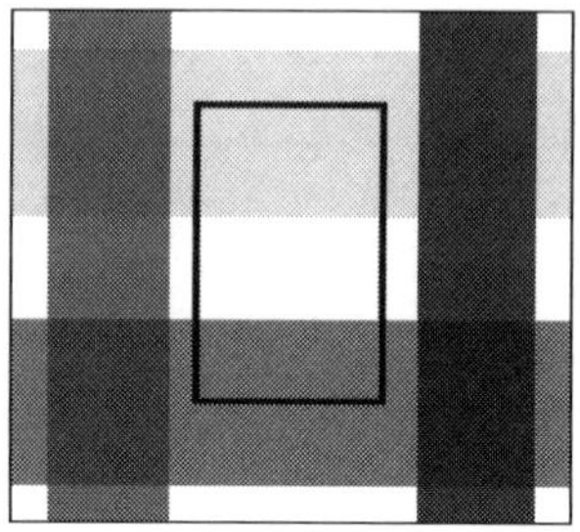

How it works...

The **Multiply** mode is most often used by digital artists. This is because it makes the white areas of a layer "transparent" but keeps the black areas opaque. This makes it the ideal selection for something like a scanned ink image. By setting the scanned image to **Multiply**, digital colors can be applied beneath the line art to finish the illustration. **Multiply** also makes the colors darker by combining them with the colors below them. In the preceding example, where the blue and the yellow stripes overlap, they change to a dark green color. Where the red and light purple stripes overlap, they change to a dark burgundy color.

Using the Color burn mode

How to do it...

This simple recipe will show you how to change a layer mode to the **Color burn** mode:

1. In the **Layer** palette, click on the layer to edit (if the **Layer** palette is not visible, go to **Window** | **Layer** to open it).

2. In the top-left corner of the **Layer** palette, click on the drop-down menu. Then, click on the **Color burn** mode.

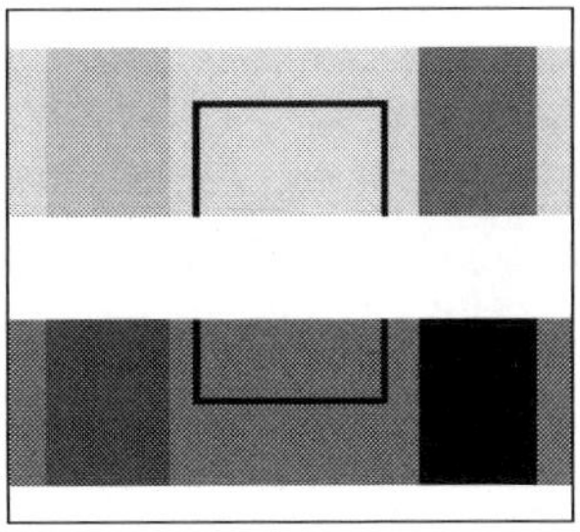

How it works...

In this mode, the colors from the bottom layer are darkened to increase the contrast and are then combined with the colors on the top layer. Only the areas where the colors overlap are visible, leaving a white stripe in the center. The area where blue and yellow overlap gets a dark golden color. The dark red and yellow colors become a bright, vivid red, the blue and light purple colors combine to become a bright royal blue, and the area where purple and dark red combine is almost black.

Using the Linear burn mode

How to do it...

This simple recipe will show you how to change a layer mode to the **Linear burn** mode:

1. In the **Layer** palette, click on the layer to edit (if the **Layer** palette is not visible, go to **Window** | **Layer** to open it).
2. In the top left corner of the **Layer** palette, click on the drop-down menu. Next, click on the **Linear burn** mode.

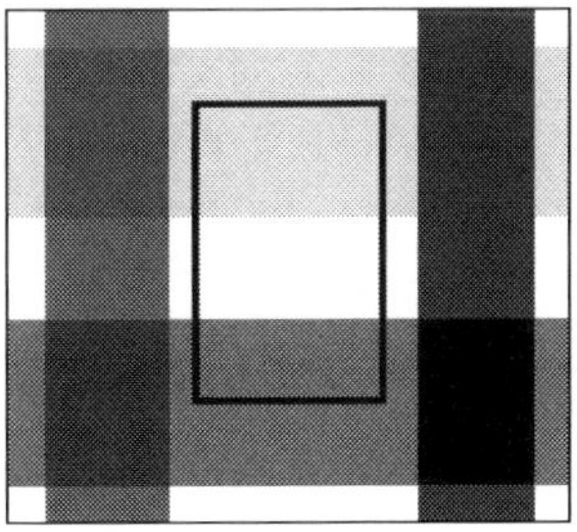

How it works...

This mode is less dramatic than the **Color burn** mode. The bottom layer's colors are still darkened for contrast, and then combined with the upper layers wherever they overlap. However, the areas where the vertical lines cross the transparent areas of the underlying layer are still visible. The blue and yellow overlap area is green, while the blue and purple overlap is dark blue. The dark red and yellow overlap has barely changed, and the dark red and purple area has become a darker burgundy (but not quite as dark as in the previous mode).

Using the Subtract mode

How to do it...

This simple recipe will show you how to change a layer mode to the **Subtract** mode:

1. In the **Layer** palette, click on the layer to edit (if the **Layer** palette is not visible, go to **Window** | **Layer** to open it).
2. In the top-left corner of the **Layer** palette, click on the drop-down menu. Then, click on the **Subtract** mode.

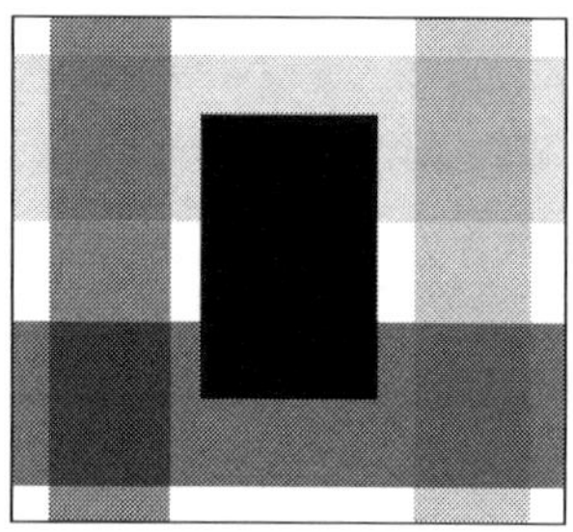

How it works...

The colors in the top layer (the layer being adjusted) are subtracted from the layer below it. Our white-filled rectangle has changed to solid black. The blue vertical line has become light orange where it overlaps the white paper color; where it overlaps yellow, it has become medium orange; and where it overlaps purple, it has changed to a purple-red color. The dark red vertical line has become light blue where it overlaps the white areas, and where it crosses the yellow stripe, it is light green. Where it crosses the purple line, it has become medium blue.

Using the Lighten mode

How to do it...

This simple recipe will show you how to change a layer mode to the **Lighten** mode:

1. In the **Layer** palette, click on the layer to edit (if the **Layer** palette is not visible, navigate to **Window** | **Layer** to open it).
2. In the top-left corner of the **Layer** palette, click on the drop-down menu. Next, click on the **Lighten** mode.

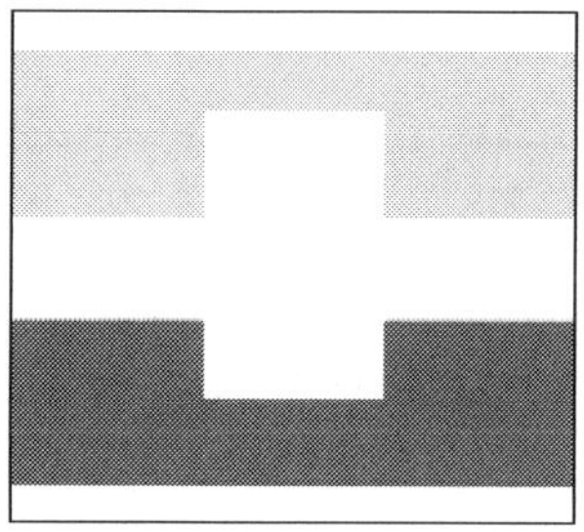

How it works...

This mode works on the colors in the top layer and the bottom layer, and combines the color in the bottom layer with a brighter color. In our preceding example, the blue and red stripes have all but disappeared. In fact, only a lighter yellow rectangle remains where the blue and yellow lines overlap in the upper-left corner. The black outline of the central rectangle has disappeared and only the white fill remains, leaving a void in the center of the image. Because the **Paper** color is white, wherever the vertical stripes overlap the **Paper** color, they turn white as well, causing them to disappear.

Using the Screen mode

How to do it...

This simple recipe will show you how to change a layer mode to the **Screen** mode:

1. In the **Layer** palette, click on the layer to edit (if the **Layer** palette is not visible, go to **Window** | **Layer** to open it).

2. In the top-left corner of the **Layer** palette, click on the drop-down menu. Then, click on the **Screen** mode.

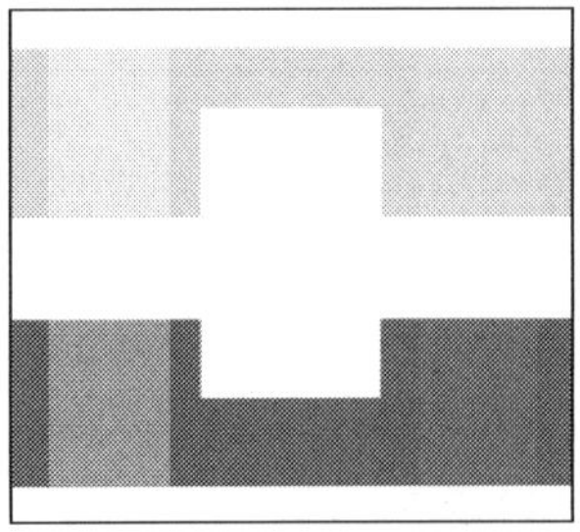

How it works...

Again, the black outline of the rectangle has vanished, leaving just the white fill as a void in the yellow and purple stripes. The areas where the blue and red vertical stripes crossed the white now have no color to them. Where the blue and yellow stripes cross is almost white; it's so pale! The region where the blue and purple colors meet has become light blue. The red stripe has had almost no effect on the yellow one, while the red and purple overlap has turned into a lighter violet color.

What the program is doing is inverting the colors below, and then multiplying them with the layer being configured. The colors become brighter after this configuration. Because the **Paper** color is white, wherever the vertical stripes overlap the **Paper** color, they turn white as well, making them disappear.

In my own work, I tend to use this mode or the **Lighten** mode for the highlight areas of my color images.

Using the Color dodge mode

How to do it...

This simple recipe will show you how to change a layer mode to the **Color dodge** mode:

1. In the **Layer** palette, click on the layer to edit (if the **Layer** palette is not visible, go to **Window** | **Layer** to open it).

2. From the top-left corner of the **Layer** palette, click on the drop-down menu. Next, click on the **Color dodge** mode.

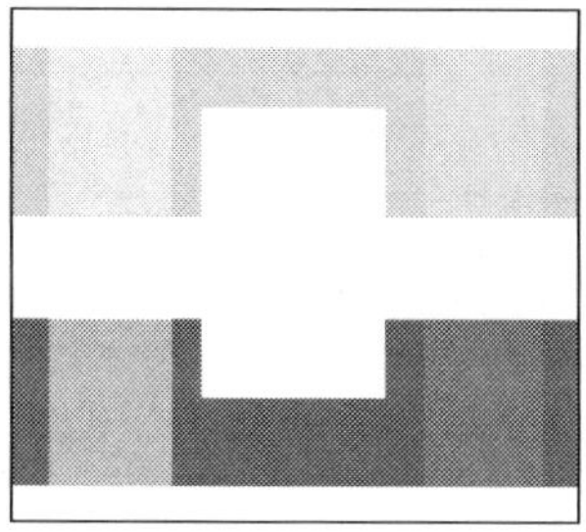

How it works...

Again, this mode lightens the colors being combined, much like the **Screen** mode in the previous example. This time, however, the blue vertical stripe has changed to a brighter, lighter yellow color where it intersects the yellow stripe, and has become a much paler and brighter blue over the purple stripe. The vertical red stripe has become golden over the yellow stripe and bright pink over the purple stripe. The black outline around the central rectangle has disappeared, and the white color of the inside fill is leaving a white space where it crosses the horizontal stripes of the colors.

Because the **Paper** color is white, wherever the vertical stripes overlap the **Paper** color, they turn white as well, causing them to disappear.

This mode also has a **Glow dodge** mode, which interacts in the same way but produces a stronger effect on the semi-transparent areas of the layer.

Using the Add mode

How to do it...

This simple recipe will show you how to change a layer mode to the **Add** mode:

1. In the **Layer** palette, click on the layer to edit (if the **Layer** palette is not visible, go to **Window** | **Layer** to open it).

2. From the top-left corner of the **Layer** palette, click on the drop-down menu. Then, click on the **Add** mode.

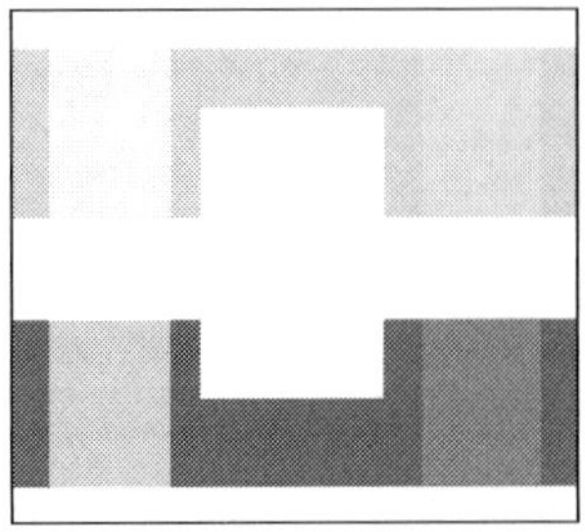

How it works...

As we can see, this mode is similar to the three modes before it. It also lightens the colors on the adjusted layer and only affects the regions where there is a color on the lower layer. Because the **Paper** color is white, wherever the vertical stripes overlap the **Paper** color, they turn white as well, making them disappear.

The blue vertical strip has turned almost white over the yellow horizontal stripe, but it has become light blue over the purple stripe. The red vertical stripe has changed to a brighter yellow color where it overlaps the yellow stripe, but is now a hot pink color over the purple stripe. In this mode, the colors below the adjusted layer are added to the colors above and are then brightened.

This mode also has an **Add (Glow)** mode, which interacts in the same way but produces a stronger effect on semi-transparent areas of the layer.

Using the Overlay mode

How to do it...

This simple recipe will show you how to change a layer mode to the **Overlay** mode:

1. In the **Layer** palette, click on the layer to edit (if the **Layer** palette is not visible, navigate to **Window** | **Layer** to open it).

2. From the top-left corner of the **Layer** palette, click on the drop-down menu. Then, click on the **Overlay** mode.

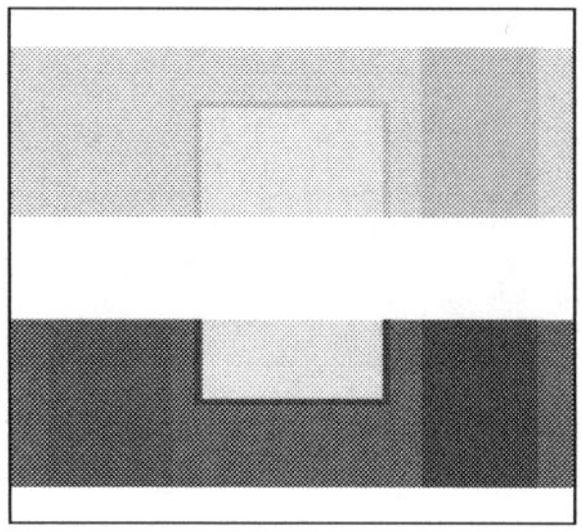

How it works...

This mode combines colors by applying either **Screen** or **Multiply**, depending on the overlapped colors. Bright areas become brighter, while dark areas become darker. In the preceding example, the central rectangle has disappeared from the region where it overlaps the white background, but it has become light yellow and golden yellow across the top stripe, and light purple and bright purple across the bottom stripe. The blue vertical stripe has all but disappeared across the top yellow stripe, and has become a medium blue in the area where it overlaps the purple one. The vertical red stripe has become golden yellow across the top stripe and bright purple across the bottom.

This mode can be used for special effects and color correction in illustrations and comic work.

Using the Soft light mode

How to do it...

This simple recipe will show you how to change a layer mode to the **Soft light** mode.

1. In the **Layer** palette, click on the layer to edit (if the **Layer** palette is not visible, go to **Window** | **Layer** to open it).

2. In the top-left corner of the Layer palette, click on the drop-down menu. Next, click on the **Soft light** mode.

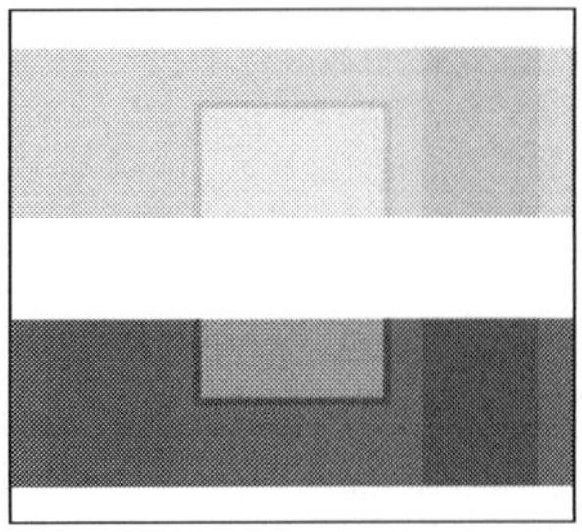

How it works...

This mode produces different results depending on the density of the colors being overlapped. When colors brighter than 50 percent grayscale are overlapped, the result is brighter than the original, much like **Dodge**. When the colors are darker than 50% grayscale, the colors are darker, much like **Burn**. When areas equal to 50% grayscale are overlapped, there is no change, and areas not overlapping with the color become white, as in the center of the preceding example.

Using the Hard light mode

How to do it...

This simple recipe will show you how to change a layer mode to the **Hard light** mode:

1. In the **Layer** palette, click on the layer to edit (if the **Layer** palette is not visible, go to **Window** | **Layer** to open it).
2. In the top-left corner of the **Layer** palette, click on the drop-down menu. Then, click on the **Hard light** mode.

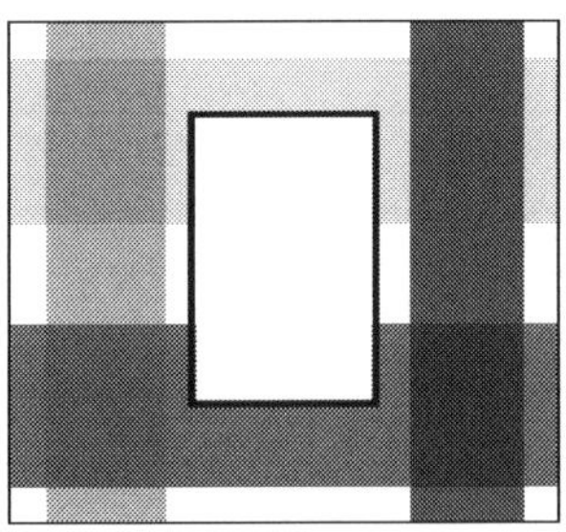

How it works...

As with **Soft light**, the **Hard light** mode's results depend on the density of the overlapped colors. Colors brighter than 50% grayscale that are overlapped become brighter, just as in the **Screen** mode. Colors darker than 50% grayscale that are combined become darker, just as in the **Multiply** mode. When 50% grayscale colors are overlapped, the lower layer remains unchanged. Areas that overlap with white become white if a color brighter than 50% grayscale is selected, and they change to the selected color if a color darker than 50% grayscale is selected.

In the preceding example, the blue and red vertical stripes still remain visible in the areas where they overlap with white. The red strip has hardly changed over the top yellow stripe, but has become a dark red in the area where it overlaps with the purple stripe. The blue stripe has become lighter overall and is green wherever it overlaps with the yellow stripe at the top. But it has got a bright, medium blue color where it overlaps with the purple stripe at the bottom.

Using the Difference mode

How to do it...

This simple recipe will show you how to change a layer mode to the **Difference** mode:

1. In the **Layer** palette, click on the layer to edit (if the **Layer** palette is not visible, navigate to **Window** | **Layer** to open it).
2. In the top-left corner of the Layer palette, click on the drop-down menu. Next, click on the **Difference** mode.

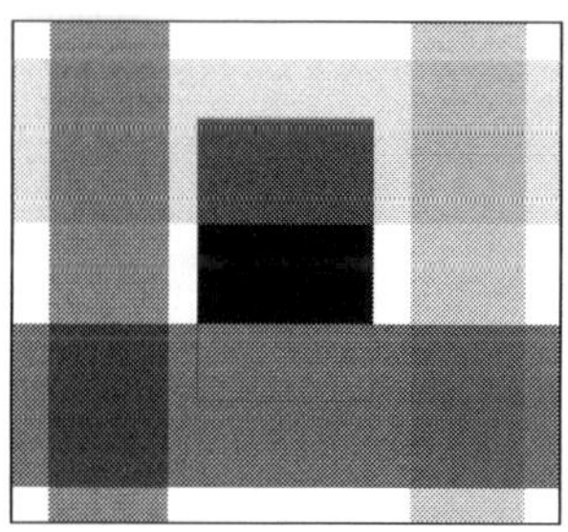

How it works...

The actual math of this one is a little hard to explain, but it does look cool! **Difference** subtracts the colors used in the lower layer from those in the layer being adjusted, and then combines the colors in the lower layer with the absolute value of the difference.

In the preceding example, the blue vertical stripe has turned orange, and the red stripe has become pale blue. Where the blue stripe (now orange) crosses the yellow stripe, it has changed to a darker orange color, and where it crosses the purple stripe, it has changed to a dark violet color. The red stripe (now pale blue) has turned green in the area where it overlaps with the yellow stripe, and has changed to a darker blue shade in the area where it crosses the purple stripe. The white rectangle in the center has no black outline now, but where the white fill crosses the yellow stripe, it has been given a very saturated blue color. It is black where it crosses the white space and medium green where it overlaps the purple stripe.

5

Making Selections and Layer Masks

In this chapter, you will learn these recipes:

- Adding a Layer Mask
- Editing the Layer Mask
- Making a quick mask using selection tools
- Using the Selection pen
- Using the Clear selection tool
- Using the Shrink selection tool

Introduction

In this chapter, we're going to explore layer masks and some of the new selection tools that are available in Manga Studio 5.0.5. In addition to the usual rectangle, ellipse, and lasso tools, there are some handy new features that are bound to make your workflow a little faster when you need to make adjustments and edits.

Let's get started!

Adding a Layer Mask

A Layer Mask is a feature that allows us to hide parts of a layer without erasing them for good. This allows us to fine-tune a drawing or a part of a drawing without losing what we've already done. Layer masks can be adjusted over and over, so we can hide part of a drawing and then bring it back later if we decide that we want it visible again.

Think of a Layer Mask like a Halloween mask. If we put a mask on, our face is still there but it can't be seen.

I find this feature to be very handy if I want to see different versions of a drawing, say, a character with a different hairstyle. The applications are pretty limitless, and it's much less nerve-wracking than completely erasing something that you may want to bring back in the future!

Getting ready

You will need a file open, with at least one layer with content (a sketch, an ink drawing, a photo, and so on) inside of it.

How to do it...

Follow these steps to add a Layer Mask:

1. Select the layer to add the mask to by clicking on it in the **Layer** palette (if the **Layer** palette is not visible, go to **Window** | **Layer** to open it).
2. Click on the **Create layer mask** icon at the bottom of the **Layer** palette. It is shown circled in white in the following screenshot:

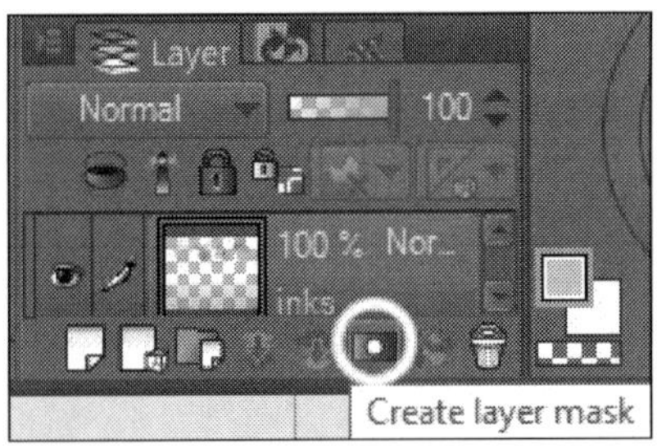

3. A new thumbnail will appear to the right of the layer thumbnail. This is the Layer Mask. A black outline will be seen around it when it is active. The selected layer, as shown in this screenshot, has an active Layer Mask:

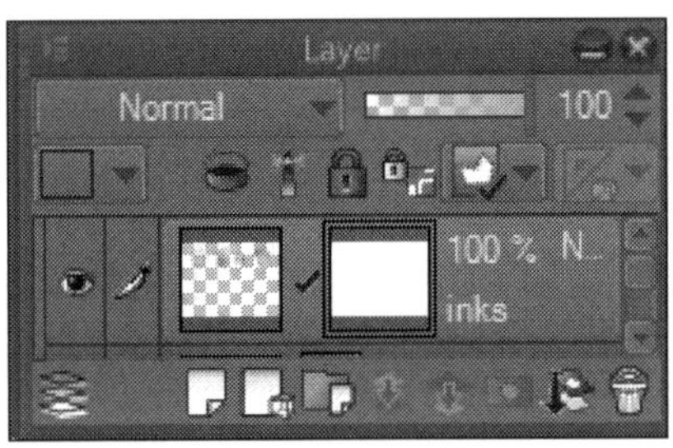

> Having trouble editing a Layer Mask or the layer that a mask is attached to? Make sure that the Layer Mask is selected, or that the layer itself is selected before you move on to other troubleshooting. I have noticed that most of the time, not having the Layer Mask selected is the problem!

How it works...

This is one way in which we can make a Layer Mask. We will explore how to make a Layer Mask from an active selection in the *Making a Quick Mask using selection tools* recipe.

This gives us a blank mask that we can start editing on. How do we do that? Find out by going to the next recipe!

Editing the Layer Mask

Now that we have a Layer Mask, it's time to learn how to hide and restore content with it!

Getting ready

Again, you will need a file open with at least one layer with content (a sketch, an ink drawing, a photo, and so on) inside of it. Follow the instructions given in the *Adding a Layer Mask* recipe to make a mask before following this recipe.

How to do it...

Here is how to edit the content on the layer with the layer mask:

1. To hide the content on the layer, select an **Eraser(E)** tool. Erase the section of the layer to be hidden. The area will show up in the layer thumbnail as black space. The following screenshot illustrates this; note the black area where artwork has been erased. This black area is the masked area.

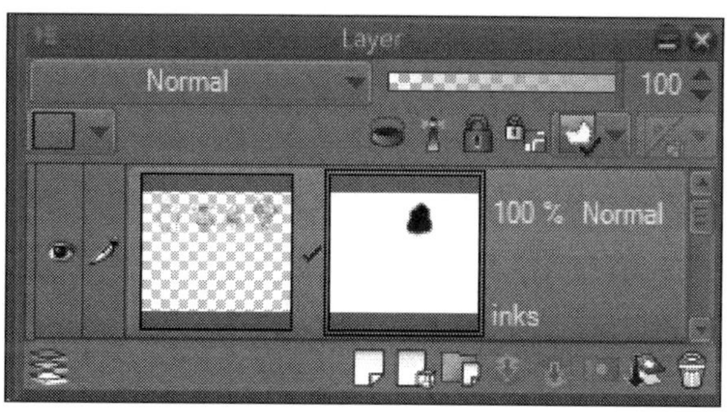

2. To make hidden content visible again, select any pen or brush tool. Draw again over the area with the **Pen(P)** or **Brush(B)** tool to bring back the hidden content. Here is a screenshot that shows a white area inside the previous black area, where the content has now been restored:

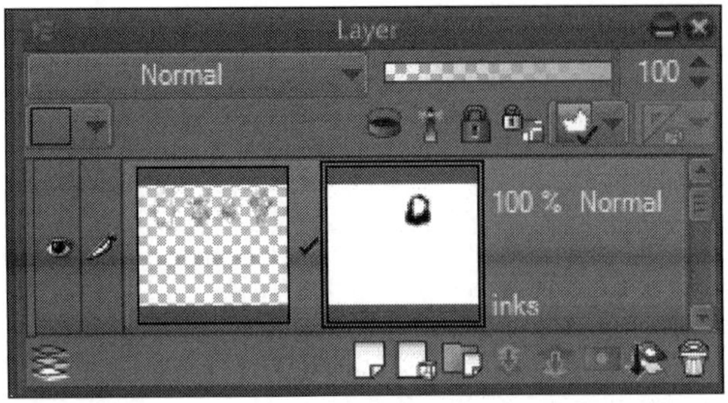

How it works...

In the case of a Layer Mask, using the eraser doesn't permanently erase any part of the drawing. Instead, it hides the content. We can see where we have the Layer Mask placed by looking at the thumbnail in the **Layer** palette and noting where the black areas are. To bring the content back, simply switch to a drawing tool and paint "white" back in the Layer Mask (though the actual color we have selected doesn't matter while working on a Layer Mask). This tells the program to show this information again.

> Want a part of your drawing to a have a ghostly, "faded" look? Use the **Soft** eraser on a Layer Mask to slowly fade out the edges of the drawing.

Making a Quick Mask using selection tools

Using selection tools and layer masks, we can quickly hide or show parts of our drawing.

Getting ready

You will need a file open with at least one layer with content (a sketch, an ink drawing, a photo, and so on) inside of it.

How to do it...

The following steps will lead us through making a mask using a selection tool:

1. First, make a selection using one of the selection tools. In the following screenshot, the details on the robot's torso have been selected using the **Lasso** tool:

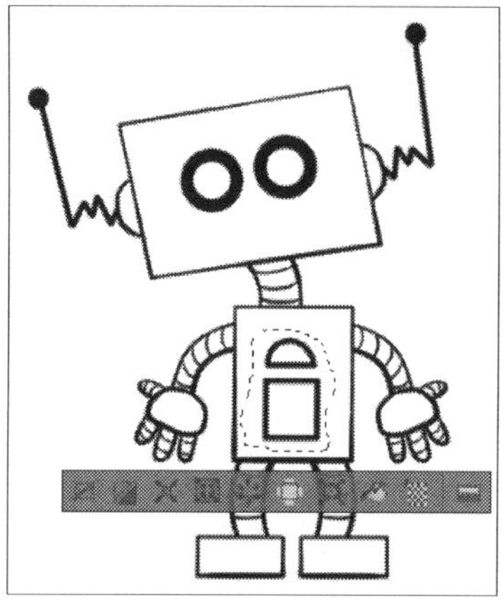

2. Go to **Layer** | **Layer Mask** | **Mask Selection(D)** to mask the *inside* of the selection. In this screenshot, the selected details on the robot have now been hidden with this option:

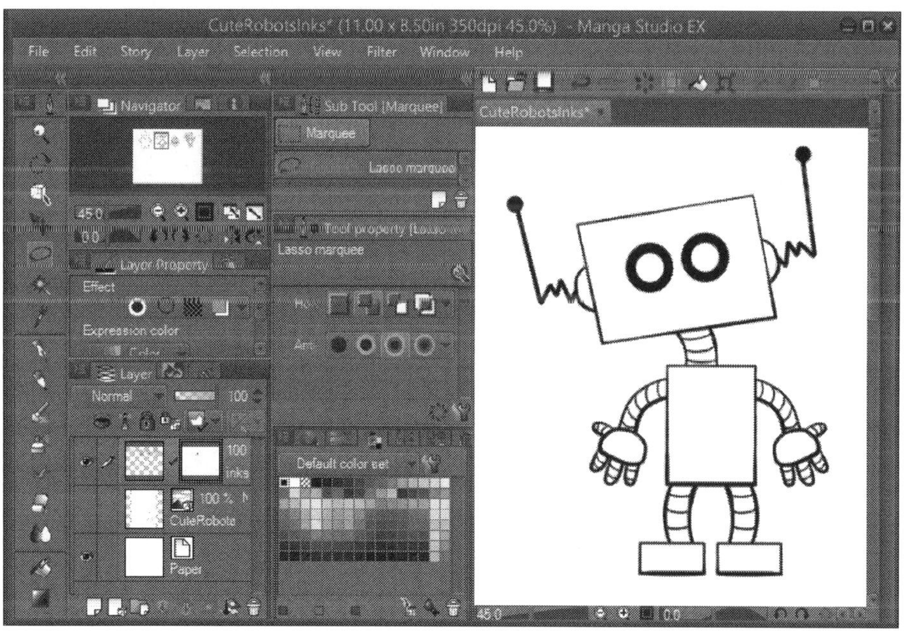

3. Go to **Layer** | **Layer Mask** | **Mask Outside Selection(V)** to hide everything *outside* of the selection. In the following screenshot, only the torso details remain, as they were inside of the selection:

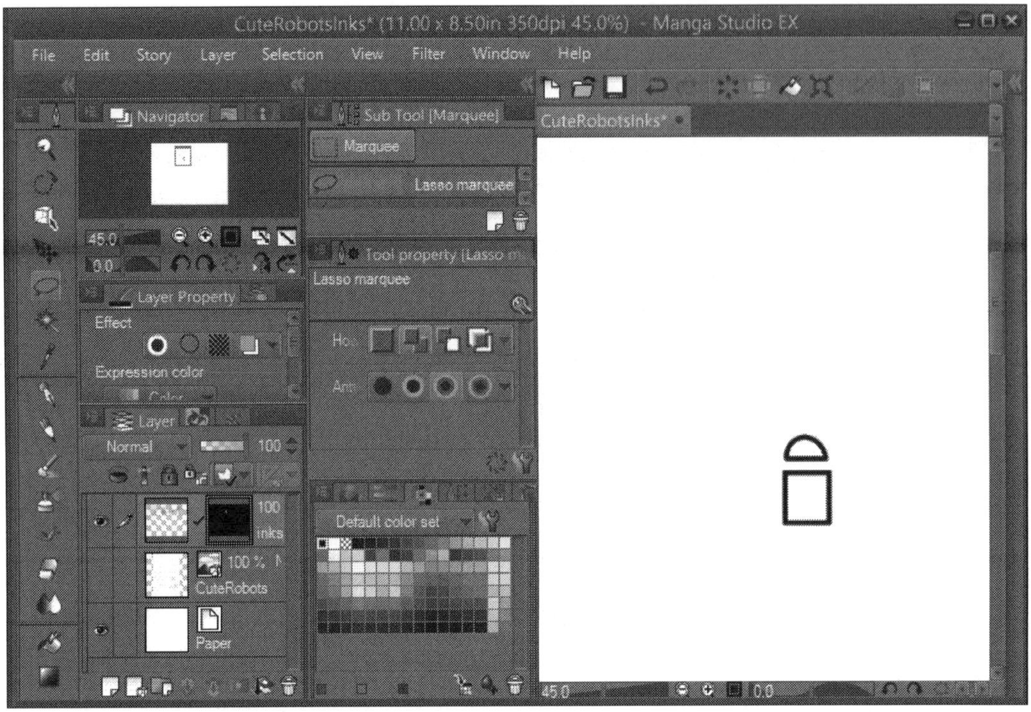

4. Make any necessary edits to the mask, as detailed in the *Editing the Layer Mask* recipe.

How it works...

Using the selection tools, we can speed up the process of masking content. Rather than having to erase large sections by hand with the **Eraser(E)** tool, we can hide or keep all the selected areas at once. This saves a lot of time; that's for sure!

> Want to **Mask Outside Selection(V)** quickly? Select the area you want to keep, and then click on the **Create layer mask** icon at the bottom of the **Layer** palette. A mask will automatically be generated for the outside of the selected area.

Using the Selection pen

The Selection pen is a quick, easy way to make organic selections.

Getting ready

Again, you will need a file open, and it should have at least one layer with content (a sketch, an ink drawing, a photo, and so on) inside of it.

How to do it...

1. Select the **Marquee(M)** tool from the toolbox, and then select the **Selection pen** subtool.
2. Draw over the area that is to be selected. The selection area will be highlighted as the pen is used, as shown in this screenshot:

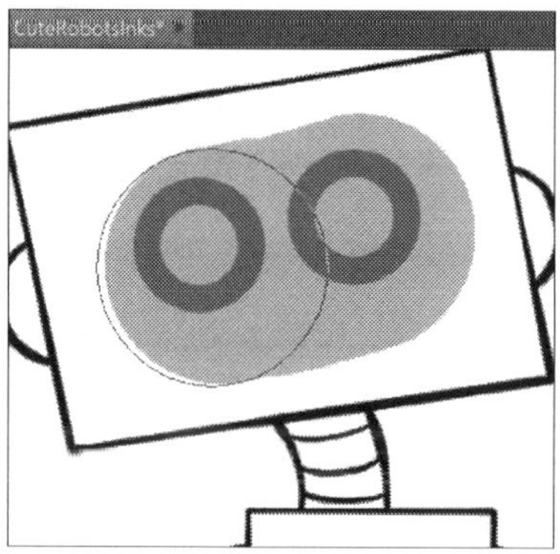

3. When the mouse button or stylus is released, the perimeter of the highlighted area will be turned into a selection, as shown here:

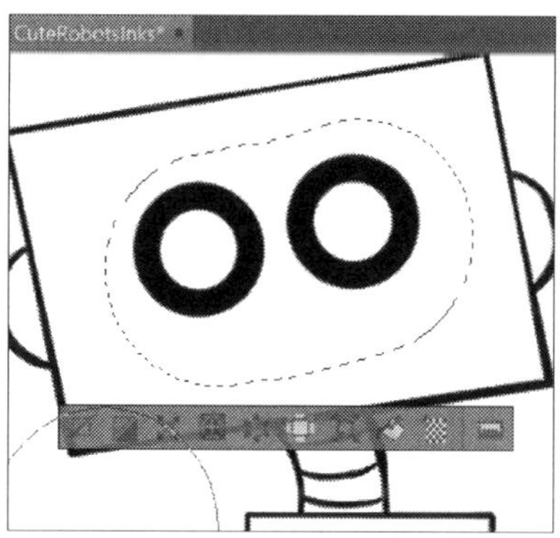

Using the Clear selection tool

Getting ready

You will need a file open, with at least one layer with content (a sketch, an ink drawing, a photo, and so on) inside of it. You will also need an active selection, such as the one made by the **Selection pen** in the *Using the Selection pen* recipe.

How to do it...

1. Select the **Marquee(M)** tool from the toolbox. Then, select the **Clear selection** subtool.
2. Draw over the area to be deselected. The area will be highlighted in green, as shown here:

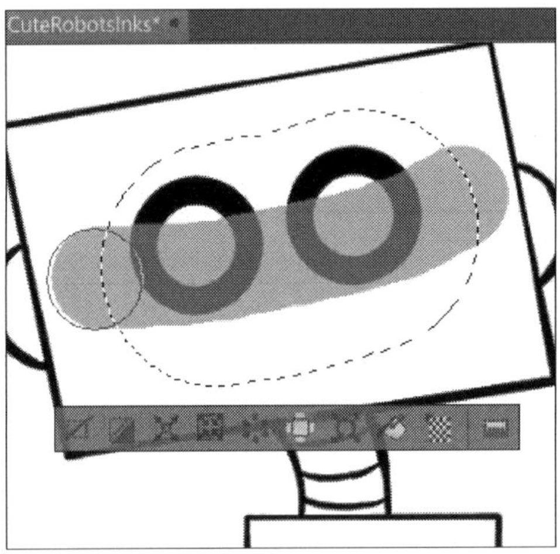

3. When the mouse button or stylus is released, the highlighted area will be subtracted from the currently active selection, as shown in the following screenshot:

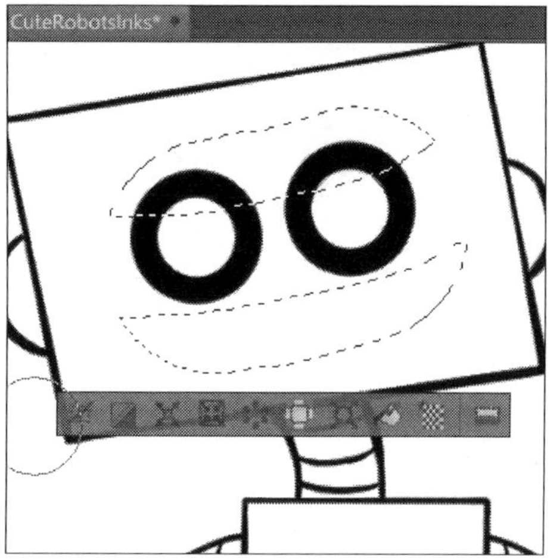

Using the Shrink selection tool

Making a precise selection can be frustrating and time-consuming. The **Shrink selection** tool solves this problem by allowing us to draw a rough selection and then having the program refine it automatically. Let's learn how to use it now!

Getting ready

You will need a file open, and it should have at least one layer with content (a sketch, an ink drawing, a photo, and so on) inside of it.

How to do it...

Follow these steps to use the **Shrink selection** tool:

1. Select the **Marquee(M)** tool from the toolbox. Then, select the **Shrink selection** subtool.

2. Using the mouse or stylus, draw around the area to be selected. In the following screenshot, the robot's facial features are what I want to select, so I've drawn a rough area around them with the tool:

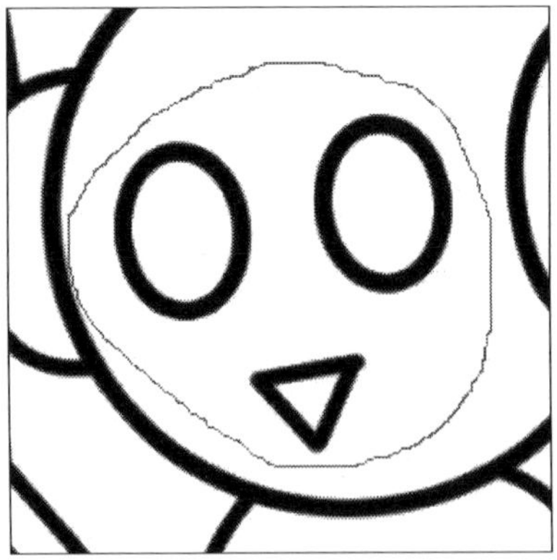

3. When the selection is completed, the tool will automatically shrink down to select the outer edges of all areas inside the area we drew around in step 2. Refer to the next screenshot and note how the facial features are now cleanly selected:

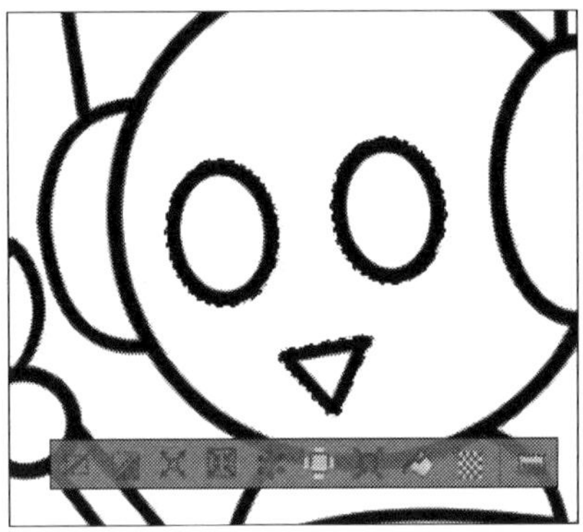

> The areas to be selected by the **Shrink selection** tool must be surrounded by transparency. In the preceding example, if we tried to use the **Shrink selection** tool to select the robot's head and move it away from the body of the robot, the tool would not work, because the black ink lines of the body intersect with the lines of the head.

6
Using New Rulers and Line Tools

In this chapter, you will learn these recipes:

- Using Symmetry ruler
- Making action lines with the Scattered stream line tool
- Making action lines with the Dark stream line tool
- Adding moods with the Gloom stream line tool
- Making rain drops with the Rain stream line tool
- Making focus lines with the Scattered stream line tool
- Making focus lines with the Dark saturated line tool
- Making focus lines with the Dense saturated line tool
- Using the Brightness tool
- Creating dark flashes with the Burst tool

Introduction

Rulers are one of the best features of several digital art programs. They allow us to simulate traditional rulers in the digital space, making it easier to draw straight lines or smooth curves. Manga Studio 5 has some special rulers, including focus lines and perspective rulers.

In this book, we're going to cover only the new rulers and line tools that are available in 5.0.5, since all the other rulers were discussed in my other book, *Mastering Manga Studio 5, Packt Publishing*.

Using Symmetry ruler

Symmetry is the quality of being made up of exactly the same parts, either facing the other, around an axis. To make a symmetrical drawing, you can draw half the object and then mirror it, or you can use **Symmetry ruler**!

Getting ready

You will need a sketch of something to mirror, of course! In this recipe, the demonstration will be of this sketch of a robot's head:

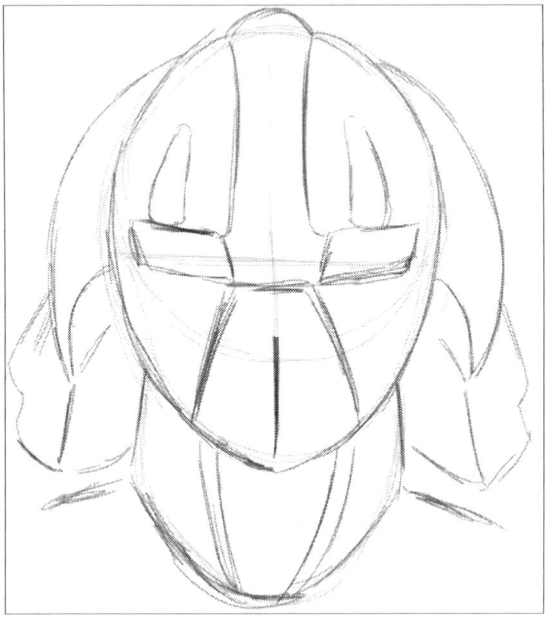

How to do it...

The following steps will walk us through the use of **Symmetry ruler**:

1. Select the **Figure** tool. Then, select the **Symmetrical ruler** subtool, which is under **Ruler**.
2. Click and hold the mouse on the drawing; then, drag out a line. This is the line that your drawing will be mirrored about. The dark line shown down the center of the face in the following screenshot is our **Symmetrical ruler**:

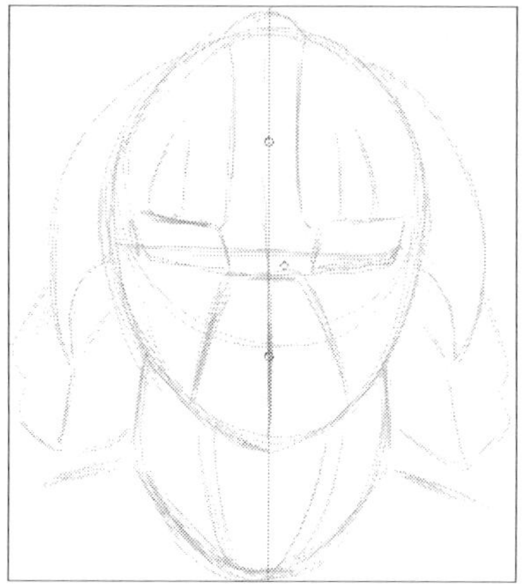

> To make the ruler perfectly straight or at a 45-degree angle, hold down the *Shift* key and drag. This will constrain the ruler.

3. If adjustments need to be made to the ruler placement, select the **Object** tool under **Operation** and click on the ruler. The circular handles control the rotation of the ruler. Clicking and dragging on the ruler line will allow you to reposition the ruler on the drawing. The diamond handle turns the ruler on or off.
4. Select the drawing tool of your choice and follow the lines. You may find that selecting one side of the drawing and only following the sketch on that side is best. The robot face shown here was completed by following the lines on the left-hand side of the ruler:

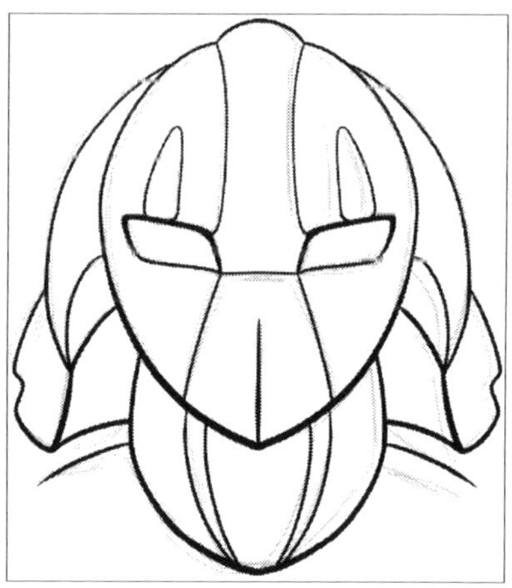

There's more...

We can add lines of symmetry to the ruler to make a kaleidoscope-like effect by performing the following steps:

1. Select the **Figure(U)** tool. Then select the **Symmetrical ruler** subtool, which is under **Ruler**.
2. In the **Tool property** palette, adjust the **Number of lines** option using either the slider or the up and down arrows to the right of the option. The following screenshot shows the settings used for this recipe:

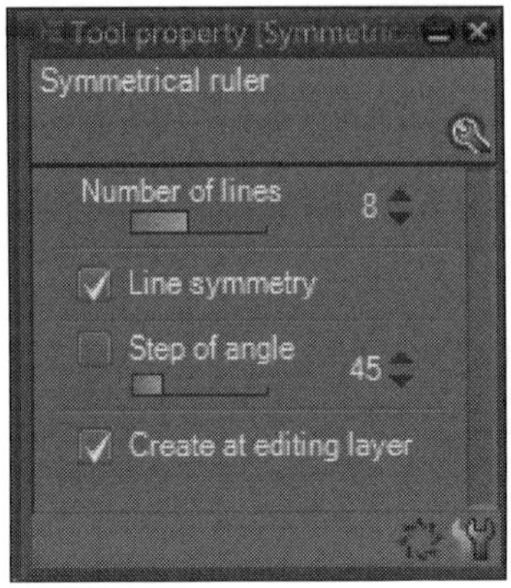

3. Click on the drawing canvas and hold the mouse button down while dragging out a line. This will determine a spoke of your ruler.
4. If adjustments need to be made to the ruler placement, go to **Operation** | **Object** and click on the ruler. The circular handles control the rotation of the ruler. Clicking and dragging on the ruler line will allow you to reposition the ruler on the drawing. The diamond handle turns the ruler on or off.
5. Select the drawing tool of your choice and finish your drawing! The next screenshot shows an image made with the **G-pen** tool. Note the lines that show where the drawing was mirrored to make the design.

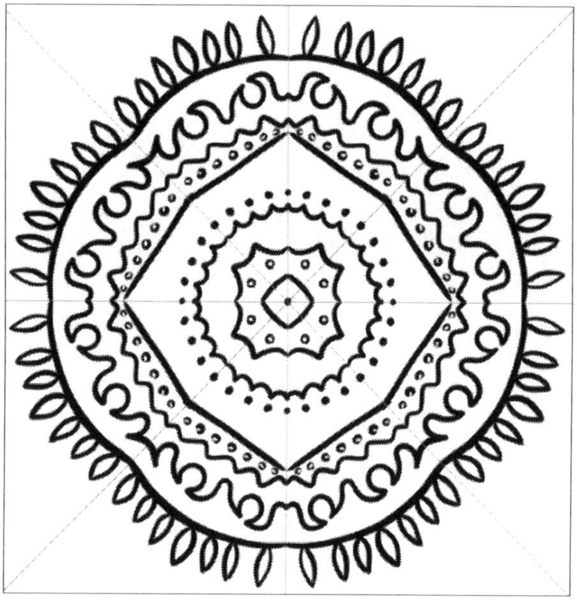

Making action lines with the Scattered stream line tool

If you read comics, you will be familiar with action lines. They show the path of an object in motion. With the **Scattered stream line** tool and the **Dark stream line** tool, we can create action lines quickly and have the flexibility to edit them—something that's not available when we draw action lines by hand!

Getting ready

You will need an open file to work in. The size and resolution don't matter. In the following recipe, the demonstration will be on the image shown here, in which we will be adding action lines behind the flying superhero:

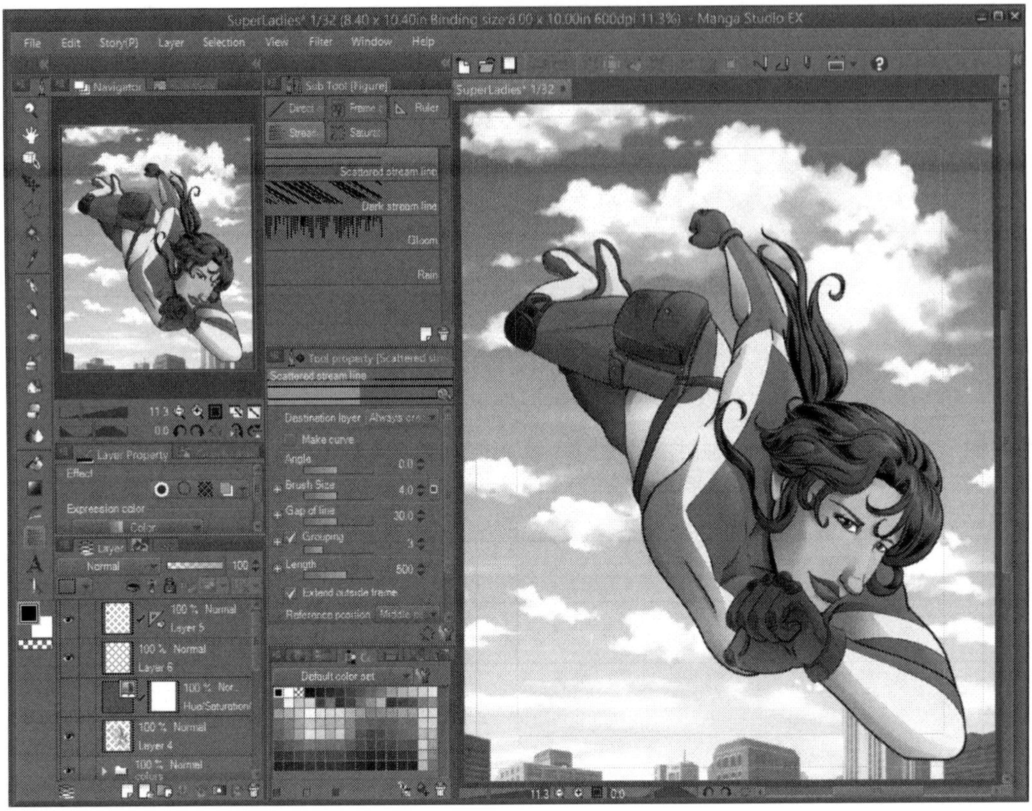

How to do it...

The following steps will show you how to use the **Scattered stream line** tool:

1. Select the **Figure(U)** tool from the toolbox. Then, navigate to the **Scattered stream line** subtool, which is under **Stream line**.
2. Click with the mouse at one point on your image. Then, double-click at another point. In the case of the hero image, these points were spaced diagonally and at the width of the character's body.

3. After you have double-clicked, the program will automatically generate action lines based on the settings of the tool. Note, as shown in the following screenshot, that these lines are horizontal instead of following the angle of the character, and we'll need additional editing:

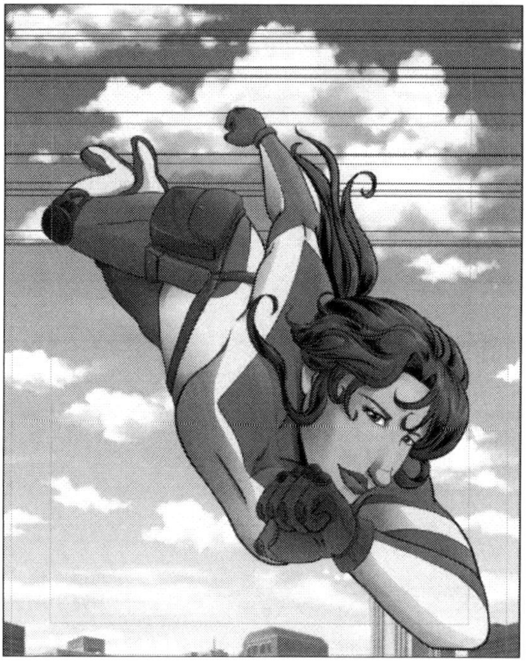

4. Select the **Operation** tool and then select the **Object** subtool. Next, we click on the line that we just made for our stream lines to select them for editing.
5. Open the **Sub Tool Detail** palette, as you did in *Chapter 2, Customizing Brushes*.

6. First, we will adjust **Angle**. Here, we've changed it from a value of `0` to `58`, as shown in the following screenshot.

> To change the angle of the lines without opening the **Sub Tool Detail** palette, select the stream lines with the **Object** tool. Next, locate the red handles. Click on one of them and rotate it until the line is at the desired angle. Then, release the mouse button.

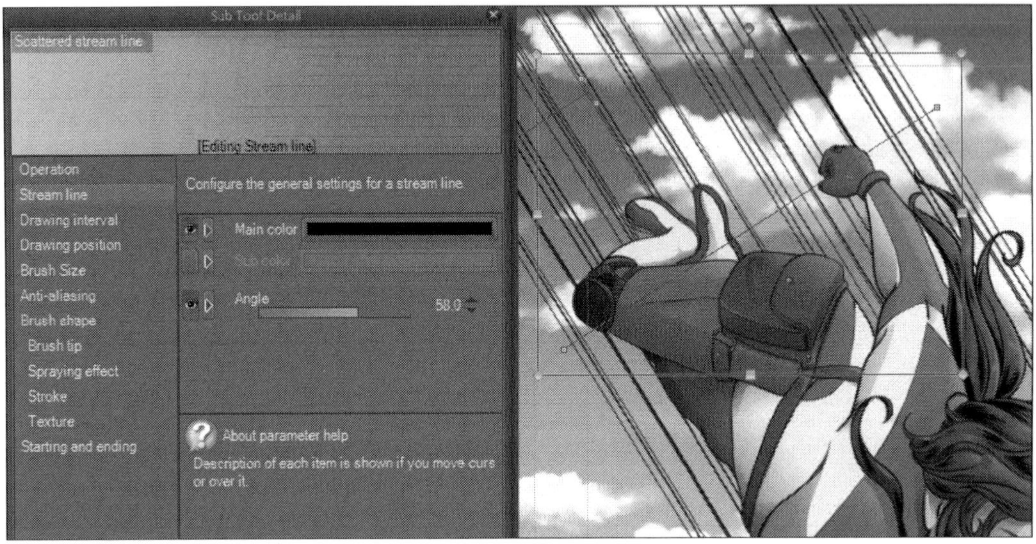

7. Next, click on the **Drawing position** option to the left of the **Sub Tool Detail** palette. In this palette, we will set **Length** to `300` to shorten the lines so that they don't extend very far beyond the character. As you can see in this screenshot, we have also moved the original blue line up toward the corner of the canvas:

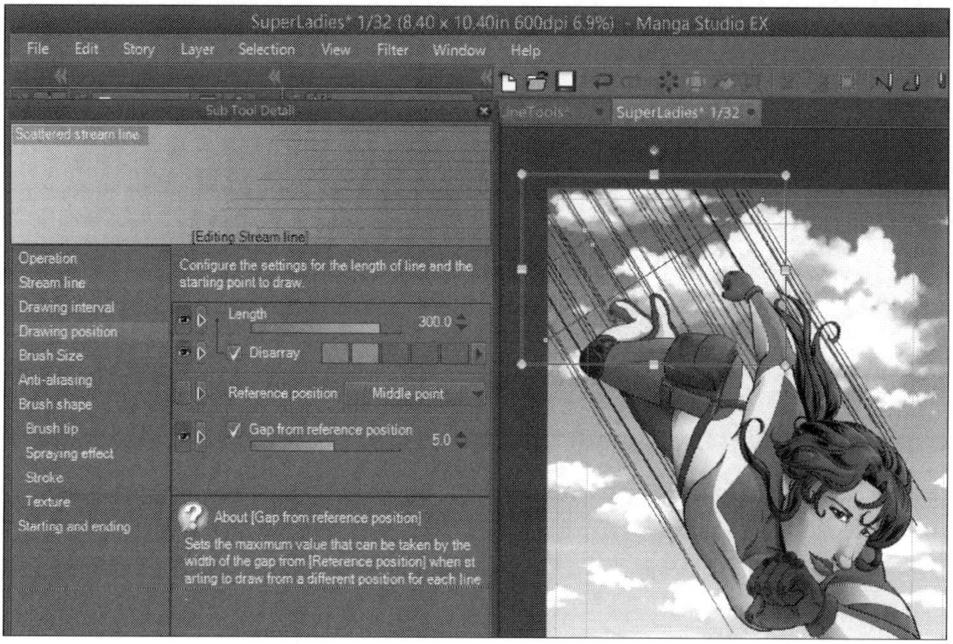

8. Next, select the **Starting and ending** option from the left-hand side of the **Sub Tool Detail** palette. Click on the drop-down menu to the right of the **Starting and ending** option on the right-hand side, and then check the box next to **Brush Size** to activate it. This will automatically taper each end of the lines, making them look more like they were hand-drawn. You can see this in the following screenshot:

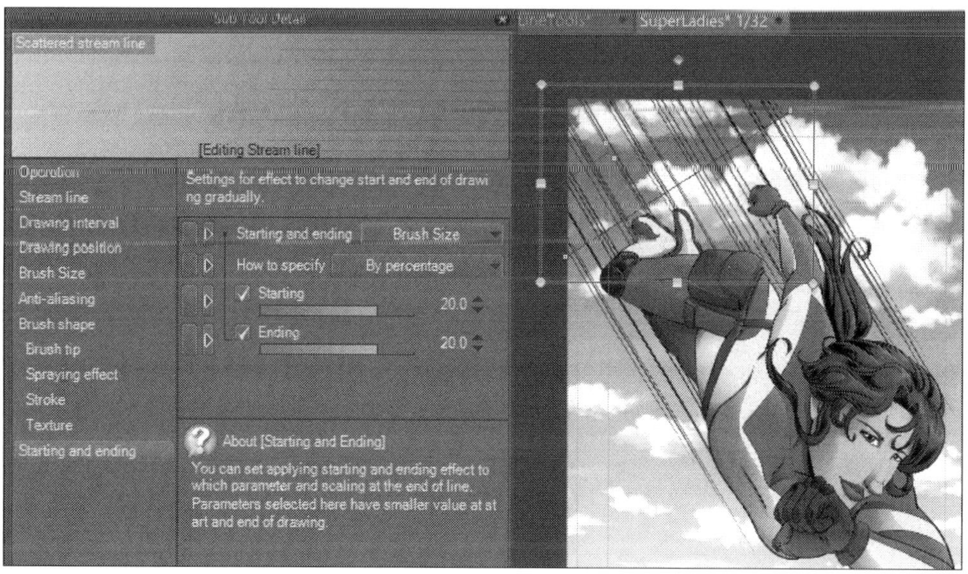

9. Make other adjustments as needed to the menu items. Refer to the *How it works...* section for more information.

How it works...

The line that we placed first is a guide for the location of our stream lines. Some of the options will be visible in the **Tool property** palette, but to see all of them, we may want to use the **Sub Tool Detail** palette as we make more edits.

Here is a brief rundown of the options specific to the **Stream line** subtools. For the other options listed in the **Sub Tool Detail** palette, refer to *Chapter 2, Customizing Brushes*.

Angle (under **Stream line**) controls the angle of the generated lines.

Under **Drawing interval**, we have the following:

- **Gap of line** is the amount of space between lines. The **Disarray** option beneath that will randomize the space between the lines, giving them a more organic look. Unchecking this box will make the space between all lines equal.
- **Grouping** alternately repeats the areas where lines are closer to each other and farther apart. The **Disarray** box makes this random, giving an even more organic and hand-drawn look.
- **Gap** is the size of the areas where the lines are not drawn. This sets the empty space between the lines.
- **Maximum number of lines** is the highest number of lines that will be displayed in this space.

Under **Drawing position**, we have these options:

- **Length** decides how long the lines are. A higher value gives longer lines, and the contrary is also true. The **Disarray** option will randomize the lengths of the lines.
- **Reference position** is where the lines will start being drawn. The options for this are **Starting point**, **Middle point**, and **Ending point**.
- **Gap from reference position** is the setting for the empty space allowed between the lines and the reference position.

Making action lines with the Dark stream line tool

In addition to the regular **Stream line** tool, there is also a subtool for a **Dark stream line**. Let's learn how to use it.

Getting ready

You will need an open file to work in. Again, the size and resolution don't matter. We will continue using the image from the previous recipe as our example.

How to do it...

The following steps will show you how to use the **Dark stream line** tool:

1. Select the **Figure(U)** tool from the toolbox. Then go to **Stream line** | **Dark stream line**.
2. Click on the canvas to create a starting point. Then double-click on another point to create an ending point. Lines will be made by the program according to the currently selected settings.
3. To make edits to the current stream lines, select the **Operation** tool and then the **Object** subtool. Select the stream lines to make them active. Next, select the **Stream line** subtool again while the existing lines are selected, and then open the **Sub Tool Detail** palette.
4. The **Dark Stream line** tool can be curved! Use the **Object** subtool and select the stream lines. Click on the center of the red control line and hold the mouse button. Drag out from the line to adjust the curve. The lines will adjust after the mouse button is released.

The following screenshot shows our hero with curved action lines:

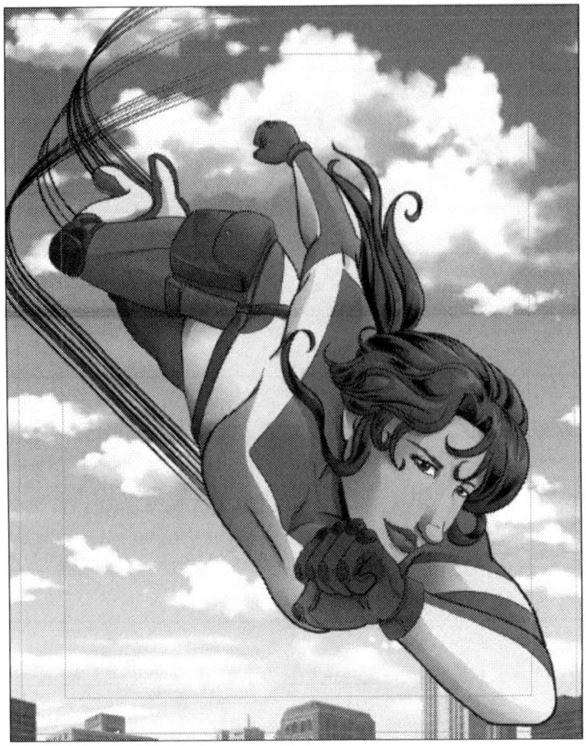

How it works...

For an overview of the options for this line tool, refer to the *How it works...* section of the *Making action lines with the Scattered stream line tool* recipe.

Adding moods with the Gloom stream line tool

Almost anyone who reads Manga will recognize the special effect of moods. A character is sad and the background will have vertical lines coming down behind them, usually ending around the shoulders or the middle of the head, depending on the desired look. The **Gloom** tool makes this effect easy to achieve with just a few clicks.

Getting ready

You will need an open file to work in. Again, the size and resolution don't matter. For this example, I have drawn a down-in-the-dumps character and filled the line art with white on the inside so that the lines won't show through the character, as shown in the following screenshot:

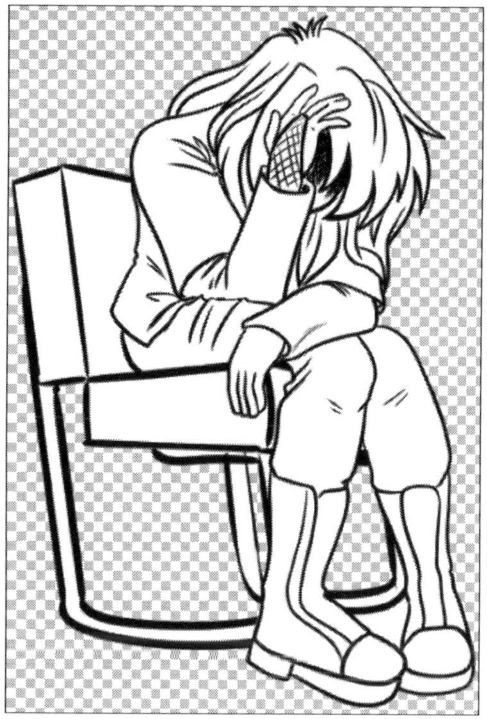

How to do it...

The following simple steps will show us how to create mood lines:

1. Select the **Figure(U)** tool from the toolbox. Then select the **Gloom** subtool under **Stream**.
2. Click with the mouse or press the stylus wherever you want the gloom lines to begin.
3. Double-click with the mouse or use the stylus on the point where you want the gloom lines to end.

The gloom lines will be generated automatically, based on the settings of the tool.

How it works...

This screenshot shows the drawing example with gloom lines added to it:

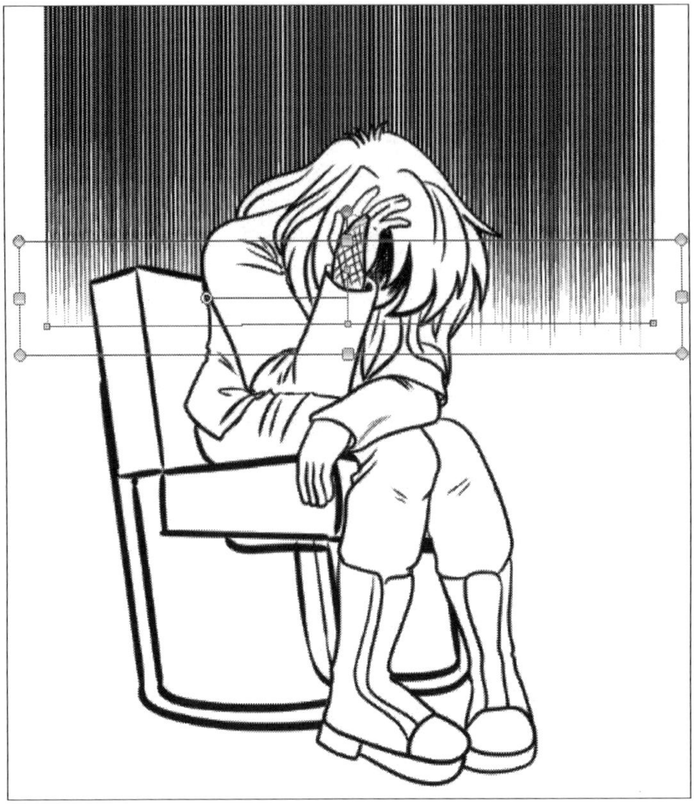

The horizontal line inside the bounding box shows where the start and end points were put on the canvas. These mark the place where the gloom lines end.

Refer to the *How it works...* section of the *Making action lines with the Scattered stream line tool* recipe for information about the different settings available for this tool.

There's more...

This tool can also create gloomy lines up to an imaginary curve! Follow the steps given here to find out how:

1. Follow step 1 and step 2 of the preceding recipe.
2. Instead of double-clicking with the mouse to end the line, click once on the place where you want the next point of the curve to be.

3. Continue clicking along the line of the curve until you have completed the desired curve shape. Double-click to set the shape.
4. Manga Studio 5 will automatically generate the lines based on the tool settings. Use the **Object** subtool to adjust the curve afterwards, if desired. The following screenshot shows the curve used around the character to create a different look for the illustration:

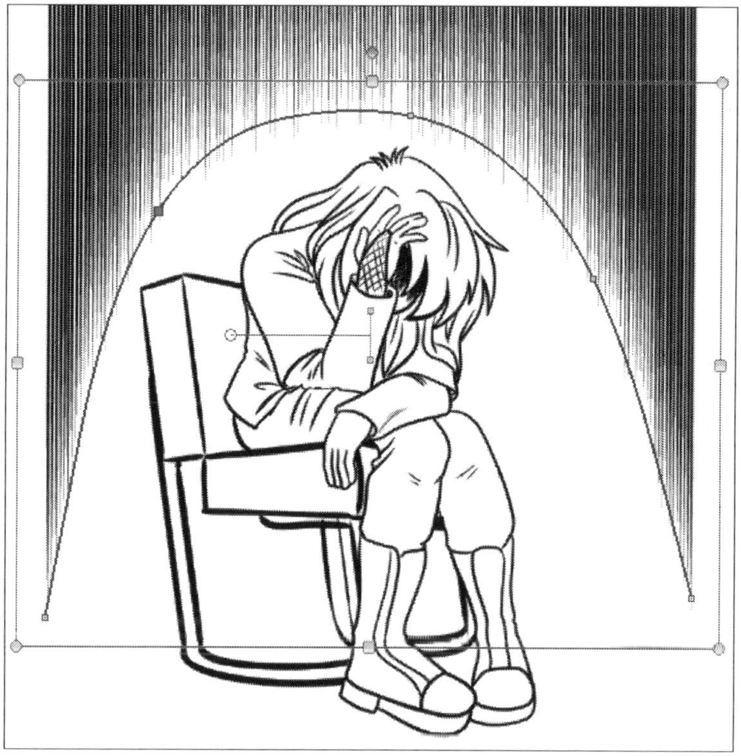

Making rain drops with the Rain stream line tool

This hand tool makes rain drops fit for a black-and-white or less detailed comic. Like the Scattered stream line and Dark stream line tools, it is easy to use!

Getting ready

You will need an open file to work in. The size and resolution don't matter.

How to do it...

The following steps will lead you through the simple process of making rain drops for your illustration:

1. Select the **Figure(U)** tool from the toolbox. Then select the **Rain** subtool, which is under **Stream line**.
2. Click on the canvas to create a starting point. Then double-click on another point to make an ending point. Lines will be made by the program according to the currently selected settings.
3. To make edits to the current lines, select the **Operation** tool and then the **Object** subtool. Next, select the stream lines to make them active. Then select the **Rain** subtool again while the existing lines are selected, and finally open the **Sub Tool Detail** palette.

How it works...

Like the previous stream tools and the **Gloom** tool, the options for the rain lines can be changed to create any look from a light shower to a heavy downpour. Refer to the *How it works...* section of the *Making action lines with the Scattered stream line tool* recipe for more information about each option.

The next screenshot shows just one of the looks that can be achieved with this tool. A Layer Mask (covered in the *Adding a Layer Mask* and *Editing the Layer Mask* recipes of *Chapter 5, Making Selections and Layer Masks*) was added to get rid of the rain drops under the umbrella. Then, details were drawn to give the appearance of rain drops hitting the top of the umbrella.

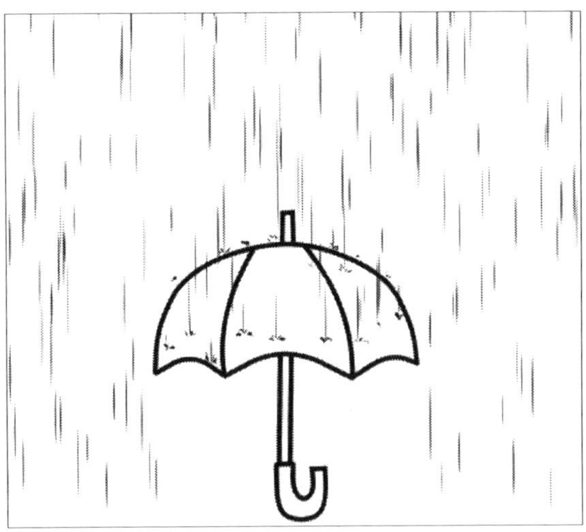

Making focus lines with the Scattered saturated line tool

Another effect used in a lot of Manga and comics is the focus line. These lines radiate from a central point and can show shock or surprise, indicate an action, or draw the eye.

Getting ready

You will need an open file to work in. The size and resolution don't matter.

How to do it...

The following steps will teach you how to use the **Scattered saturated line** tool:

1. Select the **Figure(U)** tool from the toolbox. Then go to **Saturated line** | **Scattered saturated line**.
2. Click on the spot from where you want all the lines to radiate and hold down the mouse button.
3. While still holding down the mouse button, drag out to form an ellipse around the area to focus on. In the example shown here, the lines will be focused on the character's face:

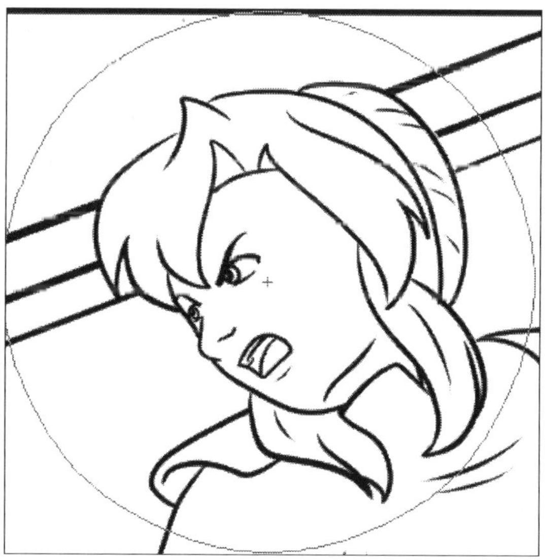

> Need a perfect circle? Hold down the *Shift* key while dragging!

4. Release the mouse button to generate the lines.

How it works...

This tool, like the line tools that we've already covered this chapter, draws lines based on the settings of the tool and the line (or in this case, the circle!) that we've already set. The focus lines radiate from the central point of the ellipse, fading at its outer edges. We can change the settings of the existing lines by selecting them with the **Object** tool, then going back to the **Scattered saturated line** tool, and opening the **Sub Tool Detail** palette, as detailed in the *How it works...* section of the *Making action lines with the Scattered stream line tool* recipe.

Here, you can see the focus lines created with the ellipse pictured in the preceding screenshot:

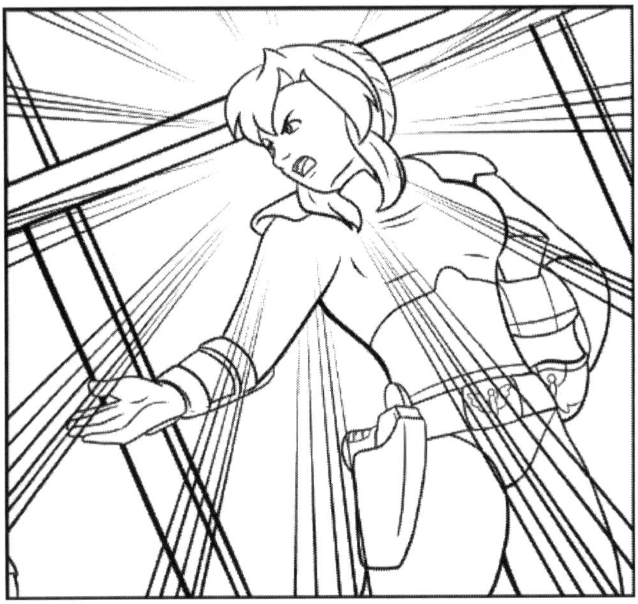

Making focus lines with the Dark saturated line tool

With this tool, we can make darker, more powerful focus lines in an instant. Instead of a circle, this tool has us placing a curve to show where to focus the lines.

Getting ready

Again, you will need an open file to work in. The size and resolution don't matter.

How to do it...

The following steps will teach you how to use the **Dark saturated line** tool:

1. Select the **Figure(U)** tool from the toolbox. Then go to **Saturated line** | **Dark saturated line**.
2. Click with the mouse button to start the curved line.
3. Continue moving the mouse and clicking to draw the curve. The following is the curve we'll be using for this example. Note that the lines will be stopping before the character's face, where we want the focus to be.

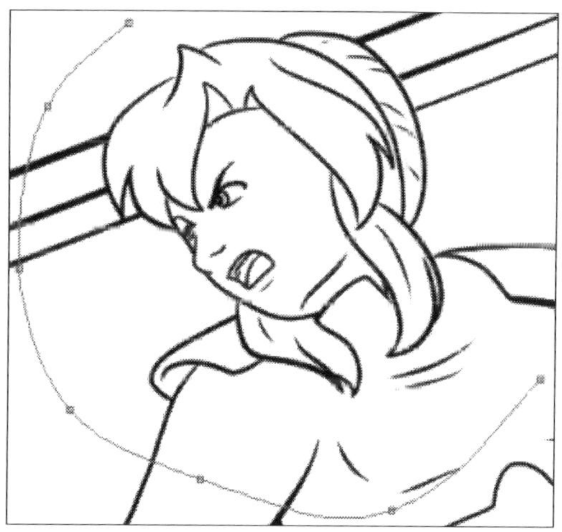

4. Double-click with the mouse on the final point to end the curve and generate the lines.

How it works...

We can change the settings of the existing lines by selecting them with the **Object** tool, then going back to the **Scattered saturated line** tool, and opening the **Sub Tool Detail** palette, as detailed in the *How it works...* section of the *Making action lines with the Scattered stream line tool* recipe.

The following are the focus lines created with the curve pictured in the preceding screenshot:

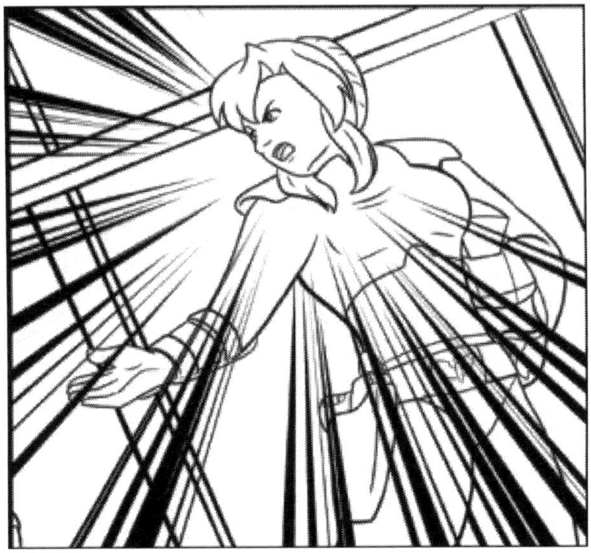

Making focus lines with the Dense saturated line tool

What if we need lots and lots of thin focus lines? The **Dense saturated line** tool is the go-to tool for that job!

Getting ready

You will need an open file to work in. The size and resolution don't matter.

How to do it...

The following steps will teach us how to use the **Scattered saturated line** tool:

1. Select the **Figure(U)** tool from the toolbox. Then go to **Saturated line** | **Dense saturated line**.
2. Click on the spot where you want all the lines to radiate from and hold down the mouse button.
3. While still holding down the mouse button, drag out to form an ellipse around the area to focus on. In the following screenshot, the lines will be focused on the character's face. Because this tool makes such dense lines, I try to go a long way around the area that I want the focus to be on so that it doesn't get obscured by the lines.

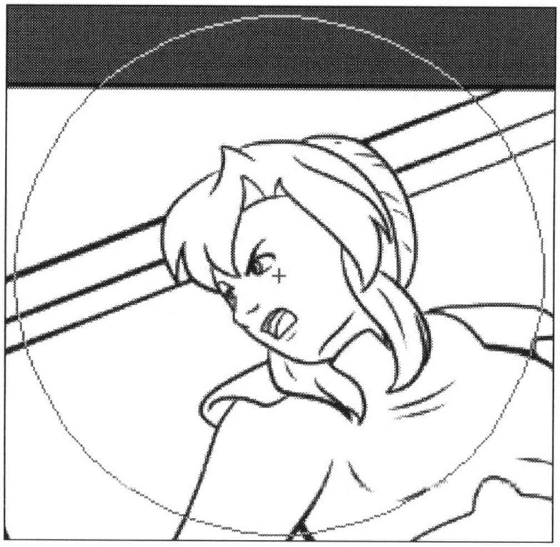

4. Release the mouse button to generate the lines.

How it works...

This tool also generates our focus lines based on a circle, just like the **Scattered saturated line** tool. The focus lines radiate from the central point of the ellipse, fading at its outer edges.

Again, we can change the settings of the existing lines by selecting them with the **Object** tool, then going back to the **Scattered saturated line** tool, and opening the **Sub Tool Detail** palette, as detailed in the *How it works...* section of the *Making action lines with the Scattered stream line tool* recipe.

Here, you can see the focus lines created with the ellipse pictured in the preceding screenshot:

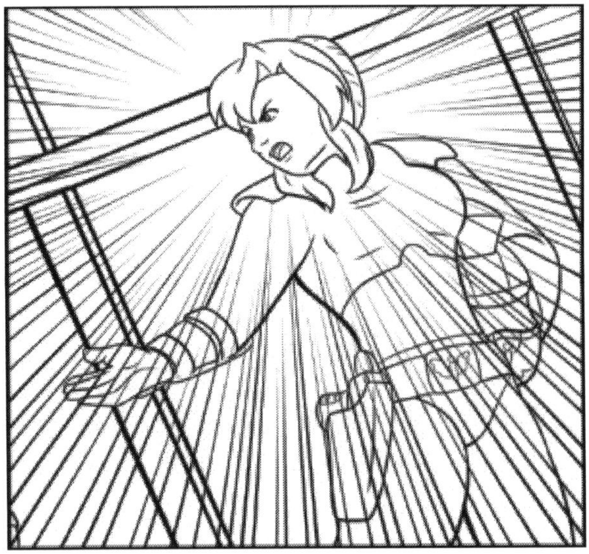

Using the Brightness tool

The **Brightness** tool can be used to add a special effect to things such as explosions or bright flashes of light. Use your imagination and you'll find lots of uses for this tool!

Getting ready

Again, you will need an open file to work in. The size and resolution don't matter.

How to do it...

The following steps will teach you how to use the **Brightness** tool:

1. Select the **Figure(U)** tool from the toolbox. Then select go to **Saturated line** | **Brightness**.
2. Click on the central point for the brightness effect and then drag out while holding down the mouse button to form an ellipse, as shown in the following screenshot:

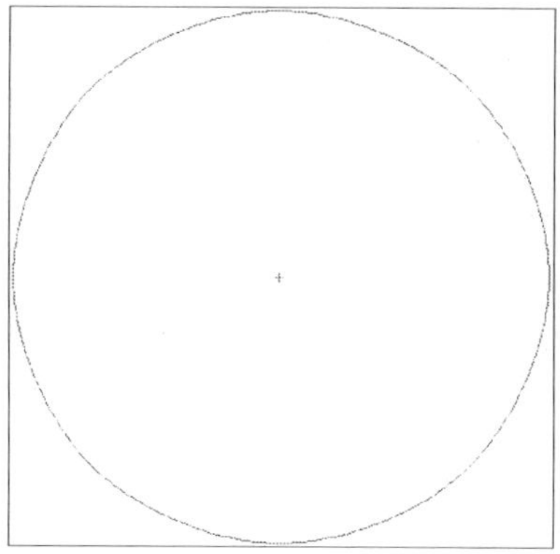

3. Release the mouse button. The brightness lines will be drawn according to the settings of the tool. This screenshot shows the result of the default settings:

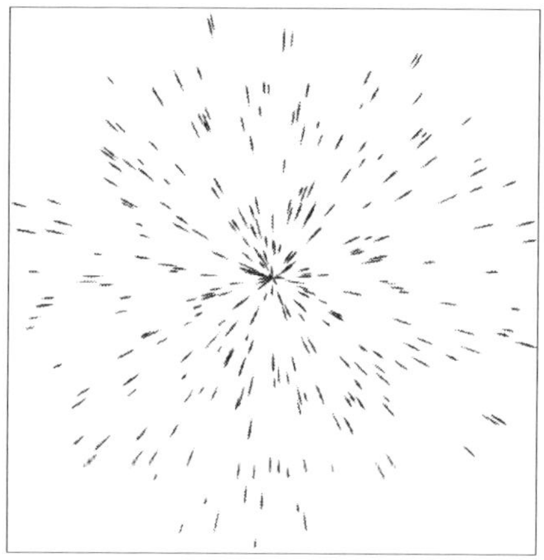

For more information on customizing the settings of this tool, see the *How it works...* section of the *Making action lines with the Scattered stream line tool* recipe.

Creating dark flashes with the Burst tool

Unlike the focus line tools, the **Burst** tool creates a series of lines emanating from the center point on the inside of an ellipse, instead of the outside.

Getting ready

You will need an open file to work in. The size and resolution don't matter.

How to do it...

The following steps will teach you how to use the **Brightness** tool:

1. Select the **Figure(U)** tool from the toolbox. Then go to **Saturated line** | **Burst**.
2. Click on the central point for the brightness effect, and then drag out while holding down the mouse button to form an ellipse, as shown in the screenshot just after step 2 of the previous recipe.
3. Release the mouse button. The lines will be drawn according to the settings of the tool. The following screenshot shows the result of the default settings:

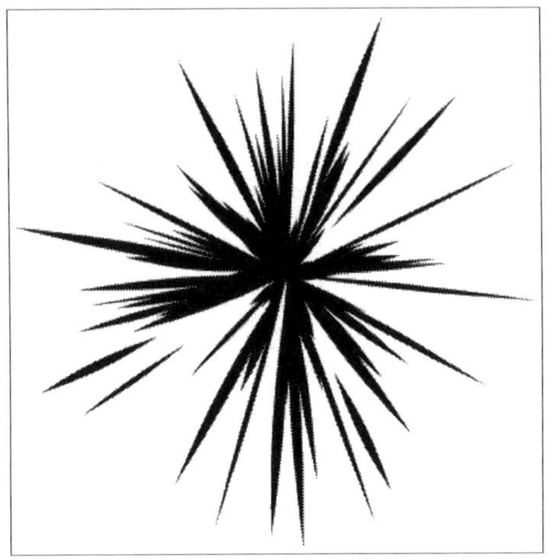

For more information on customizing the settings of this tool, see the *How it works...* section of the *Making action lines with the Scattered stream line tool* recipe.

7

Adding and Creating Tones and Materials

In this chapter, we will cover the following recipes:

- Adding a screentone to a large area
- Using a selection to apply a quick tone
- Creating and saving custom materials
- Drawing a custom fabric pattern
- Using Mesh Transformation to apply more realistic fabric patterns

Introduction

Materials are saved images that can be found in the **Material** library in Manga Studio 5. These include everything from brush tips (such as the ones we created in *Chapter 2, Customizing Brushes*) and 3D models to background images and screentones. We'll cover 3D topics in *Chapter 10, Using 3D Objects*.

Now, though, let's play with materials!

Adding a screentone to a large area

The following is the most basic way to add a screentone to an image.

Getting ready

You will need an open file. The size and resolution don't matter. For these recipes, I am using a square canvas set at `350` dpi. You will also need the **Material** library open. Go to **Window** | **Material** | **Material [Basic]** if your **Material** library is not currently open.

How to do it...

The following steps will teach you how to add a screentone or any other material to your canvas:

1. In the **Material** library, locate the material to add to the image. For this recipe, we are using the **60.0 line 40% Circle Monochrome** screentone from the **Basic** category, which is under **Monochromatic pattern**. Note that it is shown selected in this screenshot:

2. Click on the **Paste selected material to canvas** button at the bottom of the **Material** window. It is circled in the following screenshot:

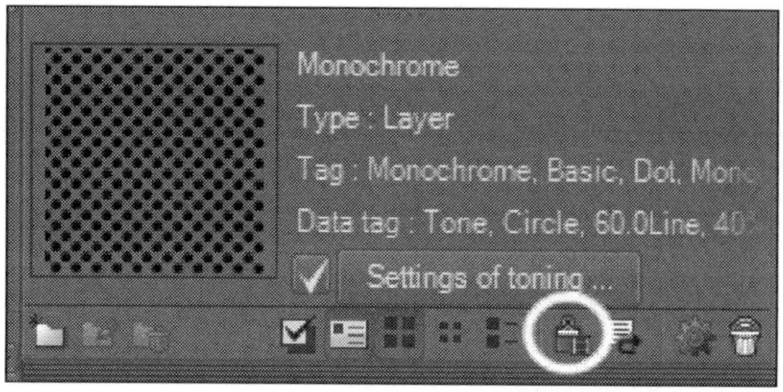

3. The selected material is added to the canvas. As shown in the following screenshot, with this method, the material fills the entire canvas instead of just a portion:

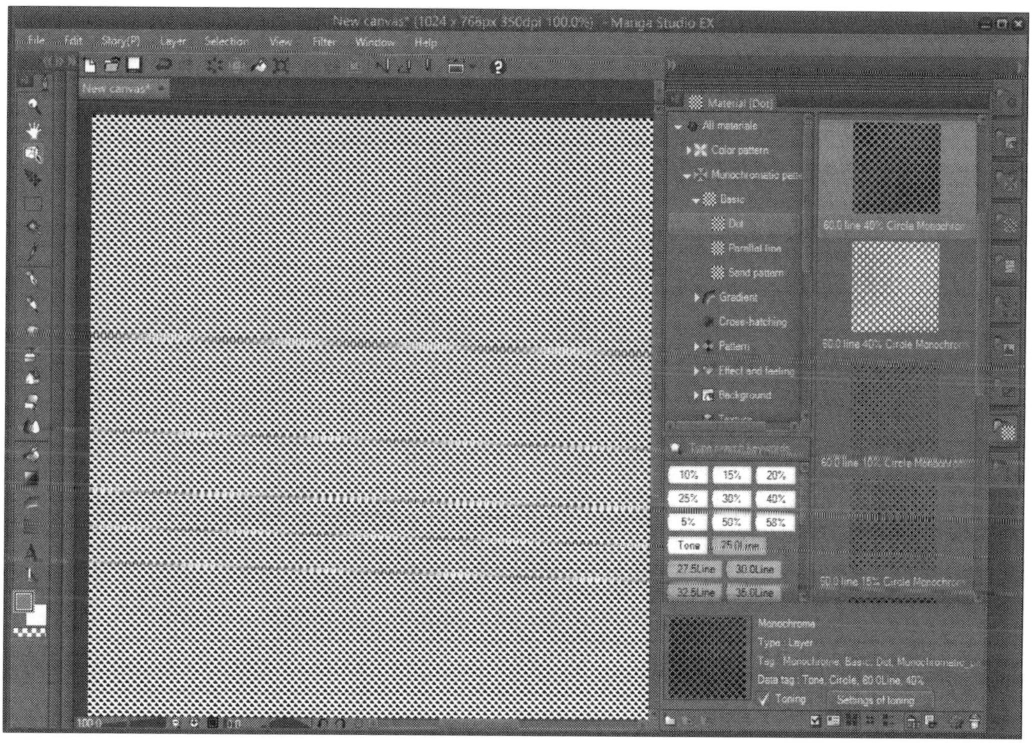

4. The new materials layer will already have an empty layer mask attached to it when you add the material in this way. Use the layer mask to shape the screentone or material image, as shown here:

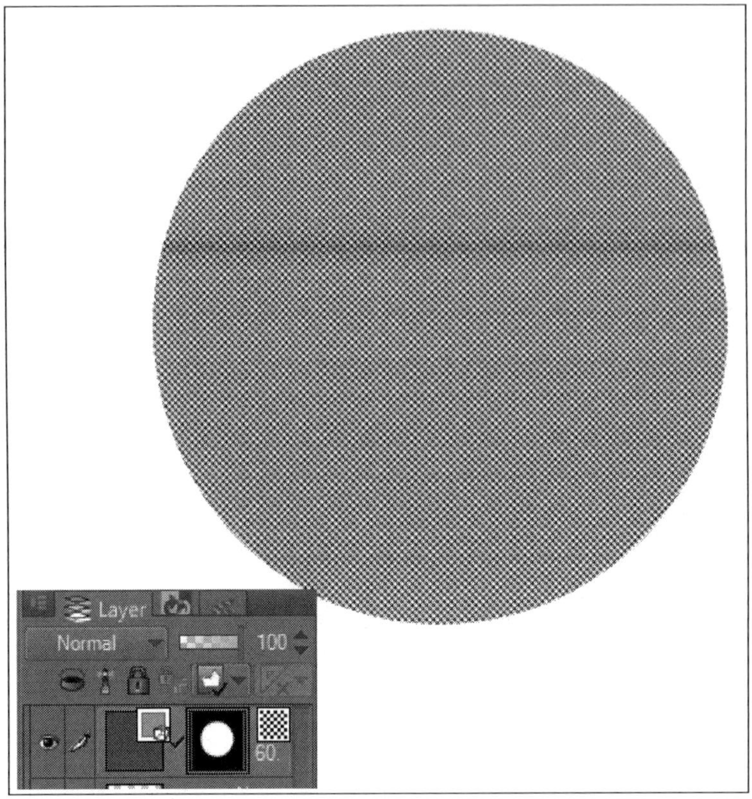

Using a selection tool to apply a quick tone

The previous method is great for applying tones or background images to a large area. But when using traditional screentones, the tones are cut to fit a space in the drawing and then applied to that area. We can do something similar by making a selection and then filling it with a tone.

Getting ready

Again, you will need an open file. The size and resolution don't matter. In this recipe, we are using a blank canvas, but you can also do this with a drawing that you have previously completed.

How to do it...

The following steps will teach you how to add a screentone to a selected area:

1. Use a selection tool to select an area. This screenshot shows a selection made with the **Lasso Marquee(M)** tool:

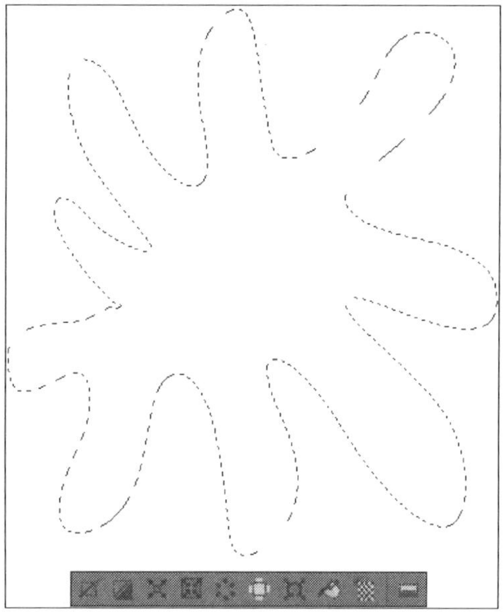

2. In the selection bar beneath the selection, click on the **New Tone** icon. It is shown circled in the following screenshot:

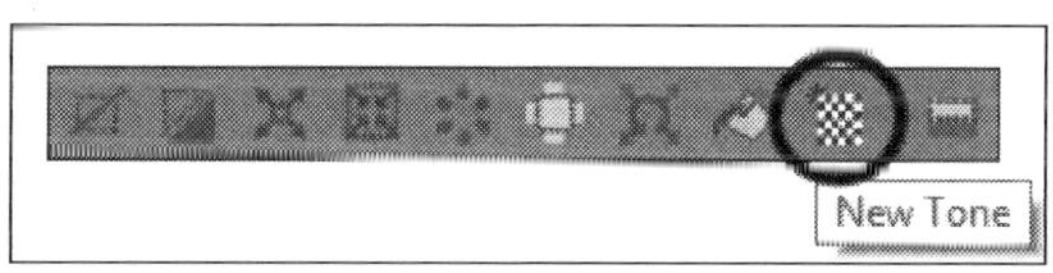

3. Choose the desired settings from the menu that appears. It is shown in this screenshot:

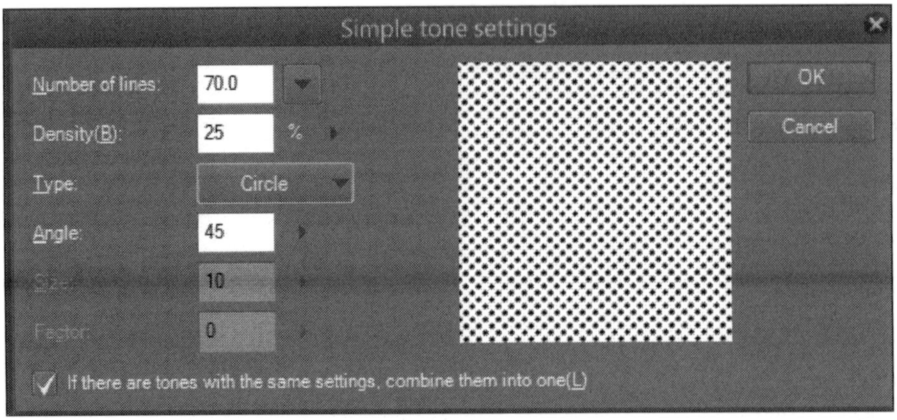

4. Click on **OK**. The selected area will be filled with the tone options from the previous step. The following screenshot shows the selection filled with a screentone of 25 percent density:

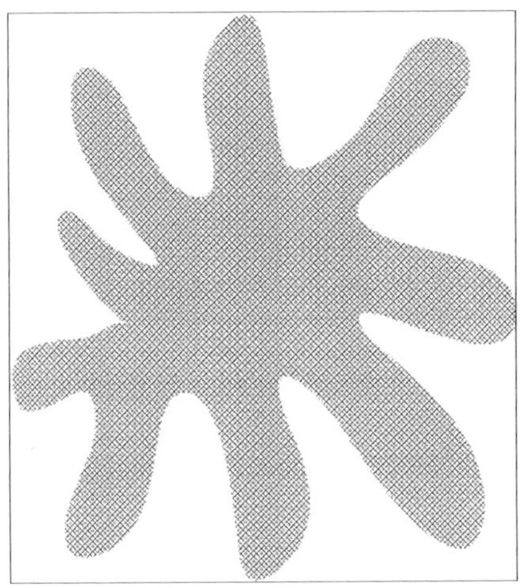

How it works...

Let's talk about the settings available in the **Simple tone settings** menu, which we looked at in step 3.

Number of lines is the number of lines in the screentone. Think of this as the dpi of the tone. A tone with 27.5 lines will be composed of much larger individual dots than a tone with 85 lines. In the recipe, we have used 70 lines, resulting in fairly small dots in the tone.

Density(B) is a measure of how dark the tone is. This can be anywhere from `1%` to `100%`; `1%` means very tiny individual dots, which are barely noticeable, and `100%` density means pure black.

Type is the shape of the dots in the tone. Our "dots" don't have to be circles! Manga Studio 5 gives us the option to use lines, flowers, diamonds, and hearts.

> Different types of tone can produce great effects. Illustrating a romantic scene and using the heart type of tone? Set a smaller number of lines so that the design is more obvious!

Angle is the angle of the lines in the tone. In this recipe, we have used `45` as our angle, so the lines of the dots run at a 45-degree angle to the page. Different angles produce different looks, so feel free to play around with the setting to see which one you like the most!

Both the `Size` and `Factor` options are available only if you are using the **Noise** type. **Size** controls the overall size of the **Noise** pattern. The higher the value of **Factor**, the more stretched the noise along the angle setting. Note that in the following screenshot, the angle is set to `45`, **Factor** is set to `100`, and the noise particles are elongated along the angle:

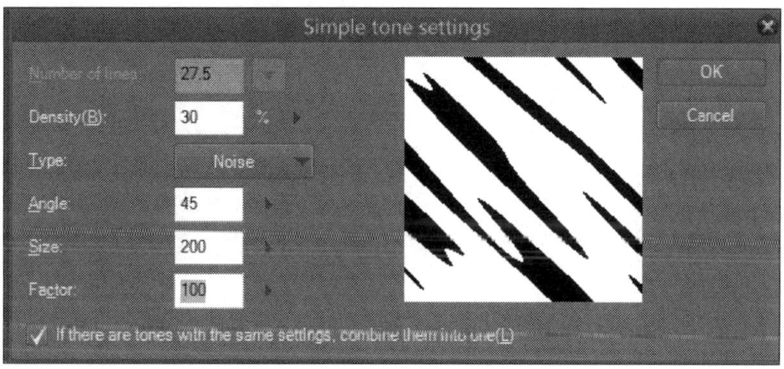

Creating and saving custom materials

In this recipe, we'll take an image and turn it into a material for use in other illustrations. This can be done with custom halftone images, photos, or drawings.

One of the many applications of custom materials is the use in your comics. Say we have a character with a design on their t-shirt. We can save the design as a material and apply it to each panel in which the character appears, without having to draw the design again.

How to do it...

The following recipe shows how to save a custom material image:

1. Open the image to be made into a material. For this recipe, I'll be using a halftone background photo, as shown in this screenshot:

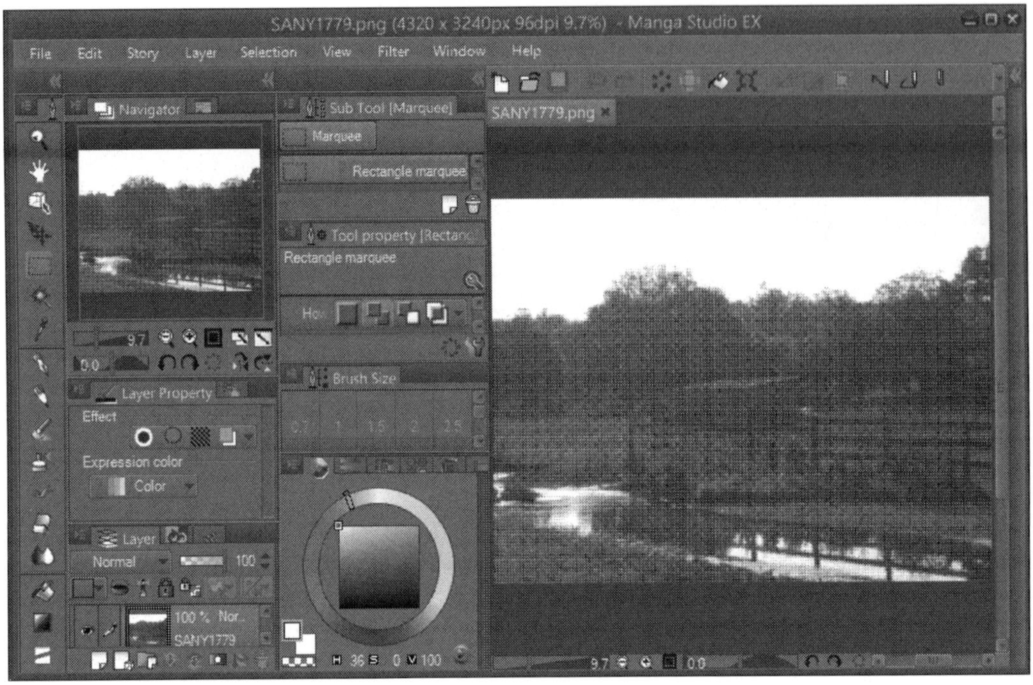

> If you are making a design for a shirt, or another image that will be used many times throughout the course of a comic, consider making it on a transparent background. In this way, it can be manipulated and transformed more easily, and the color or shading around it can be altered.

2. Go to **Edit** | **Register Image as Material**.
3. In the **Material property** window, enter a title for the new material.
4. Click on the checkbox next to **Scale up/down**, and choose the appropriate drop-down menu option.
5. Click on the checkbox next to **Tiling**, and choose the appropriate drop-down menu option if repetition of the material is desired (such as in a screentone or material pattern).

6. Click on the checkbox next to **Specify overlay**, and choose the appropriate level of the file to paste the material, using the slider beneath the box. In this recipe, we'll be using the **Background** level, since we are saving a background image.
7. Under **Location to save material**, choose the appropriate folder for the type of material being saved.
8. Add tags under the **Search tag** box by clicking on the **+** icon in the bottom-right corner. The settings used for the example material made in this recipe are shown in the following screenshot:

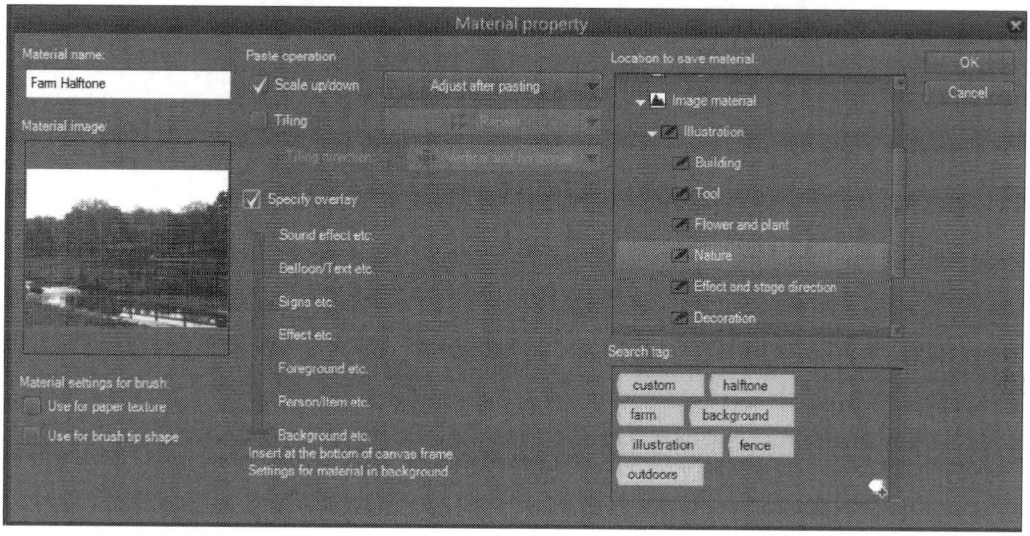

9. Click on **OK** to save the material, and close the **Material property** window.
10. Open another canvas and then open the **Material** library. If it's not already open, go to **Window** | **Material** | **Material [Manga material]**.
11. Locate the new material in the **Material** library, and click on it to select it.
12. Click on the **Paste selected material to canvas** icon in the bottom-right corner of the **Material** library window.
13. Adjust the material as needed.

How it works...

Anything can be made into a material, from photos to drawings. All the brush shapes that we made in *Chapter 2, Customizing Brushes*, can be found in the **Material** library after you have saved them.

The following is the material created in the preceding recipe, used as the background for a drawing:

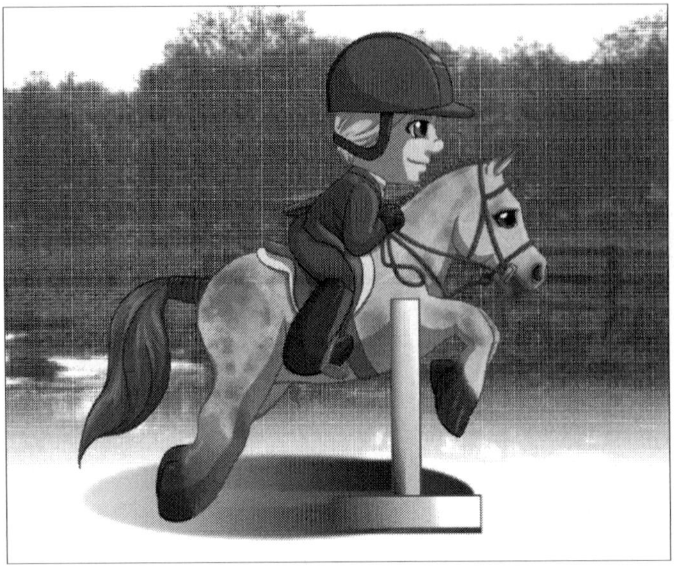

Just as we did when we made brushes, we need to name, categorize, and tag our material here. But unlike the brush tip materials, we must also specify how to tile, adjust, and paste the material when using it.

The **Scale up/down** option has five options beneath the drop-down menu. They are shown in this screenshot:

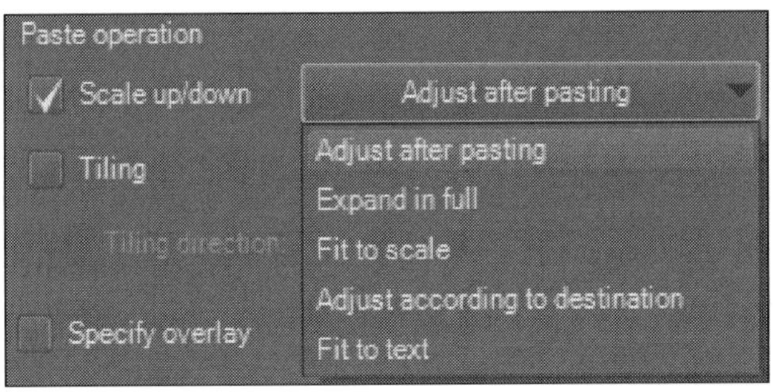

- **Adjust after pasting**: This puts a bounding box around the border of the material after it has been added to the canvas, allowing us to change the scale immediately
- **Expand in full**: This option scales the material to fit the longest side of the destination where the material is being pasted
- **Fit to scale**: This option fits the material into the destination

- **Adjust according to destination**: This option scales the material to best fit the destination
- **Fit to text**: This option is used while making custom word balloons, and can scale them according to the text they are being applied to

The following screenshot shows the same material with different **Scale up/down** options applied. They have all been pasted into comic panels of the same size to show how each option affects the way the material is sized:

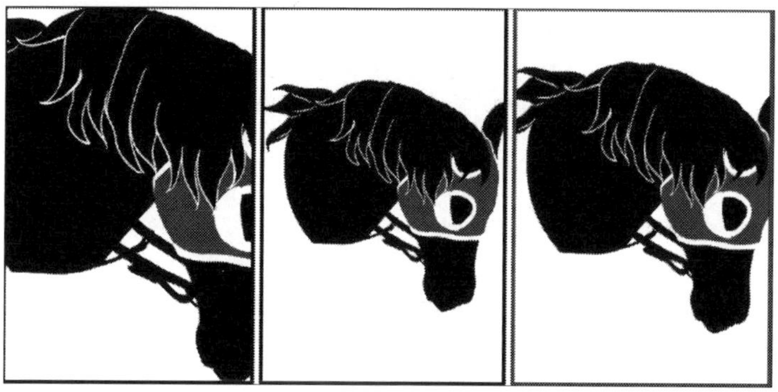

The left frame shows a material set to **Expand in full**, the central frame shows a material set to **Fit to scale**, and the right frame shows a material set to **Adjust according to destination**. Note the differences in the way each image fits the frame.

The final option for the **Scale up/down** pasting option is **Fit to text**. This can be used when you are creating custom speech bubbles. They will then scale around the text they are applied to.

Under the **Tiling** drop-down menu, there are three options. These are shown in the following screenshot:

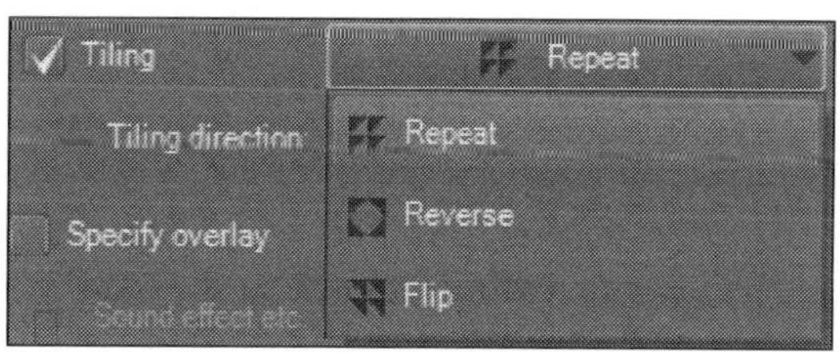

The **Repeat** option takes the material and repeats it—exactly the same material—in the selected direction. An example of **Repeat** is shown here:

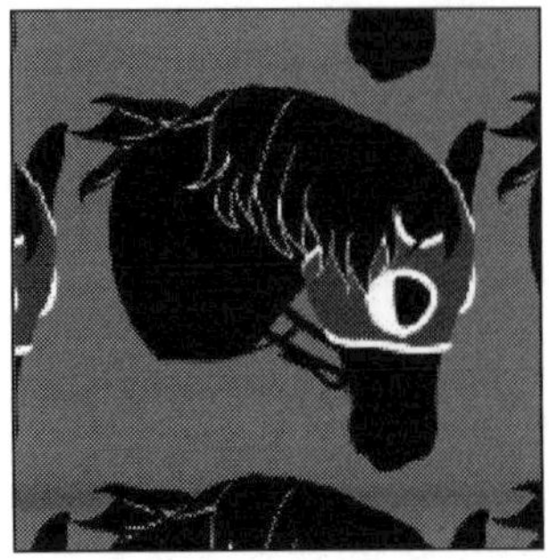

The **Reverse** option flips the material along the selected axes. An example of an image flipped both horizontally and vertically is as follows:

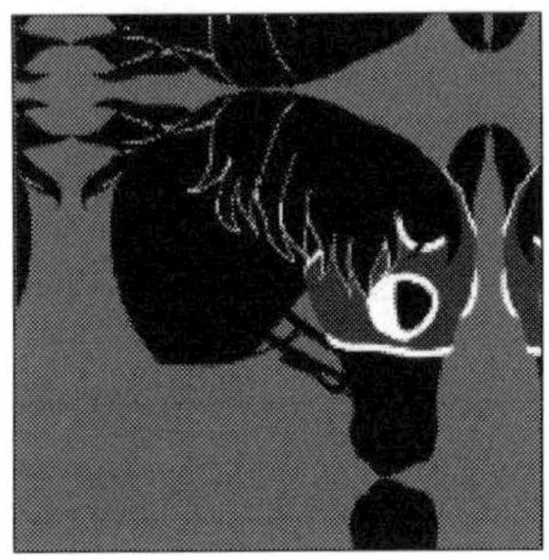

The **Flip** option reverses the material. An example of this is shown in the following screenshot:

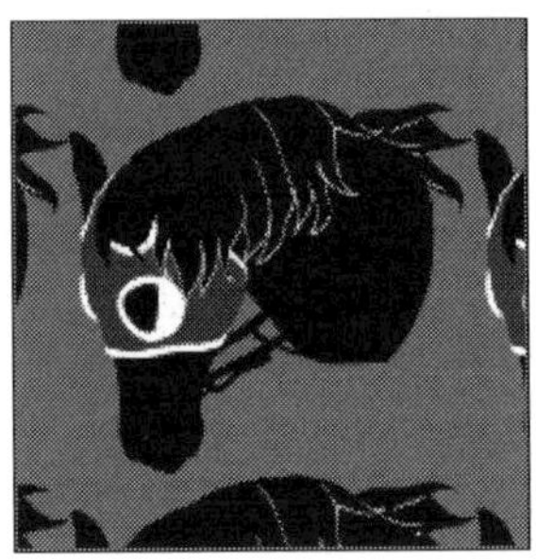

Beneath the **Tiling** drop-down menu, there is another drop-down menu for **Tiling direction**. This is where you can set the tiling to be **Vertical and horizontal**, **Only horizontal**, or **Only vertical**.

Finally, the **Specify overlay** slider allows us to set where in the stack of layers our material should show up. For backgrounds, set the level to **Background**. Text and sound effects are closer to the top of the stack, with speech bubbles beneath them.

Materials are pasted into their own layer, which can be changed later by dragging and dropping it at the desired location in the **Layer** palette.

Drawing a custom fabric pattern

In this recipe, we'll create a pattern inspired by fabric and save it as a material. Then, in the next recipe, we'll use the **Mesh Transformation** tool to make this pattern more realistic when applied to drawn clothing.

Getting ready

We'll need a pattern to look at, for inspiration, and a blank canvas. In this recipe, we'll be using the grid on a 350 dpi square canvas, and we will be making an argyle pattern.

How to do it...

The following steps will walk you through creating an argyle pattern and saving it as a material:

1. Go to **View** | **Grid** to turn the grid on. This will make it easier to draw a precise repeating pattern.
2. Draw one straight line horizontally and another vertically to mark the center of the canvas, as follows:

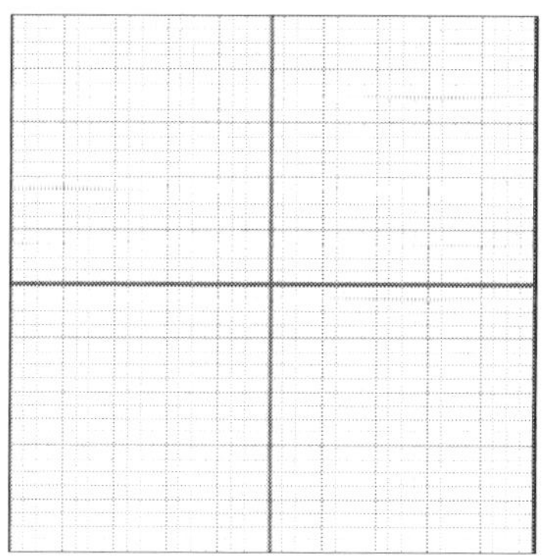

> To make working with the grid easier, turn on **Snap to Grid** in the top toolbar, or go to **View** | **Snap to Grid**. Then, any tool used will snap to the lines and intersections of the grid.

3. Create a new raster layer.
4. Select the foreground color to be used, and then select the **Straight Line** tool by going to **Figure(U)** | **Direct draw**. Draw two diamonds, one on each side of the central vertical line, touching the center of the canvas, as shown in the following screenshot. Fill them with color:

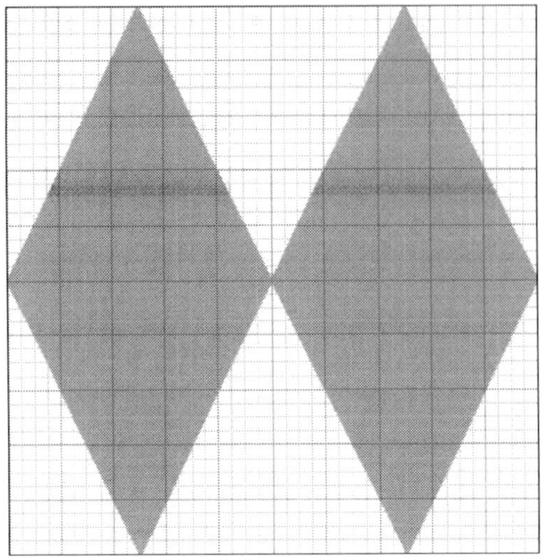

5. Make a new raster layer below the layer with the two diamonds on it.
6. On the new empty layer, fill the middle of the design with a different color, if desired.
7. Fill the outside with a third color, if desired.
8. Make another raster layer above the double diamond layer. Select the **Straight line** tool and locate the **Brush shape** option in the **Tool property** palette. Set **Brush shape** to **Dashed line**.
9. Draw diagonal lines across the design, as shown here:

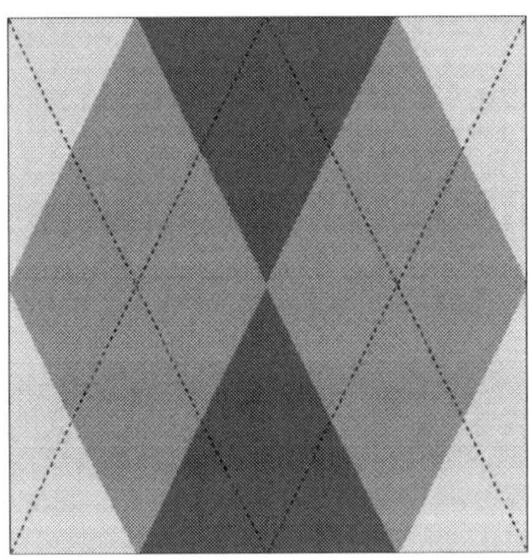

10. Flatten the design layers of the design by navigating to **Layer** | **Merge Layers(F)**.
11. Use the previous recipe (*Creating and saving custom materials*) to save the pattern as a material, with **Repeat** as the **Tiling** option and **Adjust after pasting** as the **Scale up/down** option.

Using Mesh Transformation to apply more realistic fabric patterns

Now that we have a fabric pattern, we can apply it to a character's clothing. But just pasting it in flat will look... well, flat! So, let's use the **Mesh Transformation** tool to lay the pattern a little more realistically on the drawing.

Getting ready

You will need a drawing of clothes. The example drawing for this recipe will be the blouse shown here:

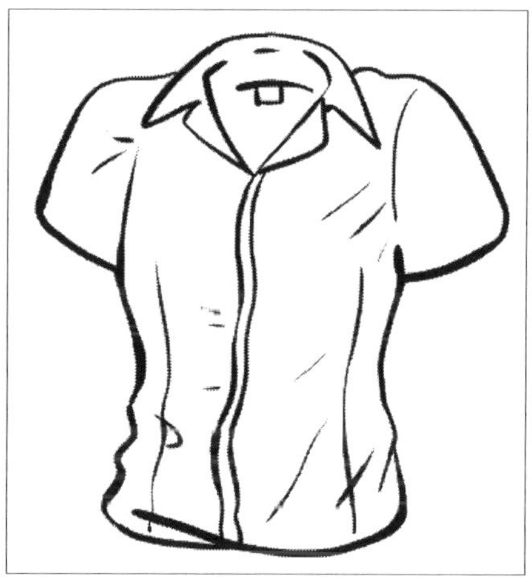

Your drawing can be a skirt, shirt, hat, or whatever you want to add a fabric pattern to!

How to do it...

This recipe will walk you through the use of the **Mesh Transformation** tool on a pattern material:

1. Make a selection around a portion of the item using the **Lasso Marquee(M)** tool. In the following screenshot, the area around the main body of the shirt has been selected:

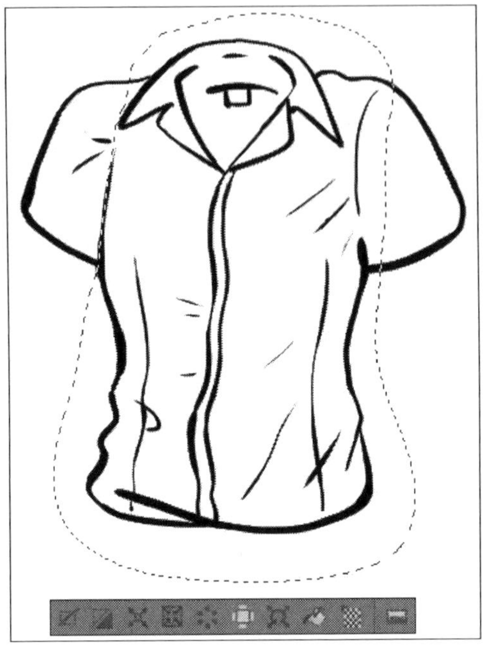

> Leave some space outside of the line art. You will need the extra space to adjust the pattern with **Mesh Transformation**.

2. Paste the desired material; in this case, we're using the argyle pattern that we created in the previous recipe. As you can see in the following screenshot, the pasted image is quite large because of the resolution we created it at:

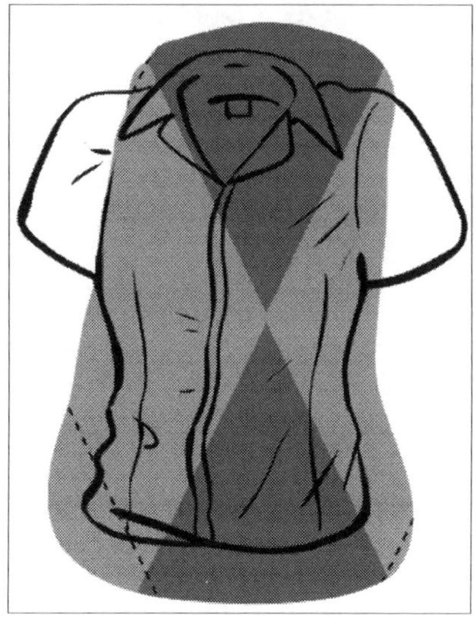

3. Use the bounding box that surrounds the material to resize the pattern, as shown here:

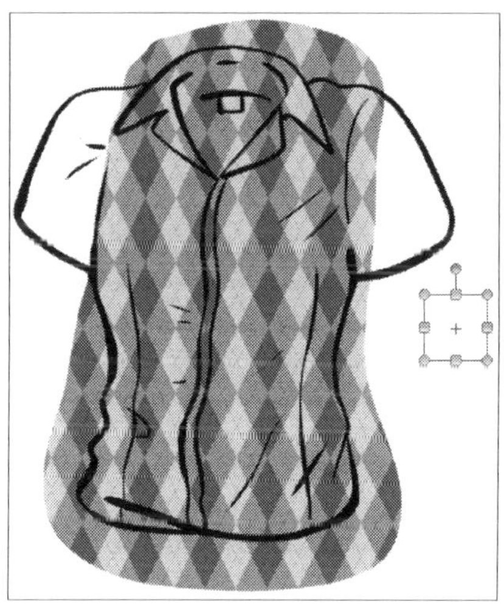

4. Once the desired scale is reached, right-click on the layer in the **Layer** palette and click on **Rasterize**.
5. Go to **Edit | Transform | Mesh Transformation**. A grid of control points will show up over the material.

6. Use the sliders in the **Tool property** palette to increase the number of control points from `4` to `8` or `10`, both vertically and horizontally. The updated lattice of control points is shown in this screenshot:

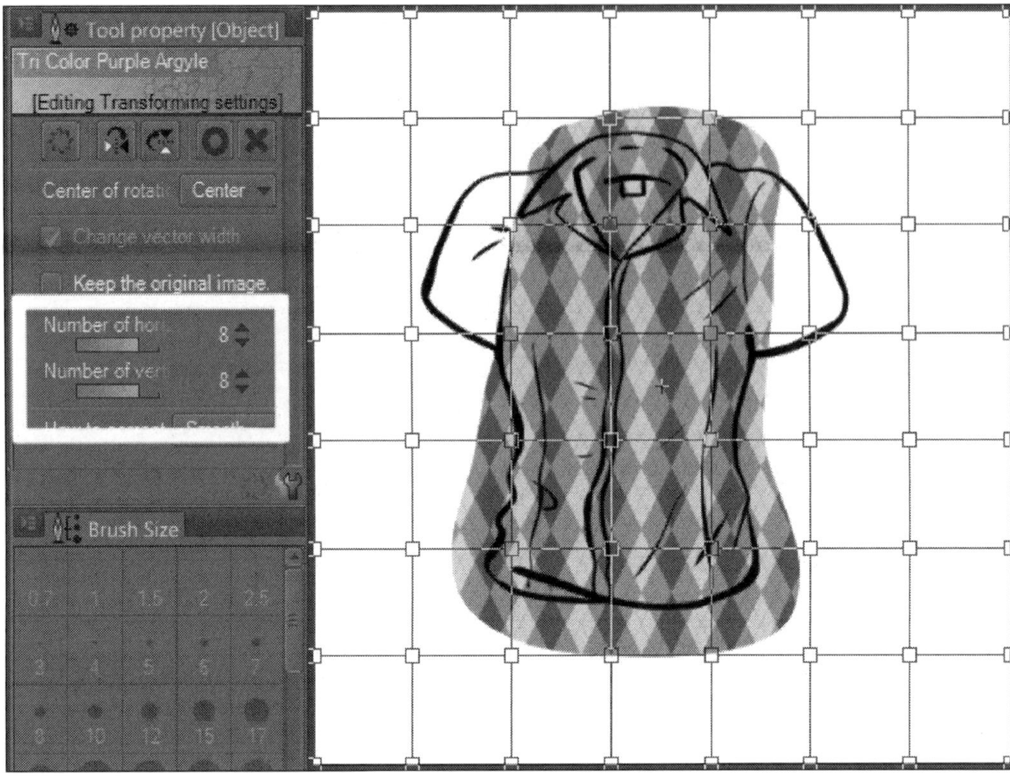

7. Use the control points to alter the pattern so that it curves with the lines of the drawing. Be sure to think about how the fabric folds and curves around! Note the way in which the control points have been altered in the following screenshot to change the bend of the pattern:

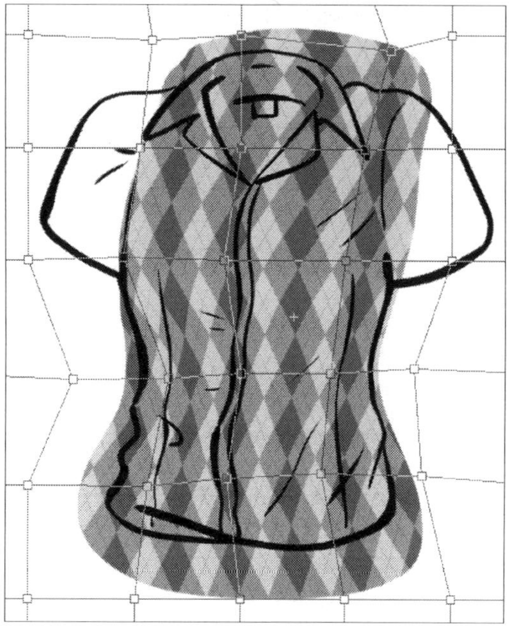

8. When you're done, press the *Enter* key to finalize the transformation.
9. Use the layer mask that is already attached to the materials layer to erase the extra pattern and clean up the edges of the material.
10. Continue designing each piece of the garment in the same way. The shirt shown next was patterned in four pieces—the main torso, the collar, and the two sleeves:

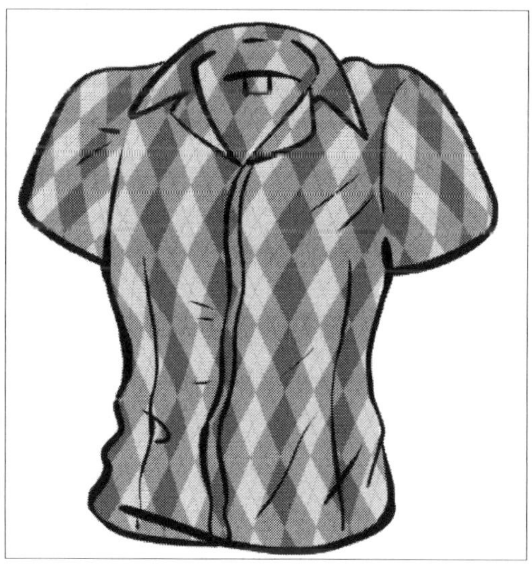

11. Add a raster layer above the material layers, set it to the **Multiply** layer mode, and add shading to the shirt to finish the drawing. The finished shirt is shown here:

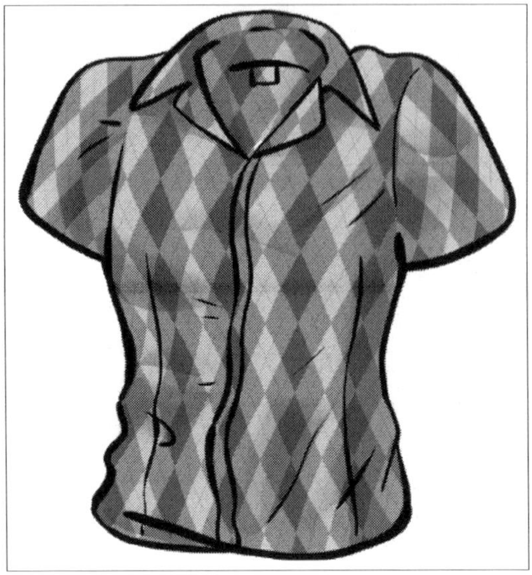

8

Playing with Color Palettes

In this chapter, you will learn these recipes:

- Importing a palette from Photoshop
- Saving a color set as a material
- Turning the color set bar on and off
- Turning the command bar on and off
- Creating harmonious color schemes using the Intermediate Color palette
- Using the Approximate Color palette
- Using the Color History palette

Introduction

Good colors can give a comic or illustration a very polished look, and while there is no one way to color, the color sets and color pickers in Manga Studio 5 can make the coloring process easier and faster.

Importing a palette from Photoshop

Perhaps you've been using Adobe Photoshop to create your art and you are just switching to Manga Studio 5. There's no reason you can't take your custom color swatches with you, though! In this recipe, we'll import Photoshop color swatches into the color sets in Manga Studio 5.

Getting ready

You'll need to save your Photoshop swatches as an `.aco` file before completing this recipe. Go to the **Swatches** palette in Photoshop and click on the menu (it will likely be in the upper-right corner, depending on which version of Photoshop you have). Next, click on **Save Swatches** in the menu. Save the `.aco` file in a folder on your computer, with a descriptive name.

At times, you can find pre-made `.aco` files available for download on the Internet.

How to do it...

The following steps will show you how to import a color swatch set from Adobe Photoshop to Manga Studio 5:

1. Open the **Color Set** palette. It can be found by navigating to **Window** | **Color Set**.
2. Click on the menu icon, circled in this screenshot:

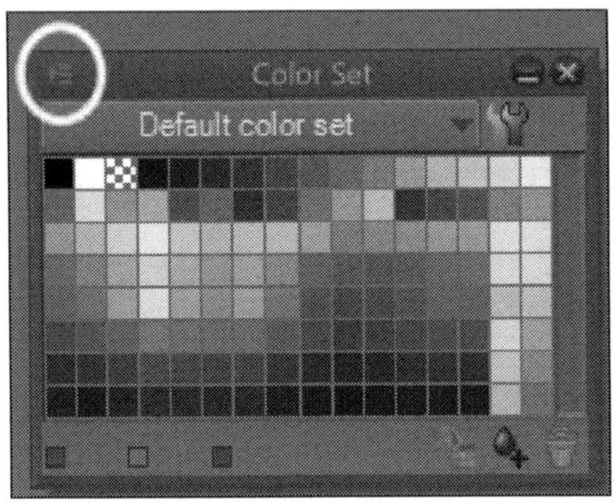

3. Then, click on **Import color set**.
4. Navigate to the folder where the `.aco` Photoshop color swatches file to be imported is saved. Click on the file to select it, as shown in the following screenshot, and then click on **Open**:

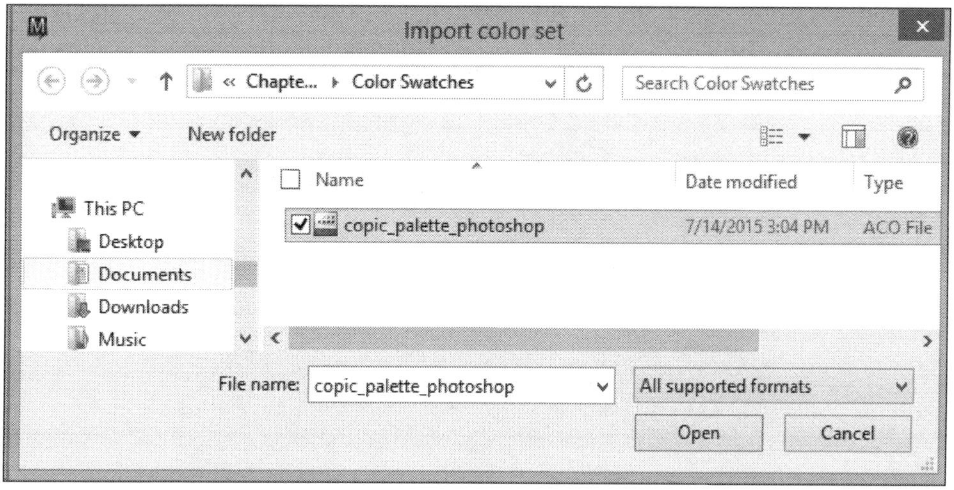

The swatches will be imported as a color set and named automatically. This screenshot shows the colors imported in this recipe:

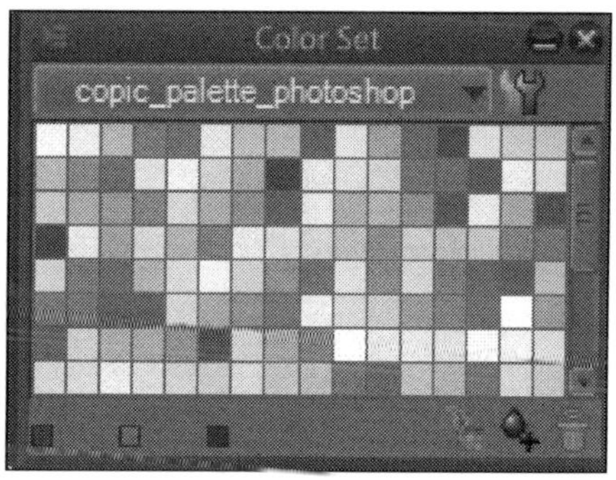

There's more...

The following instructions will show you how to rename an imported color set:

1. In the **Color Set** palette, click on the wrench icon to the right of the current color set's name. The **Edit color set** window will open.

2. Locate the color set in the list to the left. Click on it once to select it, as shown here:

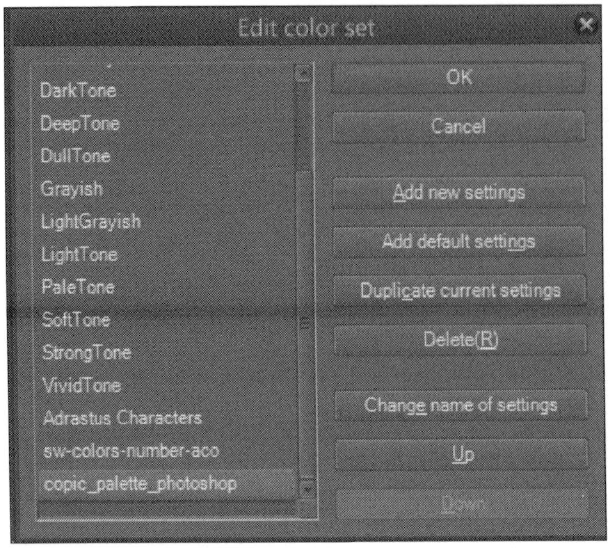

3. Click on **Change name of settings**. The name on the left will change to a text entry box. Type the new name and press *Enter*.
4. The color set's name will be changed, as shown in the following screenshot:

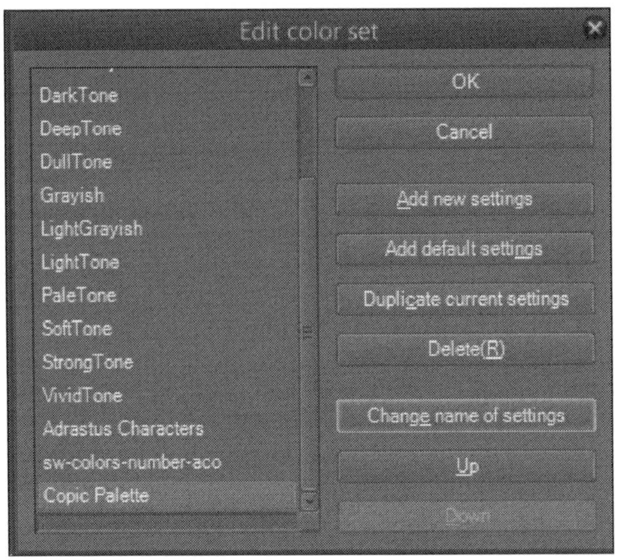

5. Click on **OK** to save the changes.

Saving a color set as a material

With this recipe, we can save a color set as an image in the **Material** library. This is an easy way to save a collection of color swatches as a new color set.

Getting ready

Make sure that the **Color Set** palette is open. If you can't locate it on the screen, go to **Window** | **Color Set** to open it.

How to do it...

Follow these simple steps to save a color set as a material:

1. In the **Color Set** palette, click on the menu icon in the top-left corner (it is shown in step 2 of the *Importing a palette from Photoshop* recipe).
2. Click on **Register color set as a material**.
3. Complete the information in the **Material property** window. For more information on saving a new material, refer to the *Creating and saving custom materials* recipe of *Chapter 7, Adding and Creating Tones and Materials*.

The color set will now be saved in the **Material** library and will appear in the list of color sets in the drop-down menu.

Turning the color set bar on and off

The color set bar is the area of the **Color Set** palette that shows the drop-down menu of the saved color sets and the wrench icon. In this recipe, you will learn how to hide or show this bar.

Getting ready

Make sure that the **Color Set** palette is open. If you can't locate it on the screen, go to **Window** | **Color Set** to open it.

How to do it...

Follow these simple steps to hide and show the color set bar:

1. In the **Color Set** palette, click on the menu icon in the top-left corner (it is shown in step 2 of the *Importing a palette from Photoshop* recipe).
2. If the color set bar is on, there will be a check mark next to **Show color set bar** in the menu. The **Color Set** palette shown in the following screenshot has the color set bar turned on:

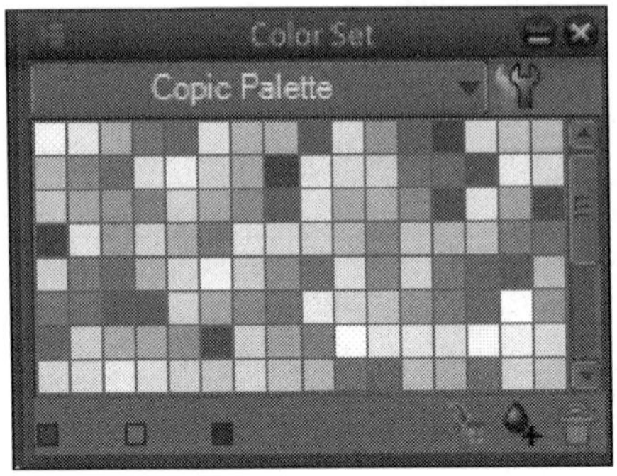

3. Click on **Show color set bar** when it is checked to uncheck the option and hide the color set bar. The **Color Set** palette shown in this screenshot has the color set bar turned off:

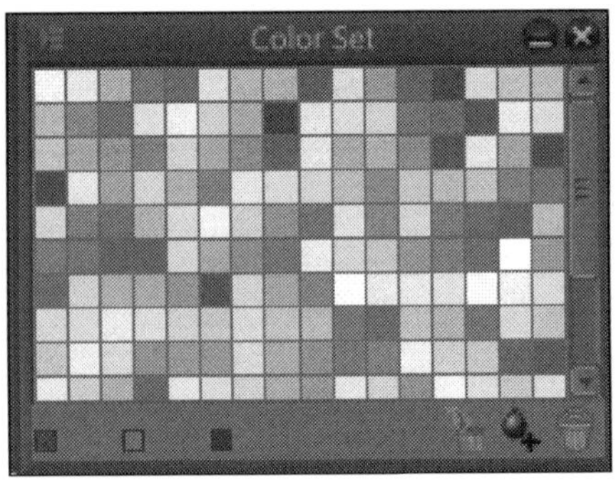

4. Click on **Show color set bar** when it is unchecked to turn the color set bar on again.

Turning the command bar on and off

The command bar is the area of the **Color Set** palette beneath the color swatches. This area shows the red, green, and blue values of a chosen color, and also has options such as **Replace color**, **Add color**, and **Delete color** for a chosen swatch. In this recipe, we will see how to hide or show these options. You may wish to hide the command bar if you are afraid that you may accidentally replace or delete a saved swatch!

Getting ready

Again, make sure that the **Color Set** palette is open. If you can't locate it on the screen, go to **Window** | **Color Set** to open it.

How to do it...

Follow these simple steps to hide and show the command bar:

1. In the **Color Set** palette, click on the menu icon in the top-left corner (it is shown in step 2 of the *Importing a palette from Photoshop* recipe).
2. If the command bar is on, there will be a check mark next to **Show command bar** in the menu. The **Color Set** palette shown in the following screenshot has the command bar turned on:

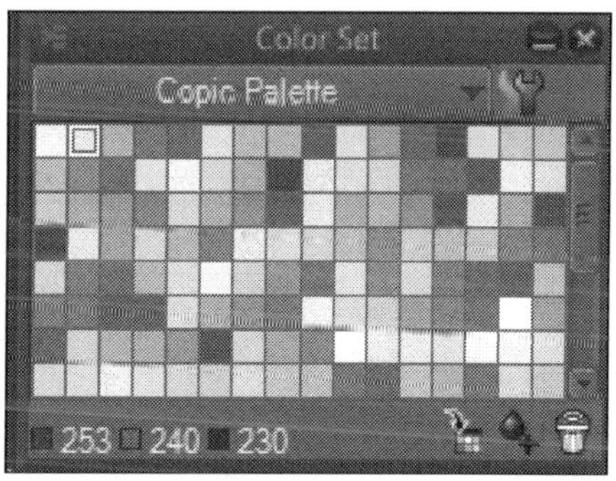

3. Click on **Show command bar** when it is checked to uncheck the option and hide the command bar. The **Color Set** palette shown in this screenshot has the command bar turned off:

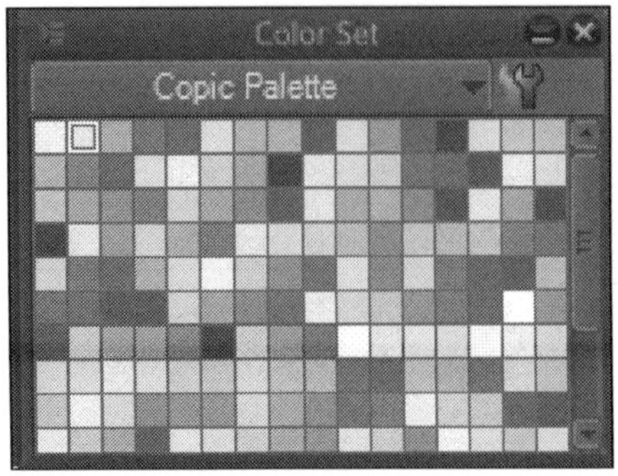

4. Click on **Show command bar** when it is unchecked to turn the command bar on again.

Creating harmonious color schemes using the Intermediate Color palette

Manga Studio has many options for making color palettes, from saving swatches to being able to *mix* colors right in the palette windows. In this recipe, we'll use the **Intermediate Color** palette to create a color scheme that works together.

How to do it...

The following recipe will walk us through the use of the **Intermediate Color** palette:

1. Open the **Intermediate Color** palette by navigating to **Window | Intermediate Color(Z)**.

> This works best if you can see the color wheel or your color sets when setting up the **Intermediate Color** palette. If the **Intermediate Color** palette is nested with other palettes, click and hold with the mouse on the tab at the top with the palette's name on it. Then, drag it to a new position and release the mouse button.

2. Choose a color from the color sets, color wheel, or color slider. Move the mouse cursor over one of the large squares in the corner of the **Intermediate Color** palette. The cursor will become a paint bucket. Click to add the color to the corner box. In this screenshot, a red color can be seen added in the top-right corner:

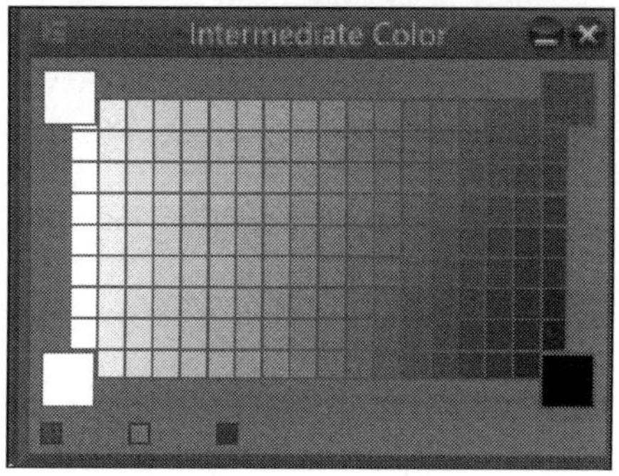

3. Repeat step 2 for any other color in the color scheme. As shown in the following screenshot, we are using red-orange, yellow-green, and blue, to make a triad color scheme. The bottom-right corner has been left black to provide darker shades:

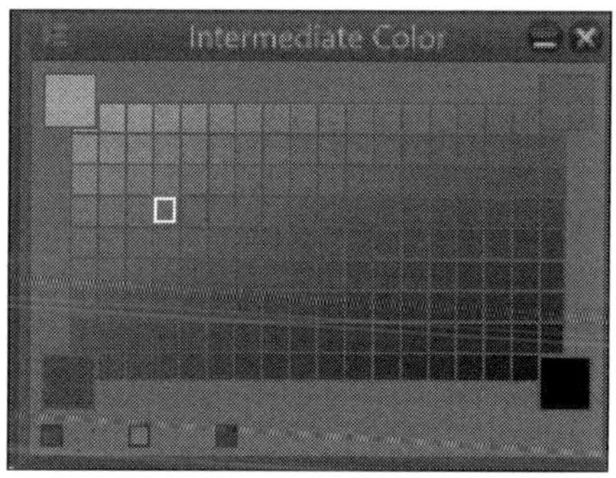

4. Use the colors in the palette to paint or color your image!

The following is an image with flat colors, mostly picked from the mixed colors shown in the preceding screenshot. Only the skin tone is not a hue mixed with the **Intermediate Color** palette:

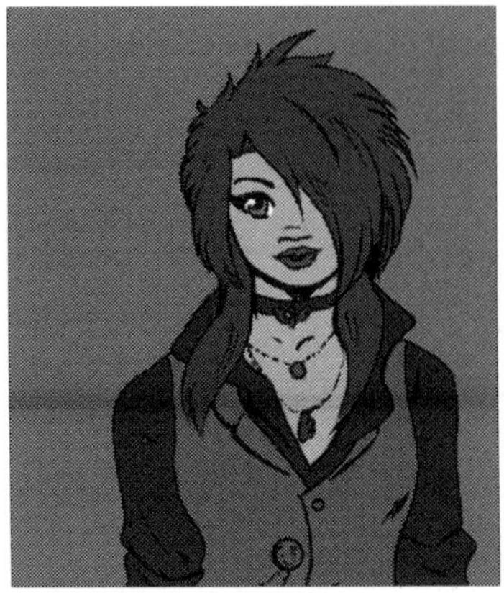

[Buy a color wheel and keep it near your computer! It will help you choose color schemes, and it is quite inexpensive.]

Using the Approximate Color palette

The **Approximate Color** palette is a different way of mixing colors and making a palette. It can require some experimentation, but once you start playing with it, you may just love it!

How to do it...

Follow these instructions to learn how to use the **Approximate Color** palette:

1. Open the palette by going to **Window** | **Approximate Color(F)**. A palette similar to the one shown here will appear:

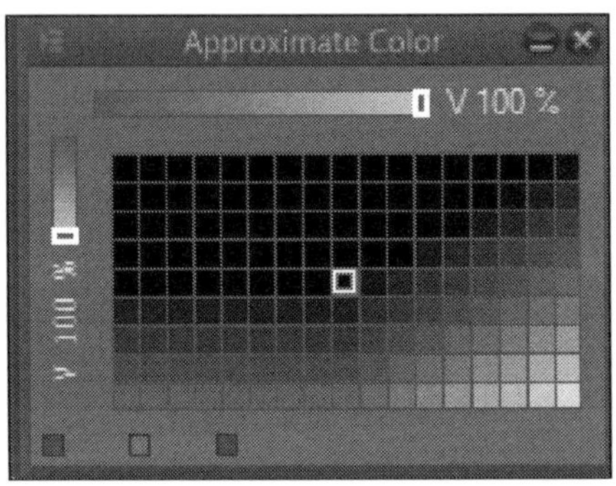

2. Select a color other than black as the active foreground color. The foreground color currently selected will change the results of the blending in the **Approximate Color** palette.
3. Click on the text to the right of the top slider. Choose an option to blend from the drop-down menu. The options will be described in the *How it works...* section of this recipe.
4. Click on the text below the slider on the left of the palette window. Choose an option to blend from the drop-down menu.
5. Adjust the top and left sliders until the desired colors are achieved.
6. Click on a color square to make it the active color and use it for drawing or painting.

How it works...

The options next to the sliders in the **Approximate Color** palette are **Hue**, **Saturation**, **Brightness (V)**, **Brightness (L)**, **Red**, **Green**, and **Blue**.

Here is what each one means:

- **Hue** is simply another way of saying "color".
- **Saturation** is the amount of color mixed in. Bright colors are highly saturated, whereas white, gray, and black are unsaturated.
- **Brightness (V)** is the value of color mixed in.
- **Brightness (L)** is the luminosity of the color.
- **Red** is the amount of red mixed in.
- **Green** is the amount of green mixed in.
- **Blue** is the amount of blue mixed in.

The sliders on each axis control how much of the selected parameter is being used. So, for instance, setting both the horizontal and vertical axes to **Hue** and setting both values to `100%` produces lots of very saturated colors when a saturated color is the active color. The following screenshot shows what the **Approximate Color** palette looks like when a saturated purple color is chosen and the horizontal and vertical axes are set to **Hue**:

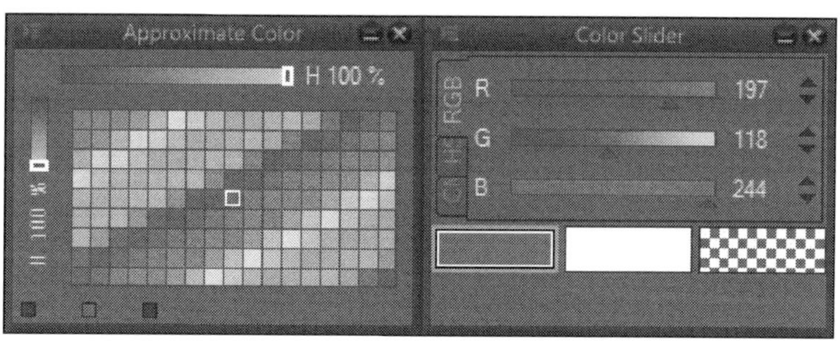

The **Approximate Color** palette is fun to play with and use! You can use it to make fun palettes for use in paintings or for character designs.

Using the Color History palette

Have you ever painted and required a color that you were using 10 minutes ago, but by now it's been so blended with everything around it that you can't get the pure color any more? The **Color History** palette is the answer to your prayers, and it's easy to use.

Getting ready

Before opening the **Color History** palette, open a blank page and scribble on it with a bunch of colors. In order for the **Color History** palette to show us anything, we must have a history of colors that we've used recently. It has to be only one click with the mouse or one stroke with the stylus, as long as the color is used somewhere on the page.

How to do it...

1. Open the **Color History** palette by going to **Window** | **Color History(Q)**.
2. The palette will open and will show any colors used recently. Click on the required color to make it active.

This screenshot shows the **Color History** palette:

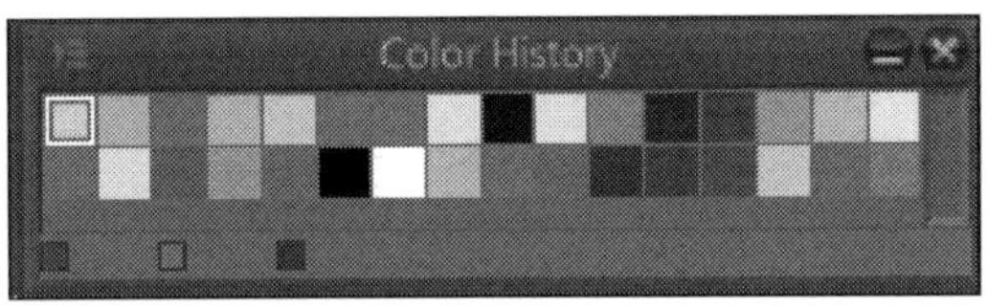

If you wish to save the colors from **Color History**, click on the icon in the top-left corner and then click on **Register to color set palette** to save them. To clear the history, click on the same icon and select **Clear color history**.

9
Creating Special Effects

In this chapter, you will learn the following recipes:

- Making colored line work
- Coloring sparkly magic effects
- Creating the look of shiny leather
- Creating a colored light effect
- Creating laser blasts
- Making lightning and electricity

Introduction

To really pull the whole thing together, you sometimes need a special effect. Whether it's as simple as coloring your line work or adding glittery magic around your magical girl, this chapter can get you started. By no means are these the only ways to create these looks. Use the following recipes as a jumping-off point and customize them to your needs.

Let's get started!

Making colored line work

Colored line work or *color holds* can be used for a variety of effects. They can highlight an area or make it blend in more with the coloring, or make a background element fade away and leave just the foreground in the spotlight. Color holds are very easy to do and can really punch up your illustration!

Getting ready

You will need line work done on a transparent layer, as shown in the following screenshot:

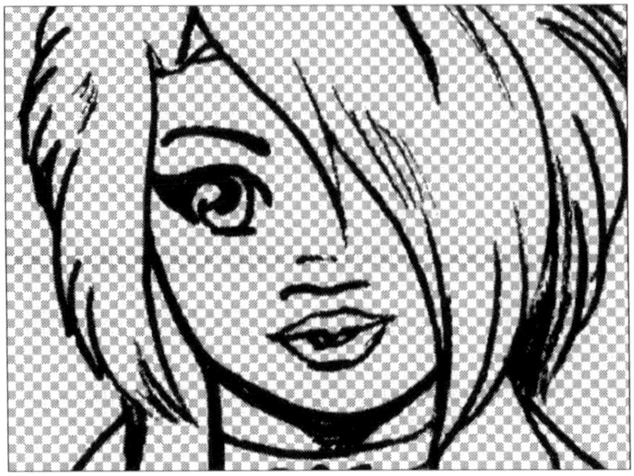

The preceding image is a scanned ink drawing, with the white from the paper taken out. Manga Studio 5 can remove the white automatically with just the push of a button, and here's how! Open your scanned drawing in Manga Studio 5. If needed, adjust the brightness and contrast to make the inked lines in the scan stand out sharply from the paper color. This will also make the conversion much cleaner. Then, go to **Edit** | **Convert brightness to opacity**. Manga Studio will make the brightest areas transparent and the darkest areas opaque.

How to do it...

Let's make some color holds with the following steps:

1. In the **Layer** palette, click on the layer with the inked lines to select it. When it's selected, it will turn blue.
2. Click on the **Lock Transparent Pixel** icon, located above the list of layers. It is shown in this screenshot:

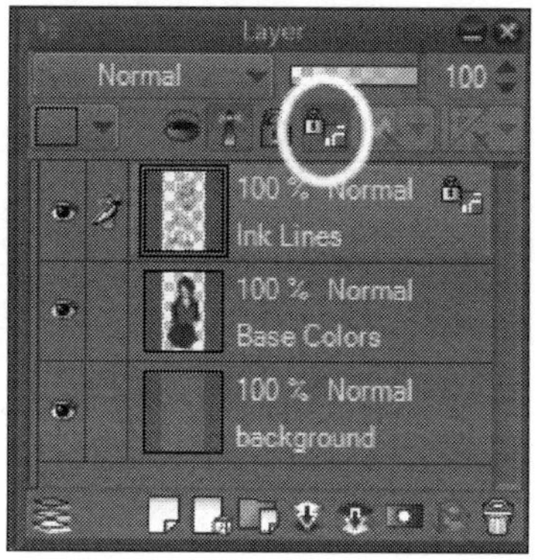

3. Select your preferred pen or brush tool.
4. Then, select the color you wish to paint your line art with.
5. Use the pen or brush over the inked lines to change the color to the active color.

How it works...

When we lock the transparent pixels of the drawing, we prevent Manga Studio from altering any pixels that are not transparent in that layer. In this case, all our ink lines are opaque, so we can only change them. Check out the following screenshot, and note that even though the hot pink scribble was made wildly, it appears on the black ink lines only:

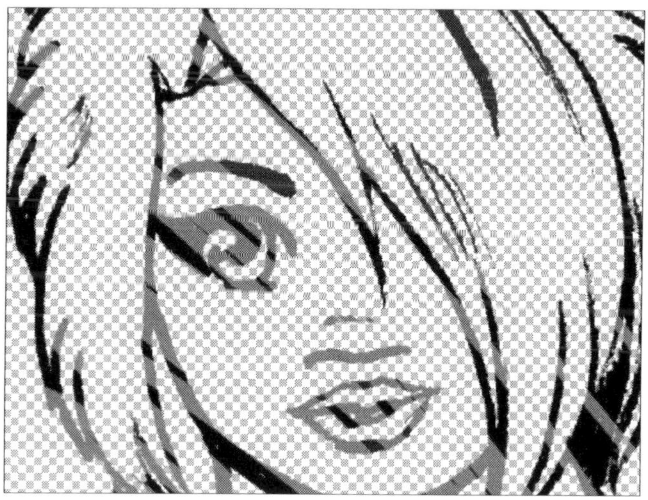

This allows us to use pens, brushes, or even the gradient tool to color our lines. Here is a drawing in which the line layer had a rainbow gradient applied:

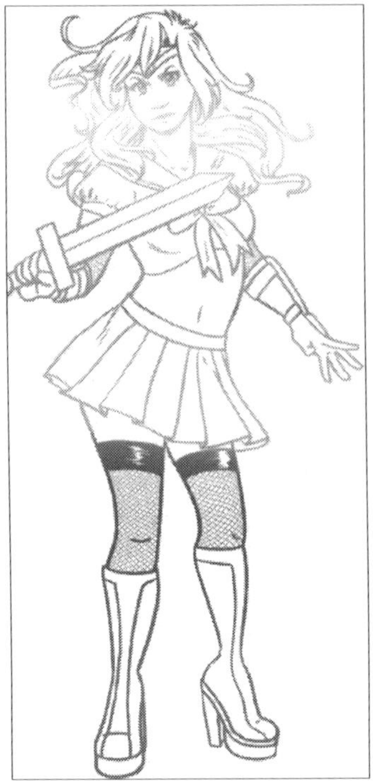

The following is another drawing with more subtle Color Holds, this time in the hair and on the face and lips to make some of the lines less "in your face":

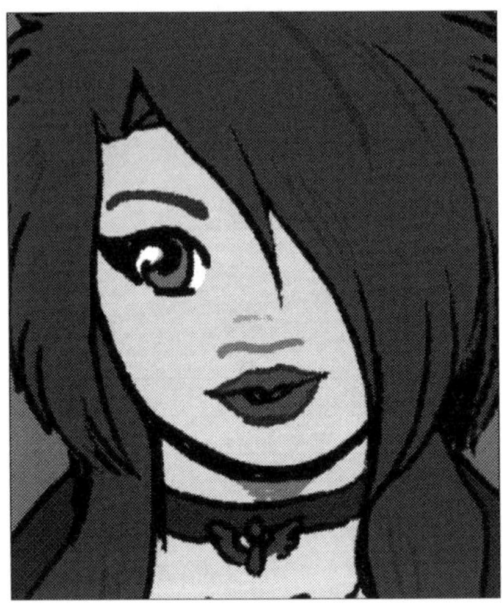

Coloring sparkly magic effects

Magic effects are useful in a variety of comics, from fantasy to magical girls. Here's one way to make sparkly blasts of magic fly from your character's fingertips!

How to do it...

Follow these steps to make some magic:

1. Start with a canvas or drawing to add your effect to. In the following screenshot, we are working on an A4-sized, 350 dpi color canvas. A hand has been drawn on it to provide a reference point for the magic effect.

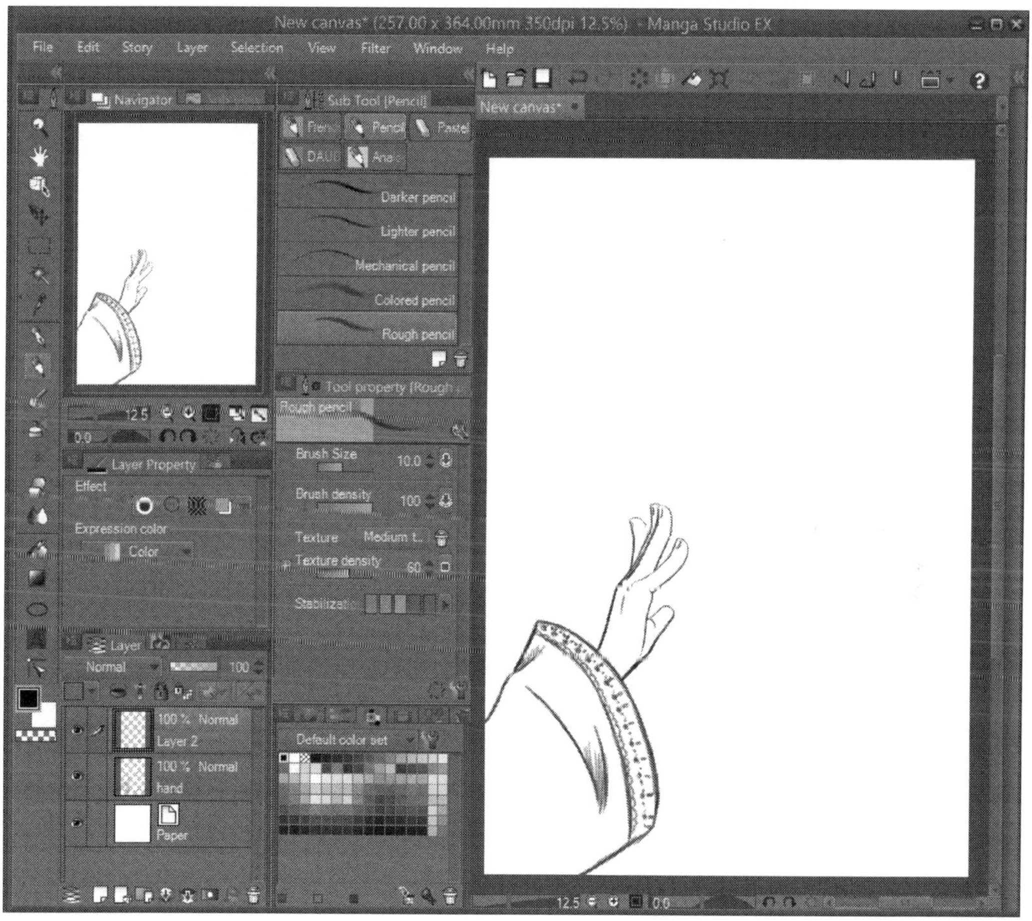

2. Make a new raster layer above or below your line art, if applicable.
3. Select the **Airbrush(B)** tool and then the **Hard** subtool. Rough out the general shape of the magic energy. As shown in this screenshot, a dark blue color has been used to complete this step:

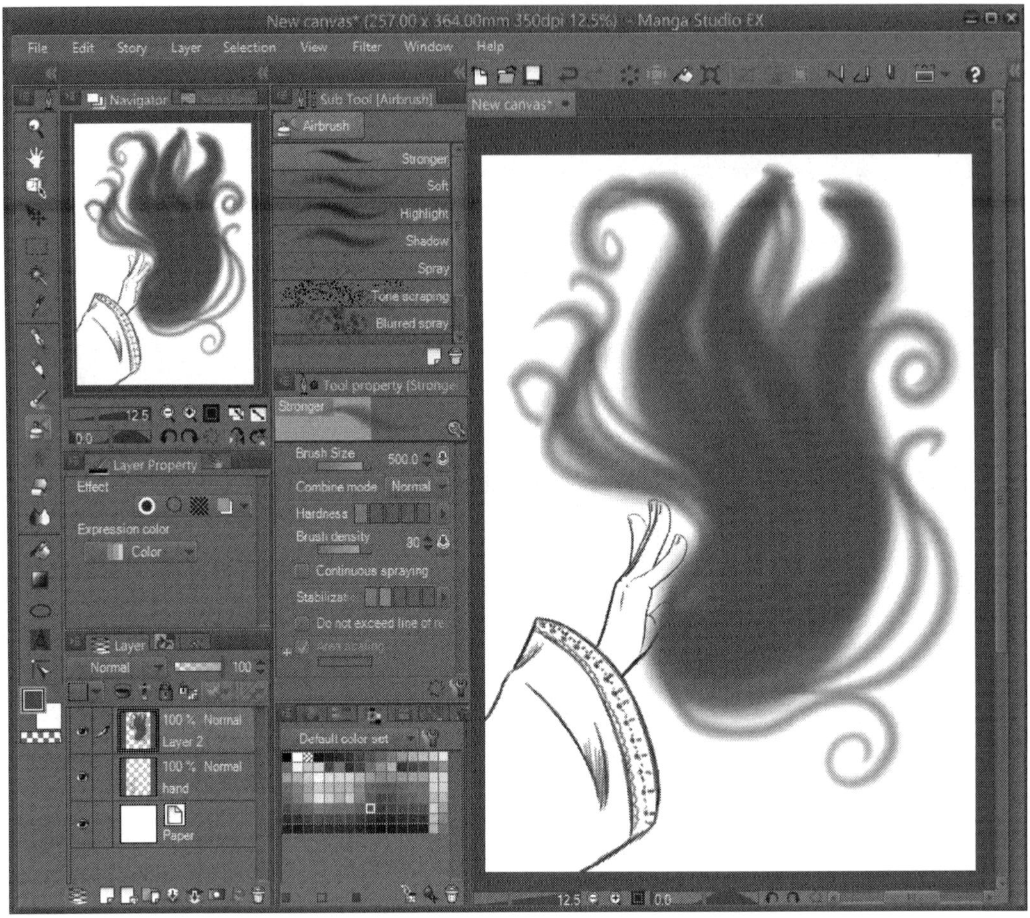

4. Select the **Highlight** subtool of the **Airbrush(B)** tool and a color lighter than the one used in step 2. Paint in some lighter areas in the center of the magic shape. As shown in the following screenshot, this has been done with a very light blue color:

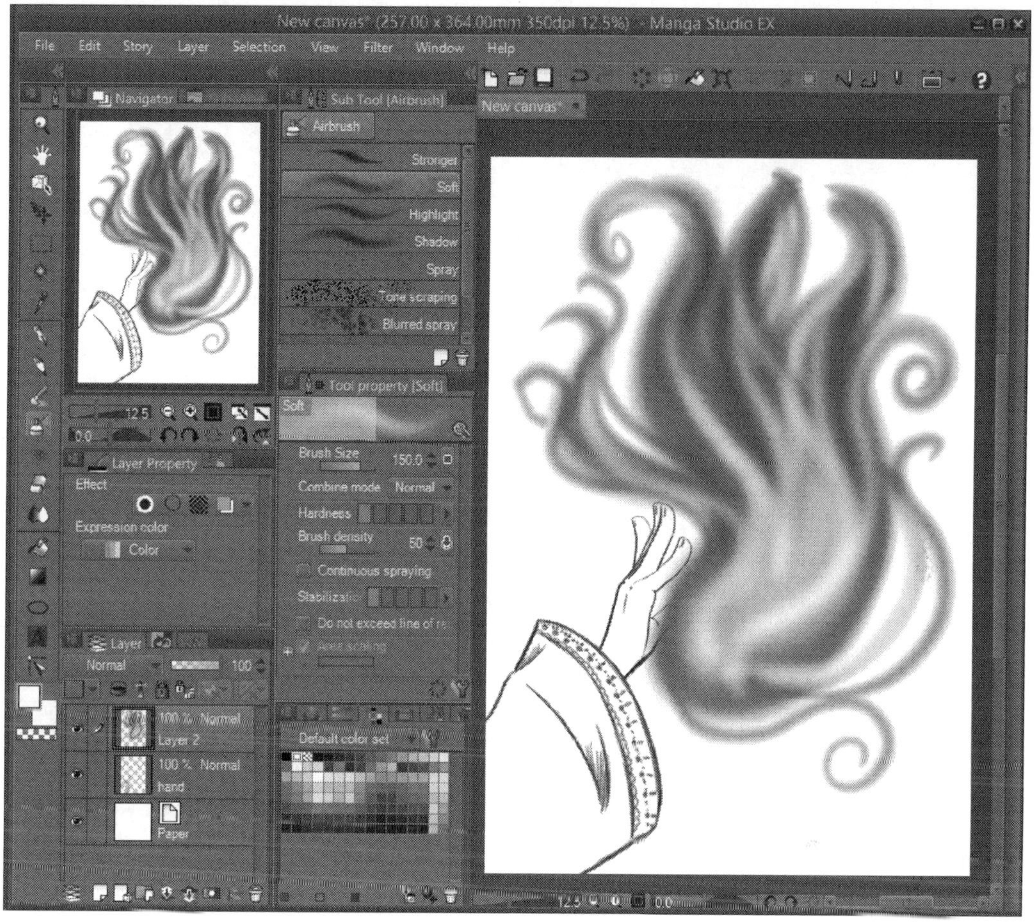

5. Now, we probably need a darker background so that we can further refine the shape and color of the magic shape. Create a layer behind the magic layer and fill it with a color darker than that of the magic effect. The hand shown in the following screenshot has also been colored, so it will show against the darker background:

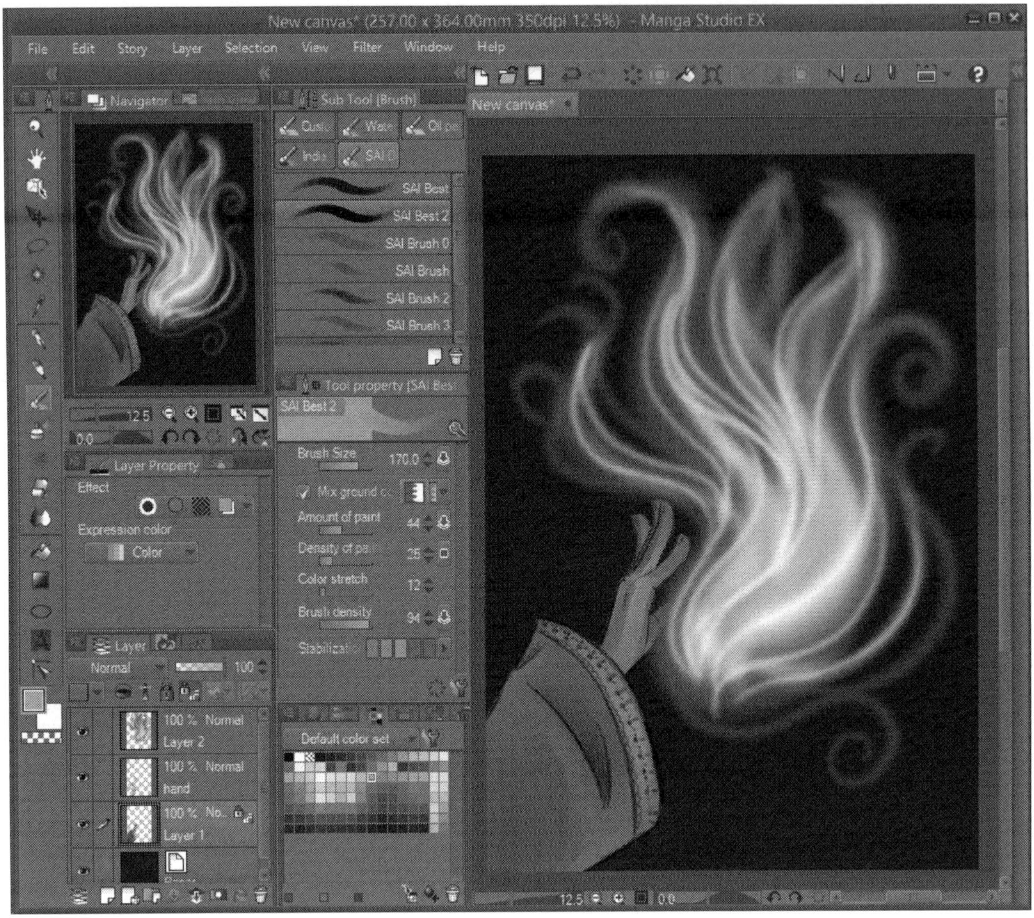

6. Continue refining the shape of the magic with the **Highlight** airbrush and a light color. Then, select the **Decoration(D)** tool and the **Sparkle A** subtool. Using white or a light color, add some small sparkles around the edges of the magic. As shown in this screenshot, the **Sparkle A** tool has been used to make the very small "glitter" areas around the edges of the curls on the magic:

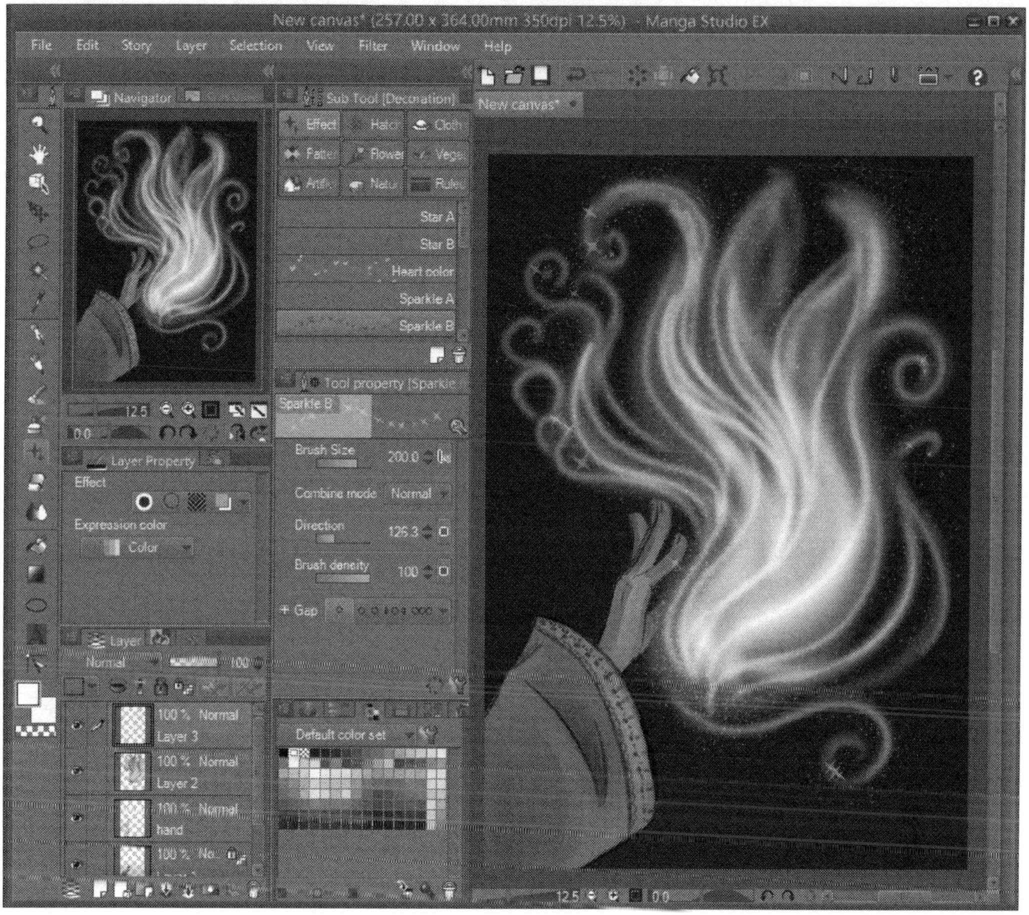

7. Continue using the **Sparkle A**, **Sparkle B**, and **Sparkle C** tools to add more sparkle to the magic. As shown here, **Sparkle B** and **Sparkle C** are the larger shine marks around the edges of the magic shape:

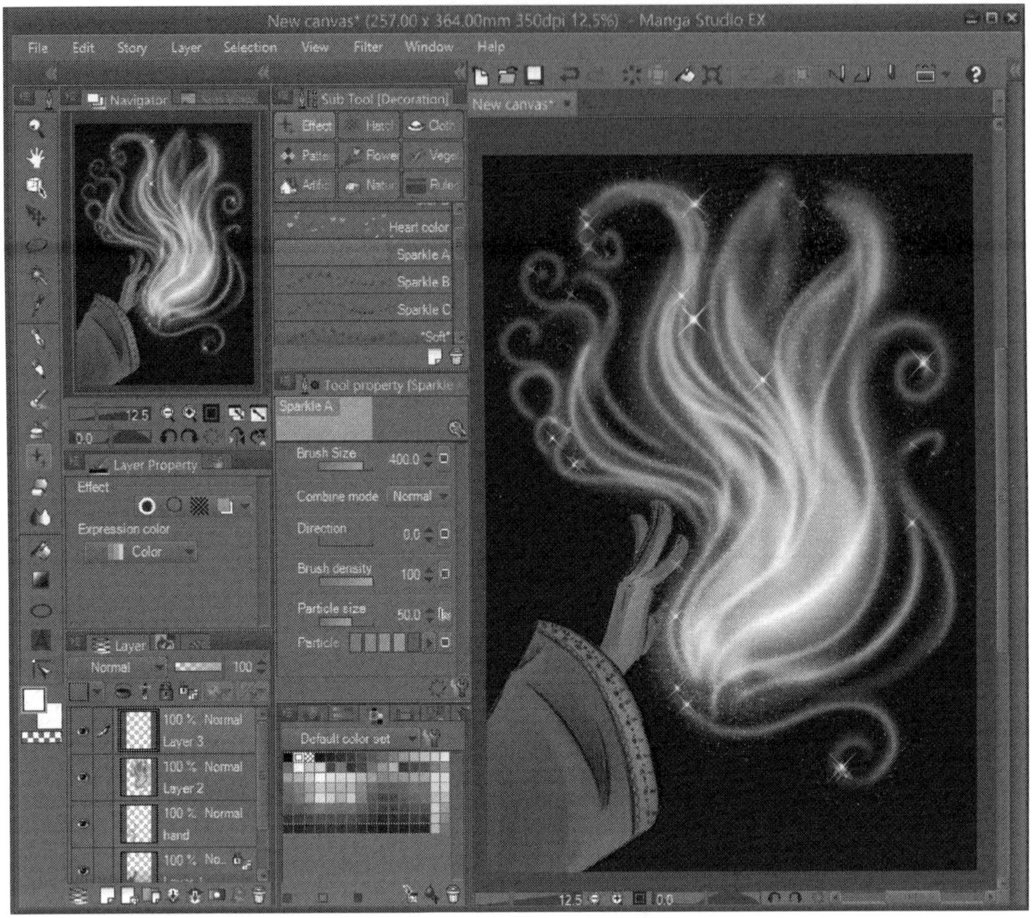

8. Create a new layer behind the magic layer and the drawing layer. Select a color lighter than that of the background but not as light as the color of the magic. Use the **Soft** subtool of **Airbrush(B)** and the lighter color, and add a lighter area around the edges of the effect, as shown in the following screenshot:

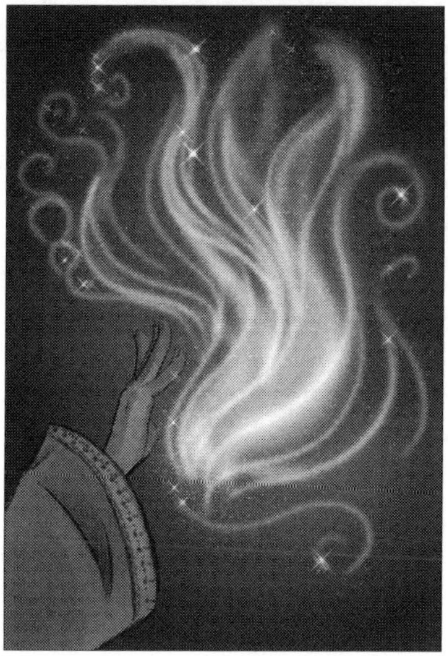

9. Refine the shape and colors as needed with the **Airbrush(B)** tools until the desired look is achieved.

Creating the look of shiny leather

It's amazing how many characters in comics wear leather, isn't it? This is my method for coloring shiny leather jackets, boots, and pants. As always, personalize this method to suit your tastes and the way you work. And the best thing that you can do is look at lots of reference photos!

This technique will work well for shiny leather, *pleather*, vinyl, and rubber. For more matte-looking leather, you may want to make the highlights less pronounced.

How to do it...

The following recipe will walk us through creating a pair of shiny leather pants:

1. Create a raster layer beneath the line art layer of your drawing. Name this layer `Base`.
2. Fill the lines with a base color. As shown in the following screenshot, we're using a dark gray color that is very close to black:

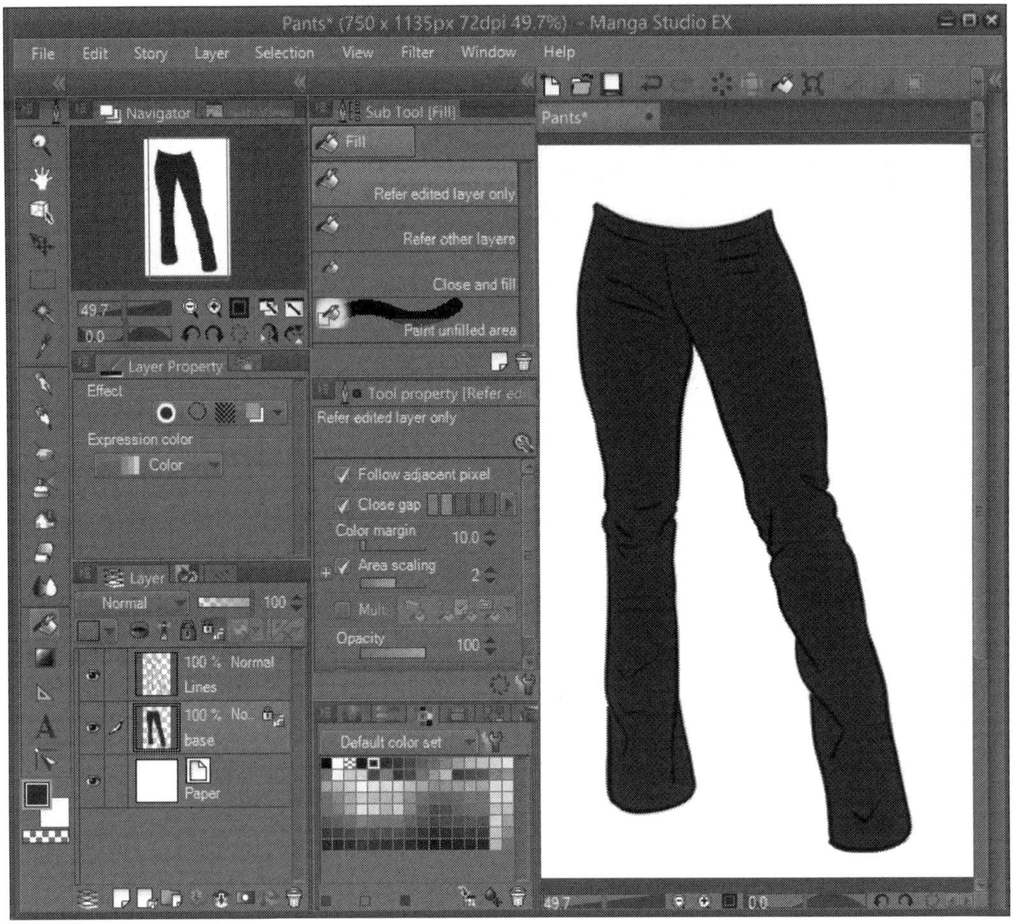

3. Create a new raster layer above the base color layer but below the lines. Name this layer `Highlights 1`.
4. Select a highlight color that is *not* white.

5. Use the **Lasso Marquee(M)** tool to mark a highlight area, as shown in this screenshot:

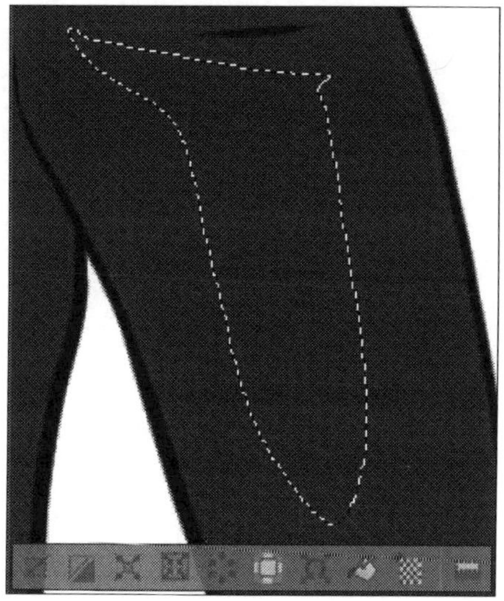

6. Select the **Gradient(G)** tool and then the **Foreground to transparent** subtool.
7. Use the **Gradient(G)** tool to fill the selection, dragging in the direction of the light source in your image. Note that the entire selection should not be a solid fill, as shown in the following screenshot:

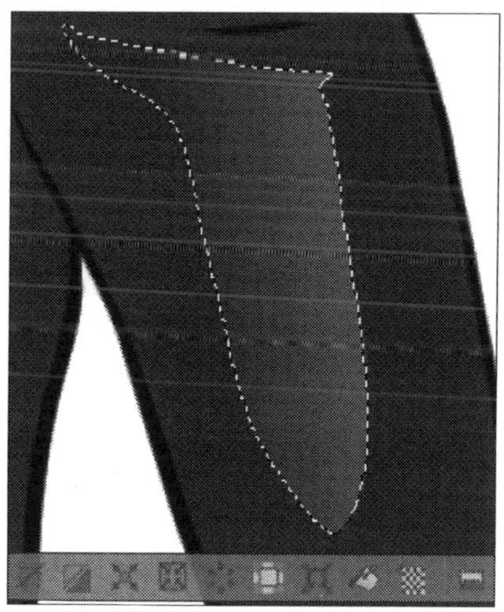

8. Continue making highlights in this manner until the initial shading is complete. This screenshot shows part of our first pass of highlights:

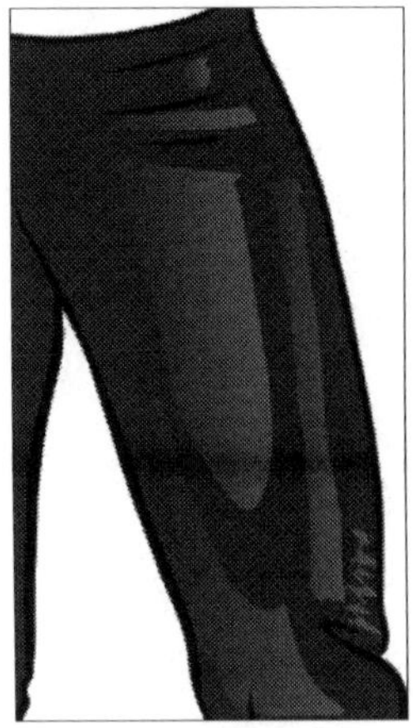

9. Create a new raster layer above the `Highlights 1` layer. Name this layer `Highlights 2`.
10. Make pure white the active color.
11. Repeat steps 5 to 8, making smaller highlights over the first highlights. These secondary highlights look best with sharper edges, so make the gradient fill more of the selection (or use the **Fill(G)** tool).
12. Adjust any part of the image as required. As shown in the following screenshot, some areas of the `Highlights 1` layer have been softened with the **Blur** subtool under the **Blend(J)** tool:

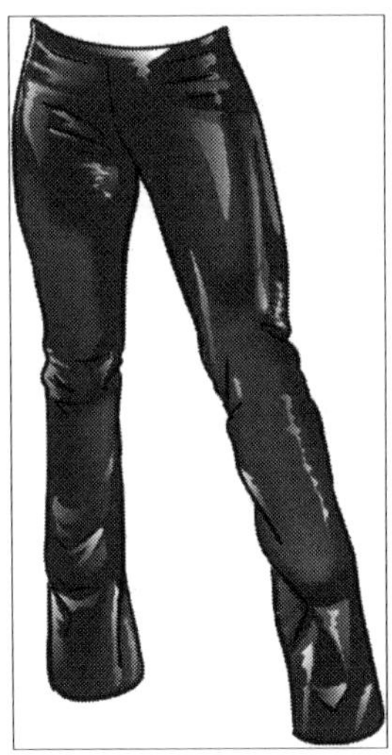

Creating a colored light effect

Getting the look of light from a fire, moonlight, or a neon sign can be tricky. This recipe will give you some tips and tricks on how to get this look!

How to do it...

The following steps will show you how to make a colored light effect:

1. Start with a drawing with flat colors laid down on their own layer, and a separate layer of line work.
2. Make a new raster layer above the flat colors but below the ink lines. Change the blending mode to **Multiply** and adjust the opacity from **35%** to **45%**. The actual number will vary depending on your personal style and the colors of the piece. The following screenshot shows the order of the layers and the settings for the **shadows** layer:

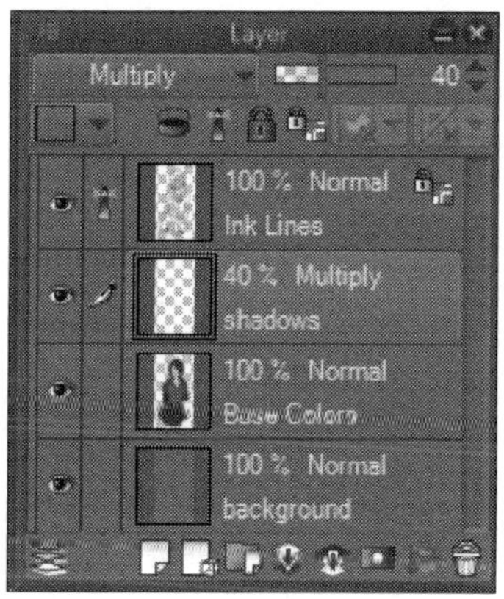

3. Select a shading color and mark in the shadows for your drawing. As shown in the following example, I decided that this will be a nighttime scene, lit by two neon signs, so I used a dark blue-violet color for the shading:

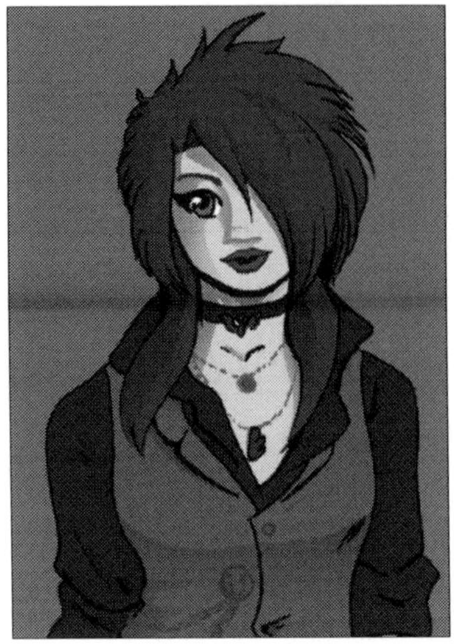

4. Once the shadows are done, create a new layer for the highlights. Change the blending mode to **Lighten** or **Screen**. As with the shadow layer, change the opacity from **35%** to **45%**. This screenshot shows the order of the layers and the settings for the new layer:

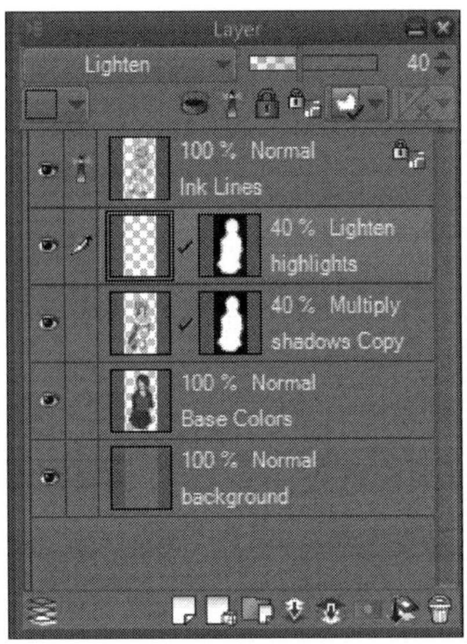

5. Choose a light color and highlight the drawing. For this piece, the highlight color will come from a yellow-green neon sign on the right-hand side of the character. Because of this, a yellow-green color was chosen for the highlights on the girl, as shown here:

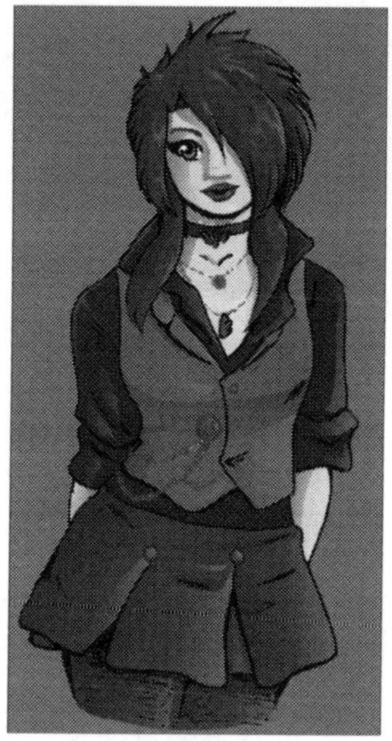

6. Now, our work on the background starts. In the following screenshot, a brick texture has been imported and added behind the character. A new layer set to **Multiply** and filled with a dark blue gradient has been added over the texture to make it match the shading of the character.

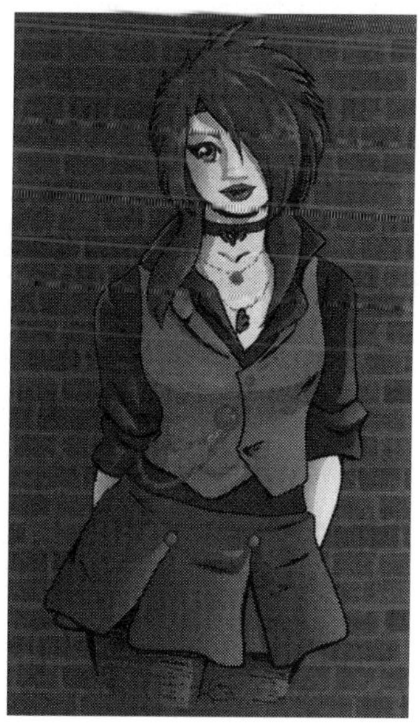

7. The visible light sources are now added to the background. The neon signs are made in a similar way to the laser blasts in the *Creating laser blasts* recipe, but an additional layer has been added behind the text. This layer has been set to the **Screen** combine mode, and the **Soft** airbrush tool has been used to add more light to the scene. Here is a screenshot of the layers used to create the **OPEN** neon sign:

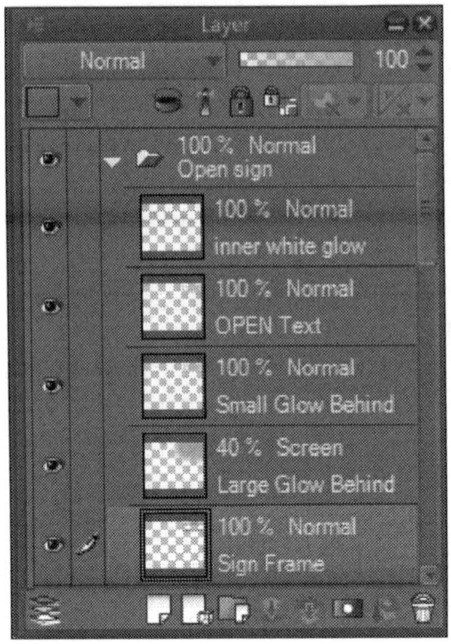

Note in the following screenshot how far out the glow extends from the signs:

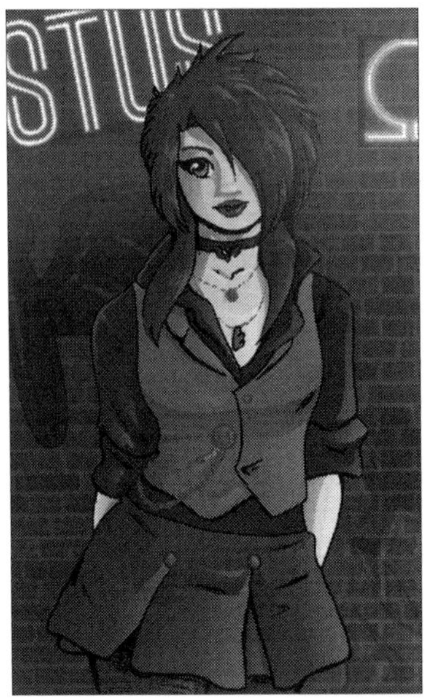

8. Now it's time to add more colored light to the edges of the character. This is called a **rim light**, and it further accentuates the character's details. Create a new layer above the inked lines layer. Select the **Screen** combine mode for this layer. Using the **Soft** airbrush tool, add thin lines of color around some of the edges of the character, as shown in the following screenshot:

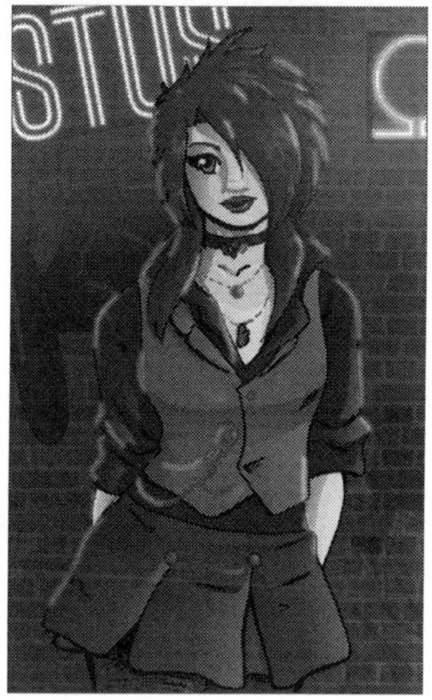

9. Adjust the opacity of the rim light layer and use the **Soft** subtool of the **Eraser(E)** or the **Blend(J)** tool to soften any areas that are too hard. This final step is shown here:

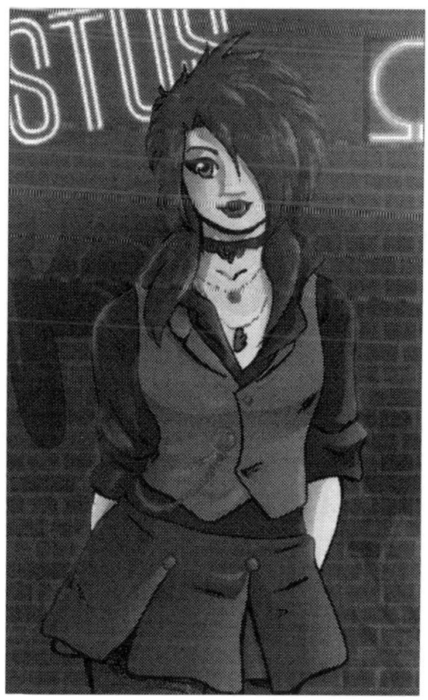

How it works...

Planning ahead goes a long way for an effect like this. Think ahead of time about what light sources you'll have in your image and where they will be coming from. Is it night time? The scene will be of blues and purples—most likely—and the light will be white and silver (provided there is starlight or moonlight). Is there a campfire nearby? Then you'll want to work with warmer colors.

For more information about light colors and working with colored light in painting, I recommend reading *Color and Light: A Guide for the Realist Painter* by James Gurney.

Also, the rim light effect goes a very long way, so don't use too much of it! I feel that this sort of intense rim light should be used sparingly to accent and bring attention to some parts of the character and punch up the look of the overall image. If we were to put a rim light on every surface of the character, it would draw the reader's eye all over the canvas and make a confusing composition.

Creating laser blasts

This recipe is best used for laser blasts coming from a gun or some other sci-fi weapon. How about a spaceship cannon? It's quite easy to do, so let's get started!

How to do it...

The following recipe will walk us through the steps of creating a laser blast:

1. Go to **Figure(U)** | **Direct draw** | **Straight line**. Select a color for the laser blast.
2. On an empty raster layer, draw a straight line with the line tool. As shown in the following screenshot, I've chosen a bright red color. I have also made the paper color black so that the laser effect is easier to see.

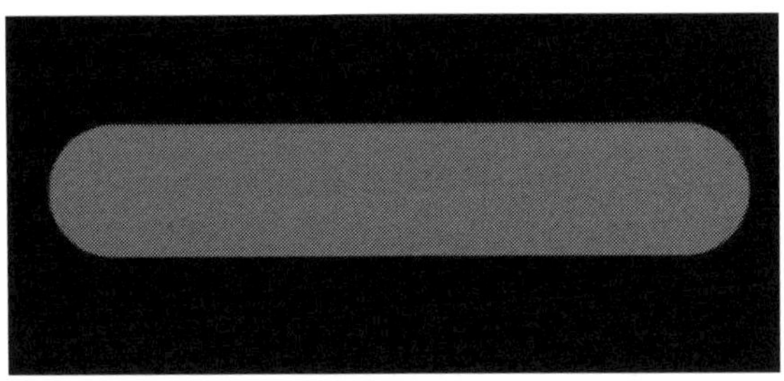

3. Lock the transparency of the layer with the straight line. For directions on how to do this, see steps 1 and 2 of the *Making colored line work* recipe.

4. Make white the active color.
5. Select the **Gradient(G)** tool. Then select the **Foreground to transparent** subtool.
6. Open the **Sub Tool Detail** palette.
7. At the top of the **Sub Tool Detail** palette, you will see a slider with the current gradient displayed. Drag the triangle below the white section into the center of the slider.
8. Click on the transparent color swatch below the foreground and background colors in the toolbar, as shown in this screenshot:

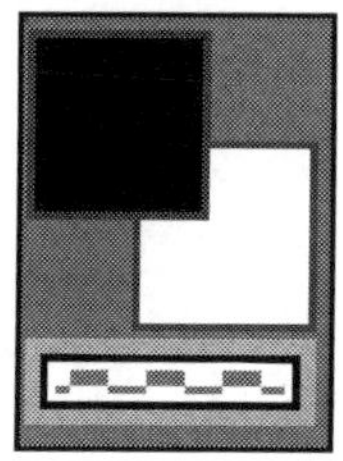

9. Move the cursor over the bottom of the gradient preview slider in the **Sub Tool Detail** palette. The cursor will show a **+** sign next to it. Click on the far left of the slider to add a transparent stop, and leave the white gradation just in the center. The following screenshot shows what the **Sub Tool Detail** palette should look like after this change:

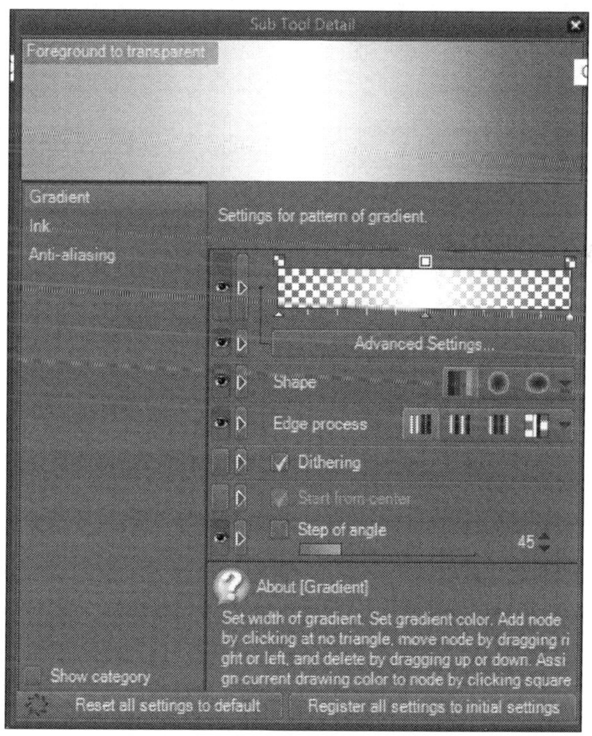

10. Close the **Sub Tool Detail** palette.
11. With the **Gradient(G)** tool still selected, click at the top of the straight line made in step 2 and hold down the mouse. Drag to the bottom of the straight line and release the mouse button. This will leave us with a colored line that has a white gradient center, as shown here:

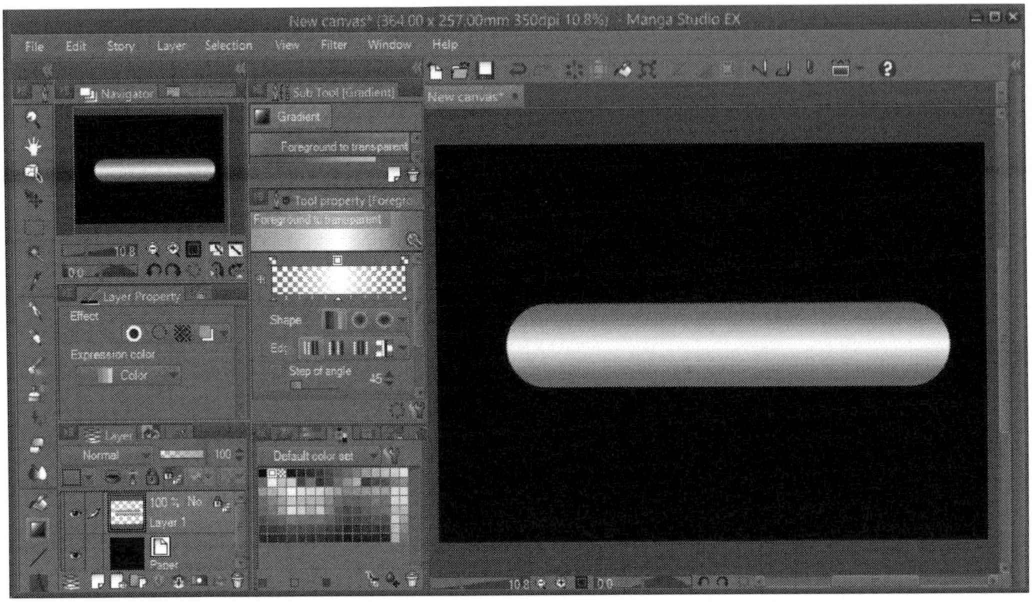

12. Copy the layer and then select the bottom copy in the **Layer** palette. This is shown in the following screenshot:

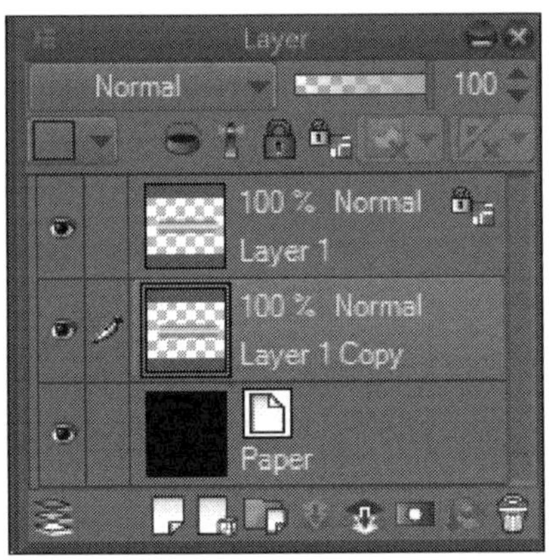

13. Navigate to **Filter** | **Blur** | **Gaussian blur** and set **Area to blur(G)** to a number that is large enough for the laser blast to get a *halo* effect around it. Click on **OK**.

14. Now the laser blast will have a blurred outline. Make a layer below the one you just blurred. Ensure that white is still the active color.
15. Select the **Airbrush(B)** tool and the **Soft** subtool. Add white around the colored edges of the laser beam to increase the glow.
16. As shown in the following screenshot, I have also used the **Soft** subtool of the **Eraser(E)** tool on the edges of the original line to blend everything together. This step is optional.

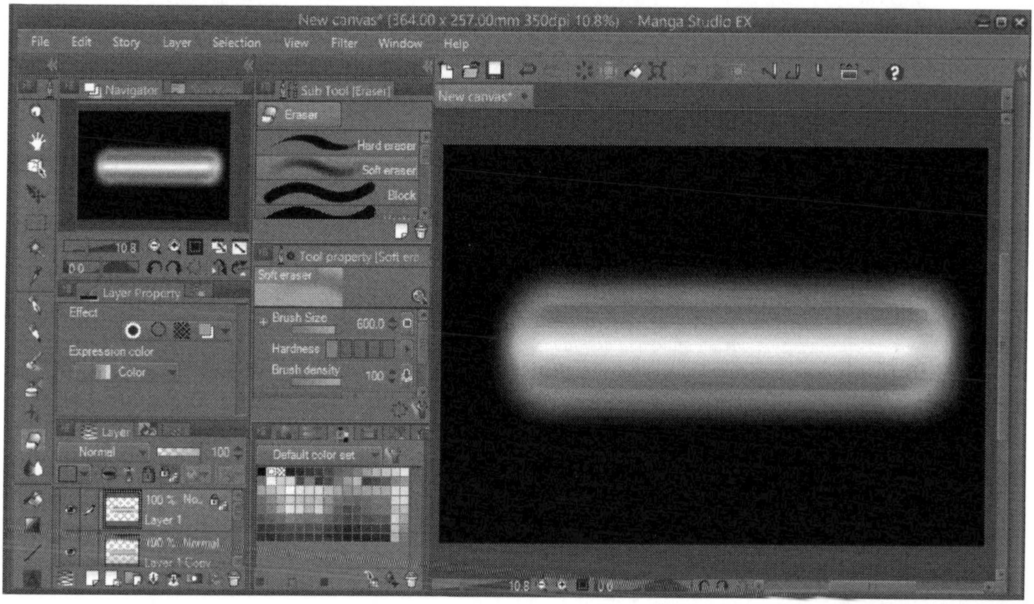

Making lightning and electricity

Another special effect that you may need for your illustrations is lightning or electricity. The results look difficult to achieve, but they're actually quite easy.

How to do it...

The following steps will teach you how to create a lightning effect:

1. Start with a light blue, gray, or yellow color as the foreground color. For this recipe, we have made the paper color black so that it is easier to see the light blue shapes.
2. Select a **Pen(P)** tool or a **Brush(B)** with a hard edge. Make the brush or pen tip large enough, and draw a rough shape of lightning on a blank raster layer.

3. Use the **Hard Eraser(E)** tool to refine the shape of the lightning. It should be angular and have areas of thick and thin lines. Here is a screenshot that shows an example of this refined shape:

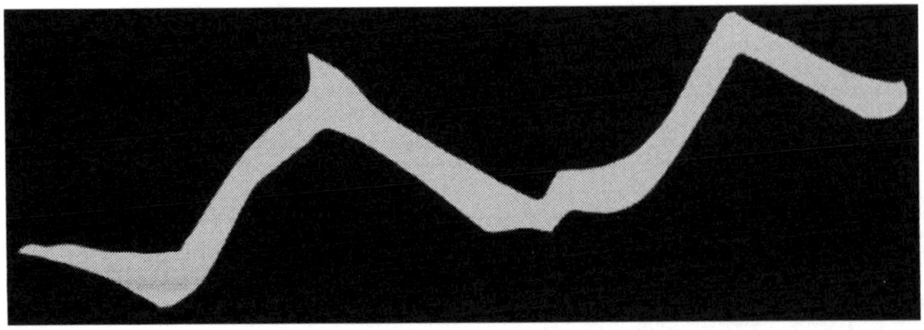

4. Using a smaller brush or pen, add another jagged line along the first one. This should not follow the main line exactly, but should overlap. Refine the line as needed with the hard eraser. The following screenshot shows an example of this:

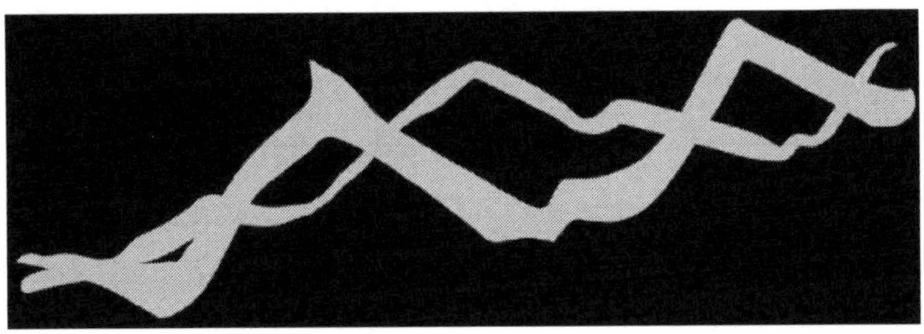

> To make refining the line easier, you may wish to create a new layer for the second line. After finalizing the shape, merge the second layer with the first one.

5. Take a very thin brush or pen, and add more crackling energy coming off and arcing between the first two lines. Refer to this screenshot for an example of what this looks like:

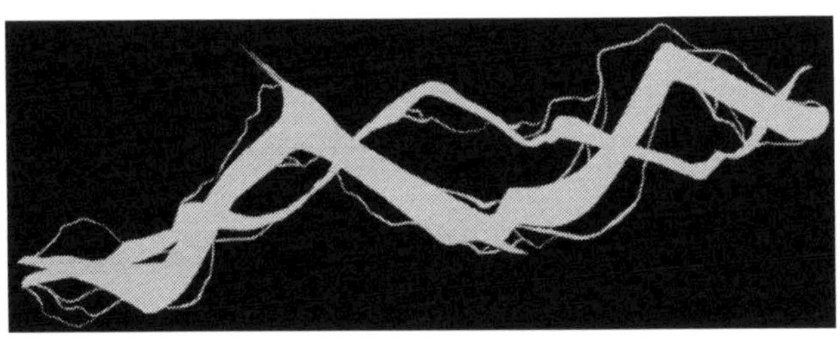

6. Copy the layer with the lightning shape once. Select the lower instance of this layer to make it active.
7. Use the steps in the *Making colored line work* recipe to change the lines in this bottom layer to white. When you're done, deselect the **Lock Transparent Pixel** icon.
8. Go to **Filter | Blur | Gaussian blur**. In the dialog box that appears, make sure that the **Preview** checkbox is marked. Then move the slider up or down to get the desired amount of blur around the lightning shape, as shown in the following screenshot:

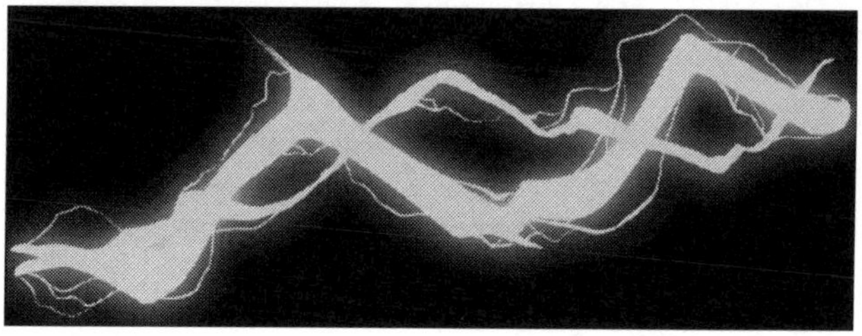

9. To finish the lightning effect, create a new raster layer above the unfiltered lightning shape. Select white as the active color, and select the **Soft** airbrush tool. Add white to the center of the lightning arcs, as shown in this screenshot:

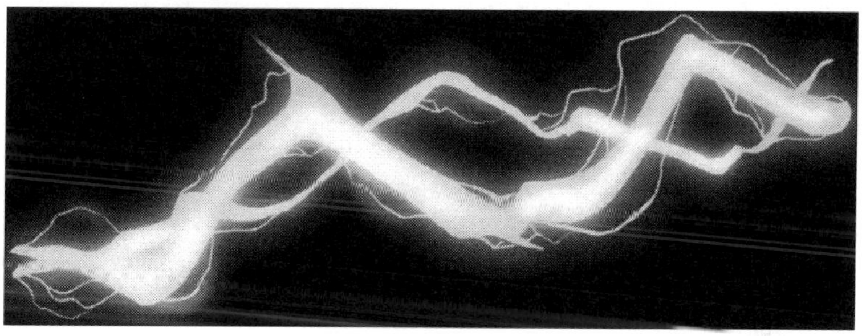

10
Using 3D Objects

In this chapter, you will learn the following recipes:

- Adding existing 3D objects to a page
- Importing a 3D object from another program
- Manipulating 3D objects
- Adjusting the 3D camera
- Using preset poses
- Saving custom information as materials
- Customizing characters

Introduction

One of the features of Manga Studio 5 that people ask me about all the time is 3D objects. Manga Studio 5 comes with a set of 3D assets: characters, poses, and a few backgrounds and small objects. These can be added directly to your page, posed and positioned, and used in your artwork. While I usually use these 3D poses as a reference (much like the wooden drawing dolls that you can find in your local craft store), you can conceivably use 3D characters and imported 3D assets from programs such as Poser to create entire comics.

Let's get into the third dimension now, and you will learn how to use these assets in Manga Studio 5.

Adding existing 3D objects to a page

Manga Studio 5 comes with many 3D objects present in the materials library. This is the fastest way to get started with using the 3D features.

Getting ready

You must have a page open in order to add a 3D object. Open a page of any size to start the recipes covered in this chapter.

How to do it...

The following steps will show us how to add an existing 3D material to a page:

1. Open the materials library. This can be done by going to **Window** | **Material** | **Material [3D]**.
2. Select a category of 3D material from the list on the left-hand side of the library, or scroll down the **Material** library preview window to browse all the available materials.
3. Select a material to add to the page by clicking on it to highlight it. In this recipe, we are choosing the **School girl B 02** character material. It is highlighted in the following screenshot:

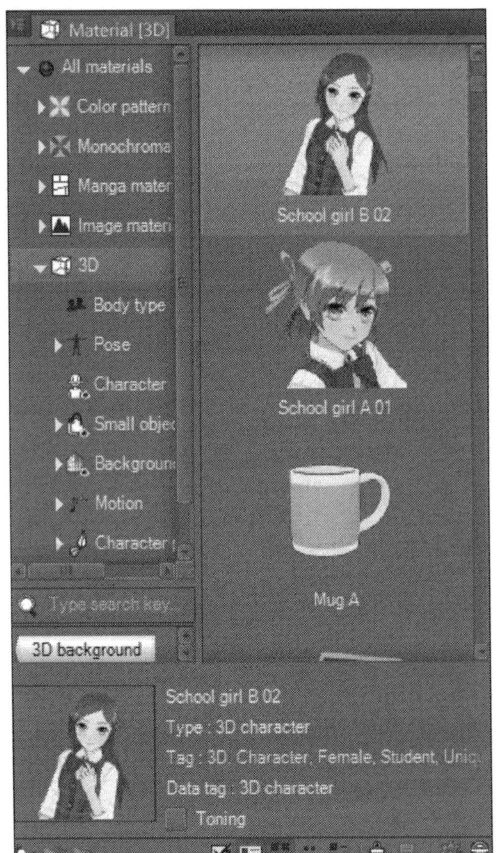

4. Hold the left mouse button down on the selected material and drag it onto the page, releasing the mouse button once the cursor is over the page, to display the material. Alternately, you can click on the **Paste selected material to canvas** icon at the bottom of the **Material** library menu.

The selected 3D material will be added to the page. The **School girl B 02** material is shown in this default character pose:

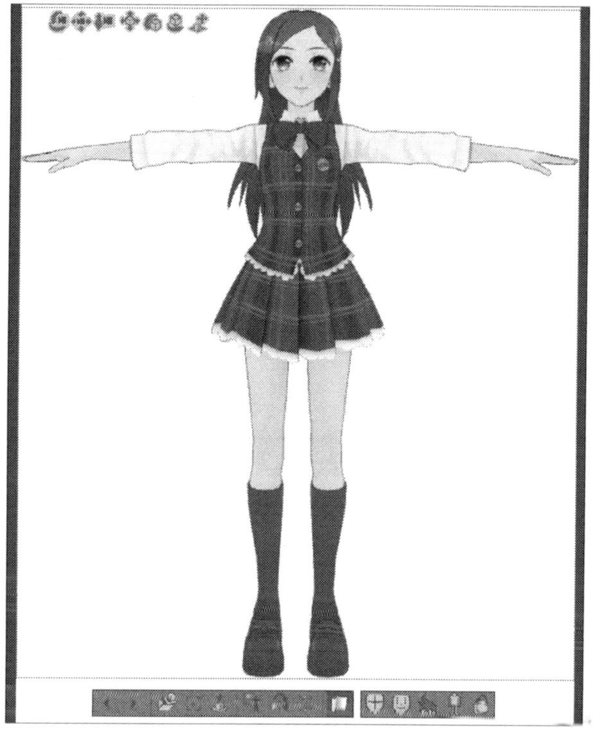

Importing a 3D object from another program

You don't have to use only the default 3D models included in Manga Studio 5. The process of importing a model is very easy.

> The types of files that can be imported into Manga Studio 5 are `c2fc`, `c2fr`, `fbx`, `lwo`, `lws`, `obj`, `6kt`, and `6kh`.

Getting ready

You must have a page open in order to add a 3D object. Open a page of any size to start this recipe. For this recipe, you will also need a model to import into the program. These can be found on numerous websites, including `my.smithmicro.com`, under the **Poser** tab.

How to do it...

The following steps will walk us through the simple process of importing a 3D model into Manga Studio 5:

1. Open the location where the 3D model that you wish to import has been saved. If you have downloaded the 3D model from the Internet, it may be in the `Downloads` folder on your PC.
2. Arrange the windows on your computer screen so that the location of the 3D model and Manga Studio 5 are both visible, as shown in the following screenshot:

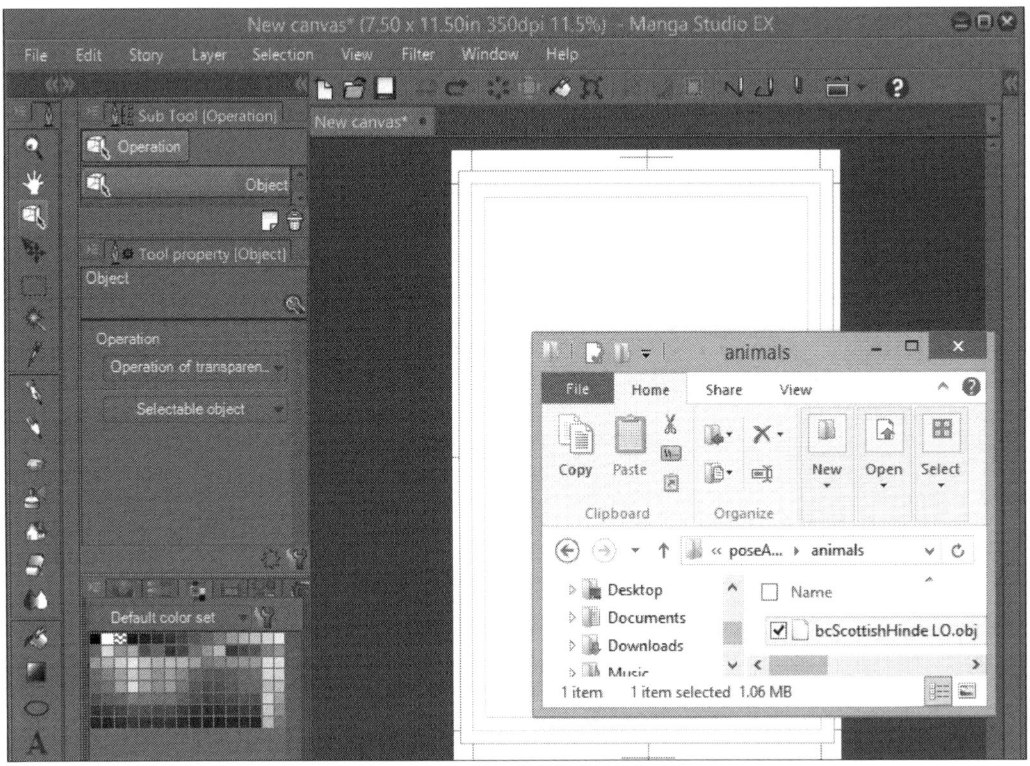

3. Click on the 3D model file and hold down the mouse button. While still holding down the mouse button, drag the 3D model file into the Manga Studio 5 window.
4. Release the mouse button.

The 3D model will be imported into the open page, as shown in this screenshot:

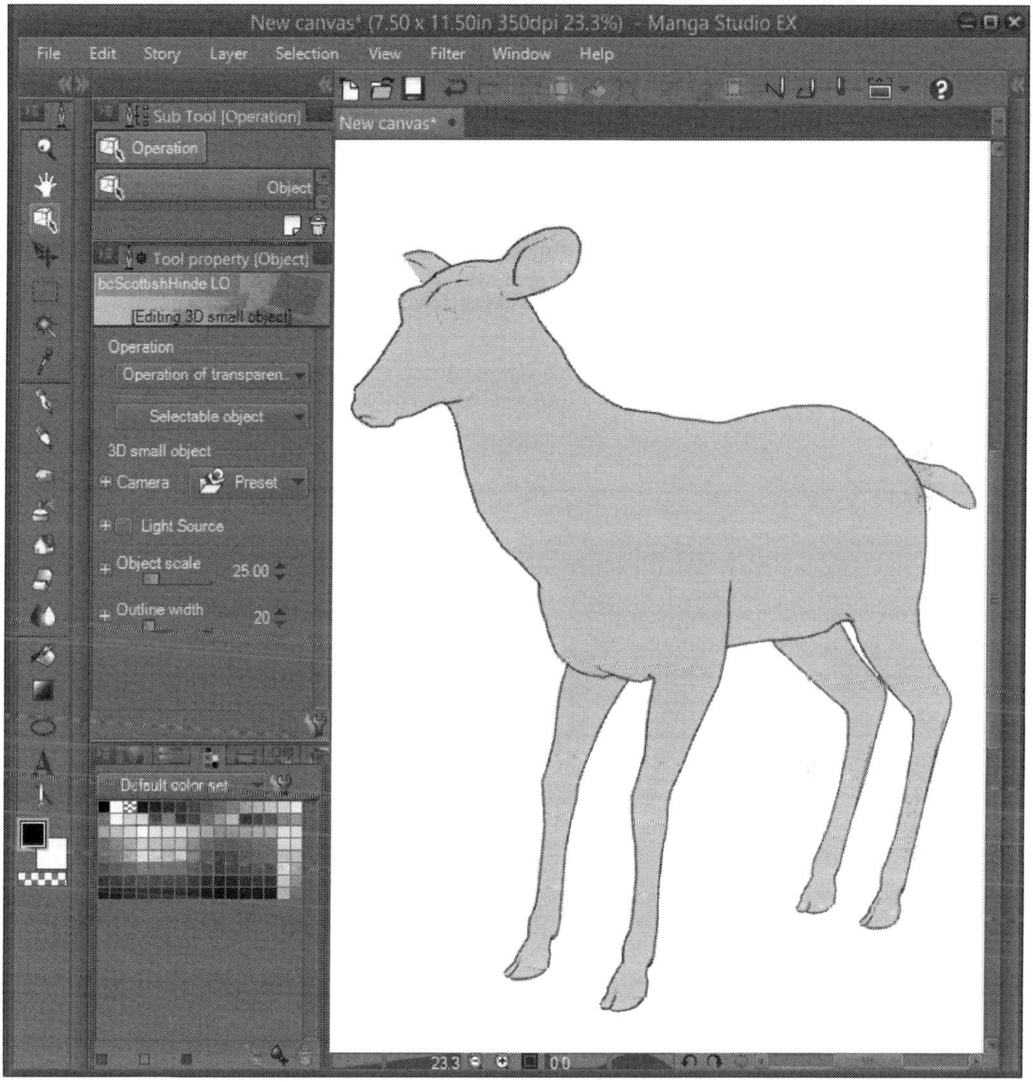

Manipulating 3D objects

You've learned how to add a 3D object to our project. But how can you pose it the way you want it to look for your scene? With a little time and patience, you'll be posing characters like a pro in no time!

Getting ready

Follow the directions in the *Adding existing 3D objects to a page* recipe before following the steps in this recipe.

How to do it...

This recipe will walk us through moving a character into a custom pose:

1. Be sure that the **Object** tool under **Operation** is selected.
2. Click on the 3D object to manipulate, if it is not already selected.
3. To move the entire object up, down, left, or right, hover the mouse cursor over the fourth icon in the top-left corner of the box around the selected object. Click and hold the left mouse button; then, drag to move the object in the desired direction. The following screenshot shows the location of the icon used to move the object up, down, left, or right. It is highlighted in pink and also shown over the 3D character.

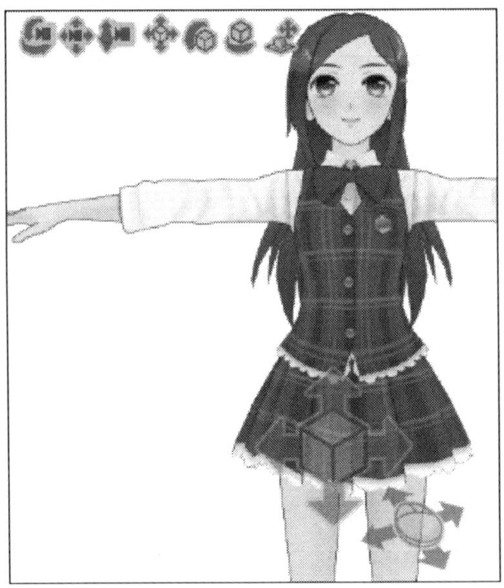

> If your models are moving very slowly, you may need to allocate more memory to Manga Studio EX 5. This can be done by going to **File** | **Preferences** | **Performance**.

4. To rotate the object along the *y* axis (or the horizon line), hover the mouse cursor over the fifth icon in the top-left corner of the box around the selected object. Click on it, hold the left mouse button, and drag. The object will rotate along the *y* axis, as shown in this screenshot:

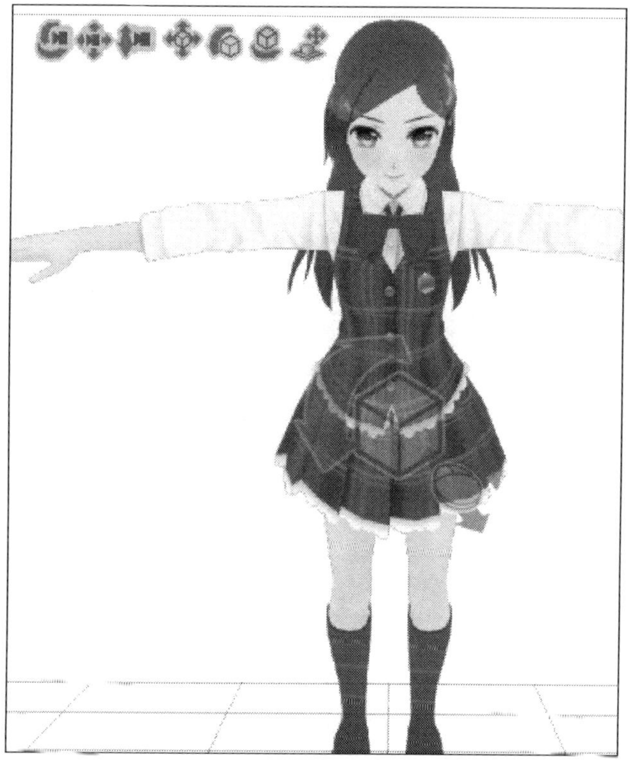

5. To rotate the object along the x axis (straight up and down vertically), hover the mouse cursor over the sixth icon in the top-left corner of the box around the selected object. Click and drag. The object will rotate vertically around its center, as shown in the following screenshot:

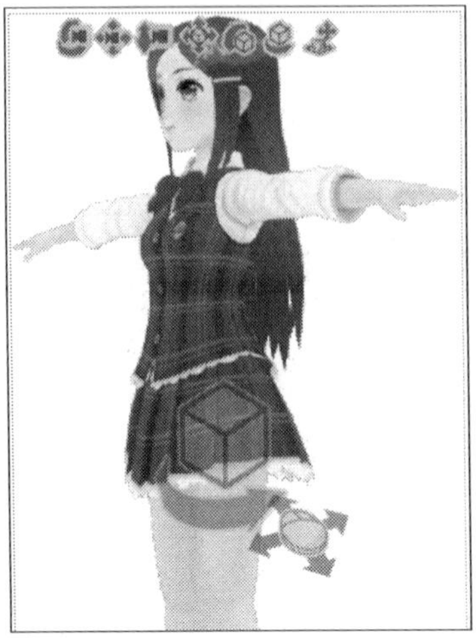

6. To move the object back and forth in 3D space, hover the mouse cursor over the seventh icon in the top-left corner of the box around the selected object. Click and hold the left mouse button; then drag it. The icon is shown as follows, highlighted in pink, and the character has been moved back—away from the camera:

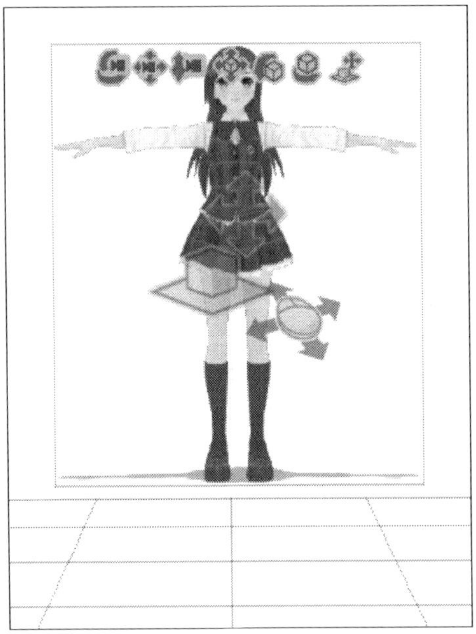

7. To move one part of a character, click on the part to be moved. For this recipe, we'll move the character's arm down. To do this, we'll click on the upper arm portion of the character to select it.
8. When a portion of the character is selected, a sphere with three lines circling it will appear. Each of these three lines represents one axis (*x*, *y*, and *z*) and controls the rotation of that portion of the character. This set of lines is shown here:

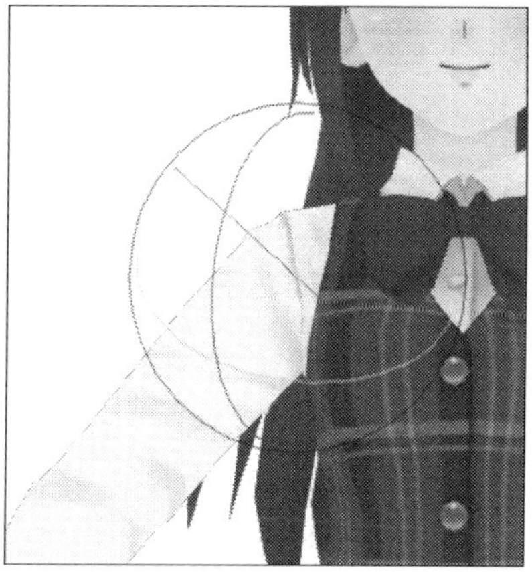

9. Use the lines of the sphere to rotate the part of the character to the desired position. For a more precise movement, the scroll wheel on the mouse can be used as well. In the following screenshot, the arm has been rotated so that it is down at the character's side:

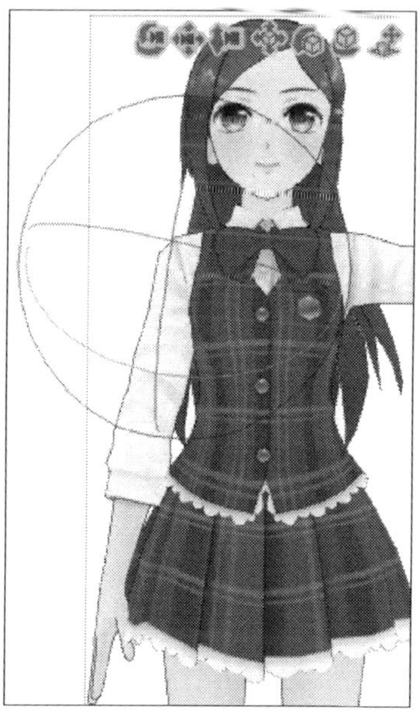

> Do you keep accidentally moving a part of the model that you don't want to move? Put the cursor over the part of the model that you'd like to keep in place, and then right-click. A blue box will appear on that part of the model, and the piece will be locked in to place. Right-click again to unlock the part.

How it works...

In this recipe, we covered how to move and rotate a 3D object and portions of 3D characters. This is the start of being able to create your own custom poses and saving them for reuse. It's also the way to pose the drawing doll models in Manga Studio to make pose references for your comic artwork. In the `3D-Body Type` folder of the materials library, you will find **Female** and **Male** drawing dolls that can be posed just as the premade characters can. These generic dolls are great for getting that difficult pose down. Then use the next recipe, *Adjusting the 3D camera*, to get the angle you need, and draw away!

The following screenshot shows a drawing doll 3D object that has been posed in a custom stance. Later in this chapter, we will save this pose as a material so that we can use it for other characters.

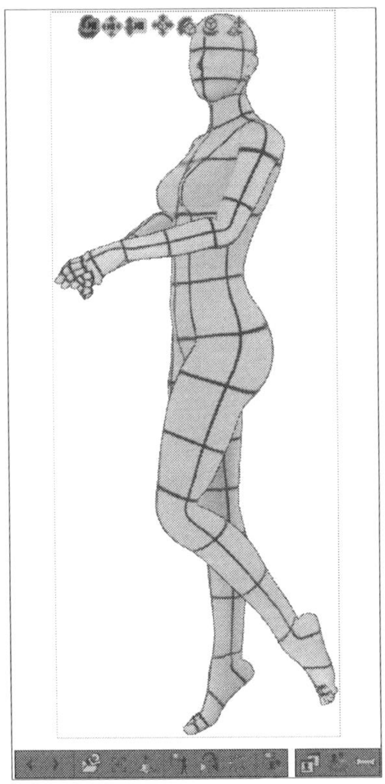

The preceding pose was relatively easy to achieve. The figure was rotated along the *x* axis, and then the head and neck joints were both rotated individually so that the doll looked toward the camera. Both its arms were rotated down and then inward. The hands were posed. The ankle joints were selected and the feet were rotated so that the toes were pointed. Then the knee of the near leg was rotated to bend it. The hip of the near leg was also rotated so that the leg was lifted slightly, giving a "cutesy" look to the pose.

> Having trouble posing a character's hands exactly the way you want them? Open the **Sub Tool Detail** palette and click on **Pose** in the left-hand-side menu. In this area, you will find a menu with a picture of a hand. This is a quick controller for the fingers. Select the hand that you wish to pose. Along the bottom of the menu are some preset hand poses for things such as closed fists. At the top of each finger on this menu is an icon that looks like chain links. Click on one of them to lock the finger that it is over and prevent it from moving. The triangle area over the large blue hand symbol controls how open and closed the fingers are. You will find this menu much easier than rotating each joint individually, I'm sure!

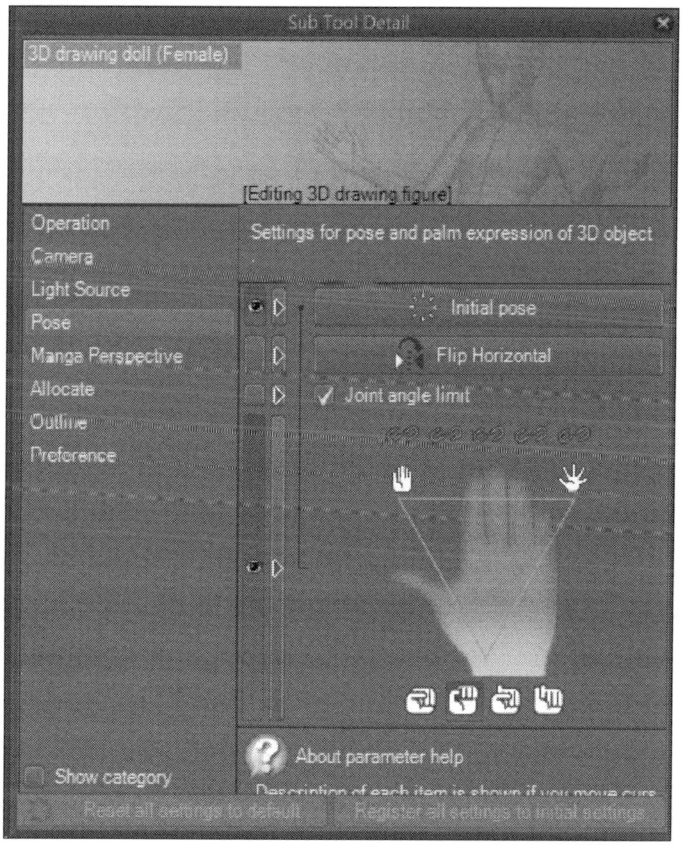

Adjusting the 3D camera

In addition to manipulating 3D objects or characters, you can also change the position of the 3D camera to get the composition that you desire for your work. Think of the 3D camera just like a camera on a movie set. It can be rotated or moved around to frame the actors (3D characters) and scenery just the way the director wants!

> Not sure whether you moved the character or the camera? Take a look at the ground plane, which is the "checkerboard" floor area underneath the characters and objects. If the character is standing straight up and down on the ground plane, it means that the camera was moved. If the character is floating above or below the ground plane, or part of the way through it, it means that the character or object was moved.

Getting ready

Follow the directions given in the *Adding existing 3D objects to a page* recipe before following the steps in this recipe.

How to do it...

1. To rotate the camera around an object (the object will remain stationary), hover the mouse cursor over the first icon in the top-left corner of the box around the selected object. Click and hold the left mouse button, and then drag. The icon and the camera rotation are shown in the following screenshot:

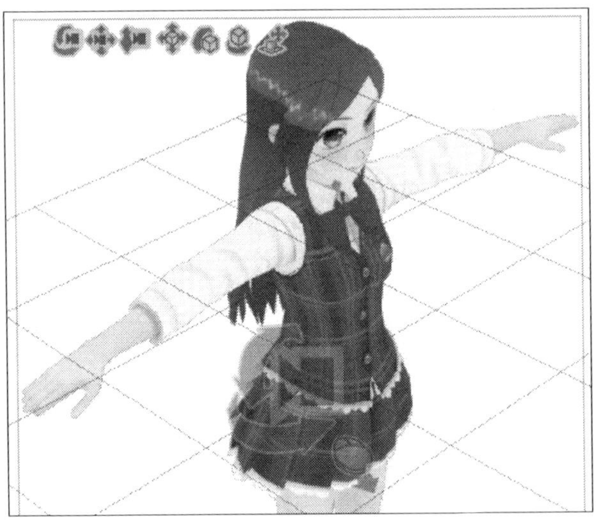

2. To move the camera up, down, left, or right, hover the mouse cursor over the second icon in the top-left corner of the box around the selected object. Click and hold the left mouse button, and then drag. The icon and camera movement are shown in this screenshot:

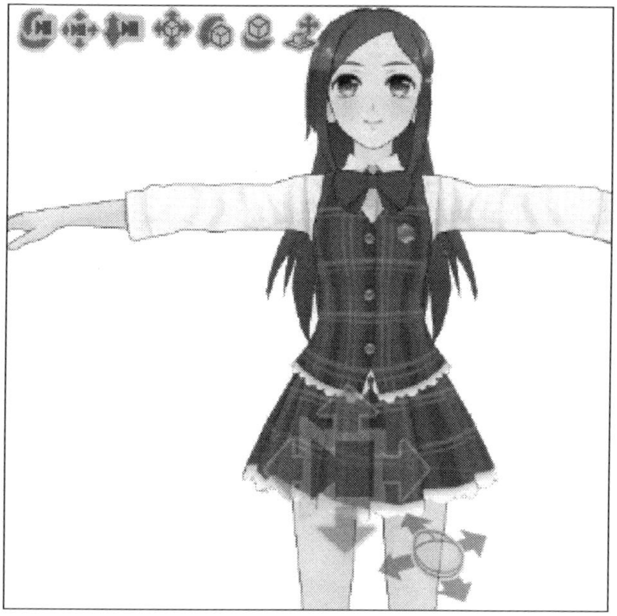

3. To move the camera back and forth in the 3D space, hover the mouse cursor over the third icon in the top-left corner of the box around the selected object. Again, click and hold the left mouse button, and then drag. The next screenshot shows the zoom icon in pink at the top and the overlay on top of the character. Note how the hand of the character and the top of the head are now out of the page, since the camera is closer to her and she appears larger on the canvas.

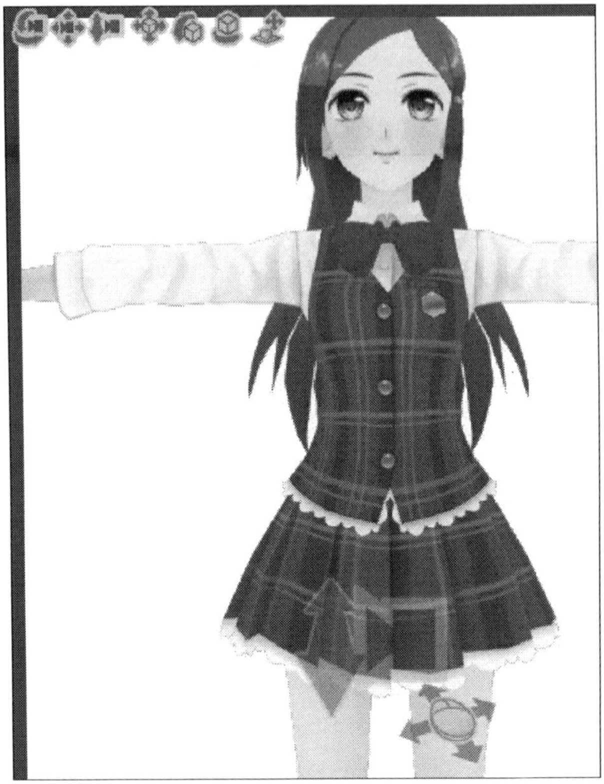

Using preset poses

The 3D section of the materials library has many pre-made poses that can be applied to characters or drawing dolls. These poses are great for getting a character quickly into position, or as starting point for a custom poses!

Getting ready

Follow the directions given in the *Adding existing 3D objects to a page* recipe before following the steps in this recipe.

How to do it...

The following steps will teach you how to use preset poses on characters or drawing dolls:

1. Go to **3D** | **Pose** | **Entire body** in the **Material** library.
2. Select a pose that you like the existing character to be in. For this recipe, we are using **P_soccer 01**.
3. Click on the chosen pose to select it. It will be highlighted in blue.
4. To add the pose to the character, click on the selected pose again and hold the mouse button down. Drag the mouse cursor over on top of the character while still holding down the button. The cursor will get a **+** symbol next to it.
5. Release the mouse button over the character.

The character will change to the new pose, as shown in the following screenshot:

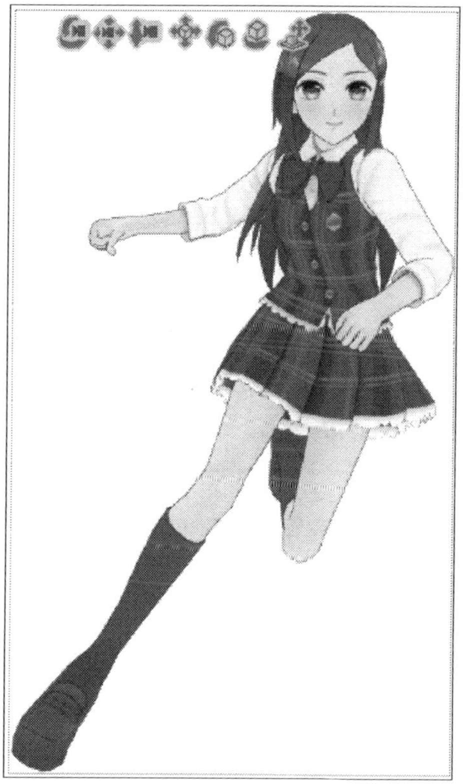

Want to use a preset pose with a drawing doll? Simply drag the pose onto the page without the character being there first. This screenshot shows the same preset pose as you just saw, but without the character model applied:

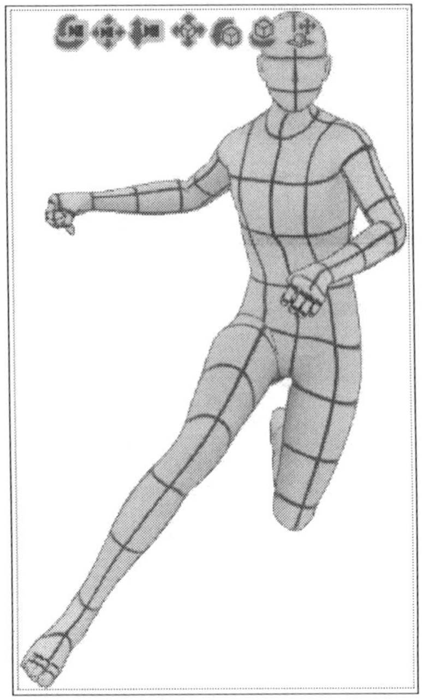

Saving custom information as materials

When you make a pose that you like and want to use again later, you can save it and apply it to other pages or character models. This is especially useful if you are creating a comic in which the characters strike the same pose a lot (think of some magical girl or martial arts comics, where the characters have special attacks or transformation sequences).

Getting ready

Follow the directions in the *Manipulating 3D objects* recipe and make a custom pose before following the steps in this recipe.

How to do it...

Now follow these steps to save your custom 3D pose:

1. Make sure that the **Object** tool, which is under **Operation**, is selected.
2. Click on the figure to be saved to select it.
3. In the menu bar below the figure, click on the **Register pose to material palette** icon, which is circled in this screenshot:

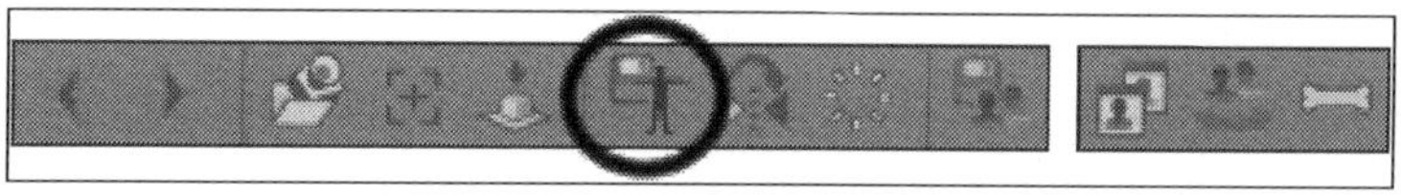

4. Fill in the **Material property** window with a title and tags. Choose the **Pose** folder under **3D** to save the material in. The following screenshot shows an example of the **Material property** window:

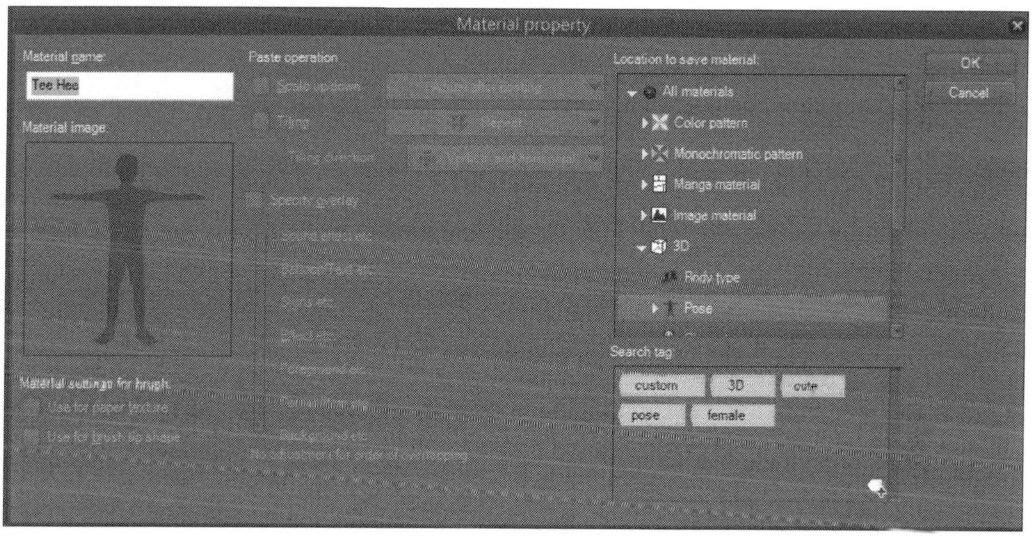

5. Click on **OK**.

6. To test the pose, load another character onto the open page. Use the instructions from the *Using preset poses* recipe to apply the newly created pose to the character. Here is the pose created in the *Manipulating 3D objects* recipe, saved as a material and applied to the **School girl B 02** character:

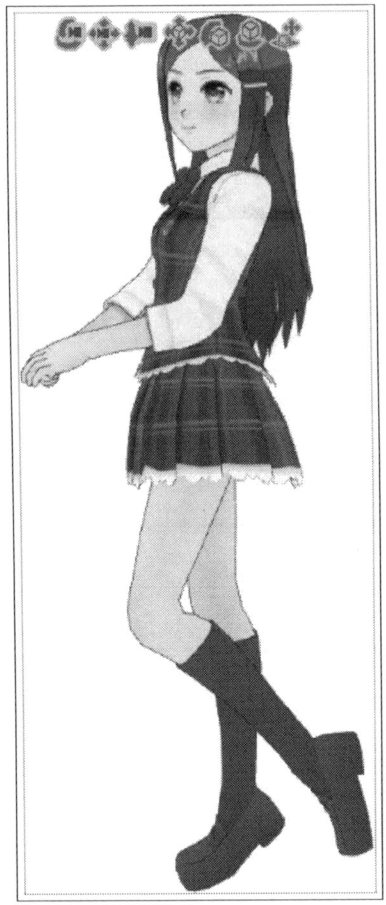

Customizing characters

So far, we've played with 3D model characters and kept them as the defaults that they come in. But what if we could customize these characters and make them unique? Manga Studio 5 has options for changing not only some of the expressions and hair of the default characters that come loaded in the materials library, but also the proportions of the character. This means that we can do much more with 3D characters and make drawing dolls for our own characters as well—complete with the correct proportions!

Getting ready

Follow the instructions given in the *Adding existing 3D objects to a page* recipe before following the steps in this recipe.

How to do it...

Let's make a custom character look with the following recipe:

1. Make sure that the **Object** tool under **Operation** is selected.
2. Click on the 3D character model you wish to change.

> The first part of this recipe works only with those character models that are included in Manga Studio 5. The **Male** and **Female** drawing dolls do not have the same facial and clothing options, of course, but they have proportion controls, which we will go over later in this very recipe.

3. Following the character, a long menu will appear. The right-hand side of this menu will look like what is shown in this screenshot:

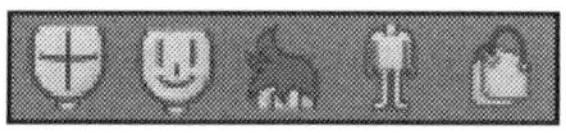

4. Click on the **Select face of character** icon to bring up any facial options for the character. The **School girl B 02** model has only a **Basic** face option, as shown here:

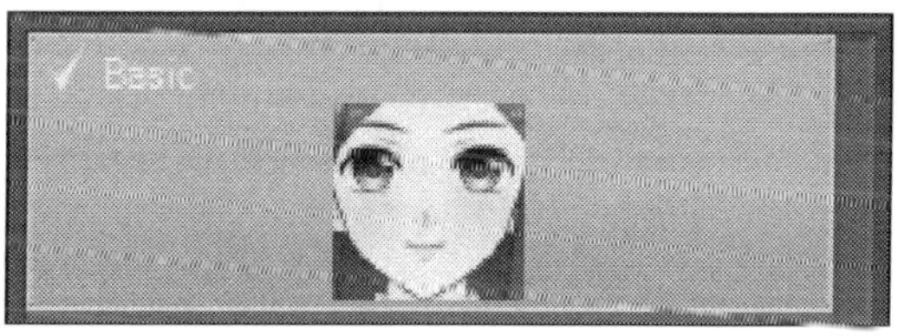

5. Click on the **Select facial expression of character** icon to show and select from a variety of facial expressions for the character. As shown in the following screenshot, each facial expression is named and has a preview image:

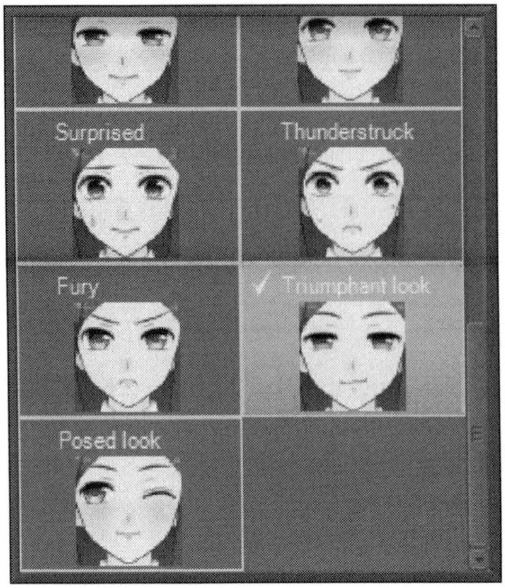

6. Click on the **Select hair style of character** icon to show the different hairstyle options available for the character model. Most of the characters have a selection of long and short styles. Click on the desired hairstyle to select it. As shown in this screenshot, each hair style has a name and a preview image to make the selection easy:

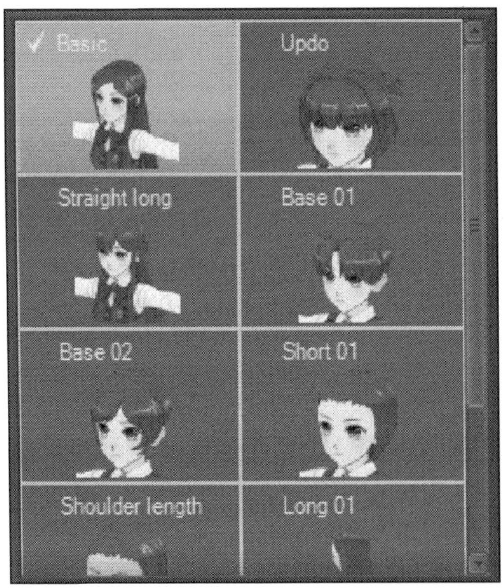

7. Click on the **Select body of character** icon to show the clothing options for the selected character. In the following screenshot, you can see that the character has three school uniform options and one street clothes option:

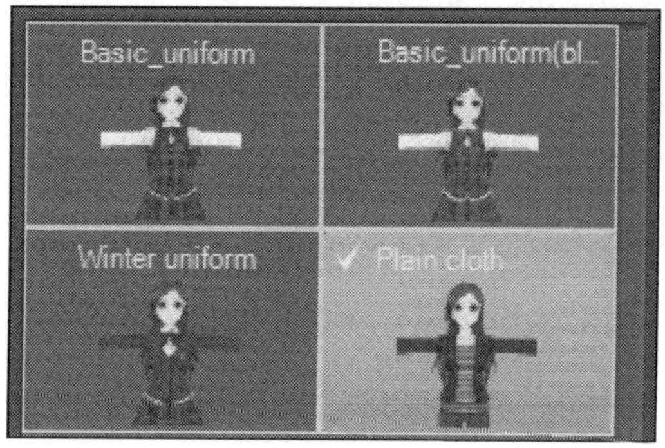

8. Click on the **Set display status of accessories of character** icon to show additional hair options (for example, more bangs, ponytails, hair bows, and so on), as well as some other fun options, such as cat and rabbit ears. Several accessories can be displayed at once, so clicking on both **Bangs 01** and **Bangs 02** will overlap the bangs one on top of the other, rather than display them one at a time. The following screenshot shows some of the extra hair options:

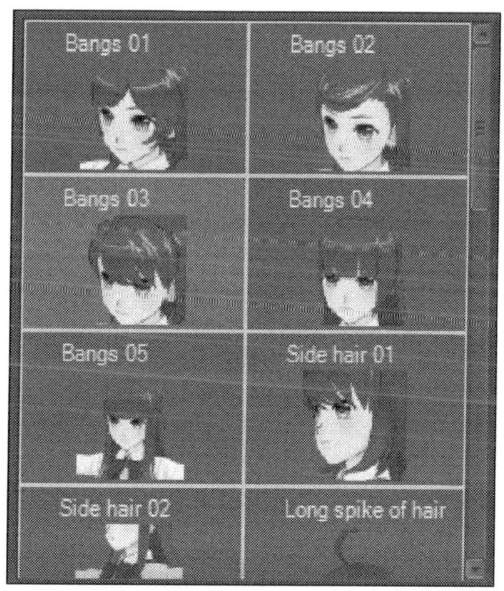

How it works...

The character customization options allow us to start with a generic school girl with long, straight hair and transform her into a character with a little more personality. Perhaps, the character in the following screenshot is a cat girl from... outer space?

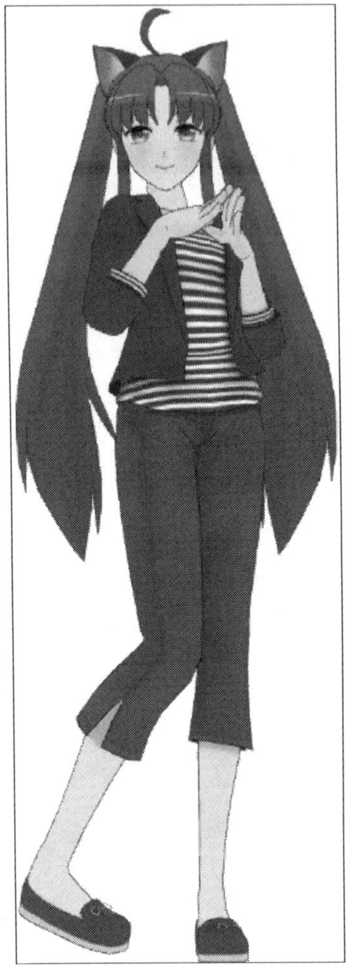

With a little work, some customization, and importing of a few other models, it's easy to see that even someone who doesn't want to draw 2D characters can make a 3D rendered comic with Manga Studio 5! But for those who are more interested in using the generic dolls as a reference to draw your own characters, read on!

There's more...

The generic **Male** and **Female** drawing dolls don't have accessories and clothes to change. However, their body types have lots of options:

1. Add a 3D drawing doll to the open page by opening the materials library and going to **3D** | **Body type**. Click on a doll to select it and add it to the page as explained in the *Adding existing 3D objects to a page* recipe.
2. With the 3D drawing doll selected, look at the lower menu bar that appears beneath the model's feet. On the right-hand side, you will see the following icons:

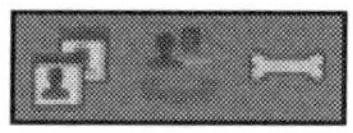

3. Click on the first icon (**Adjust body shape and size of 3d figure briefly**) to bring up this menu:

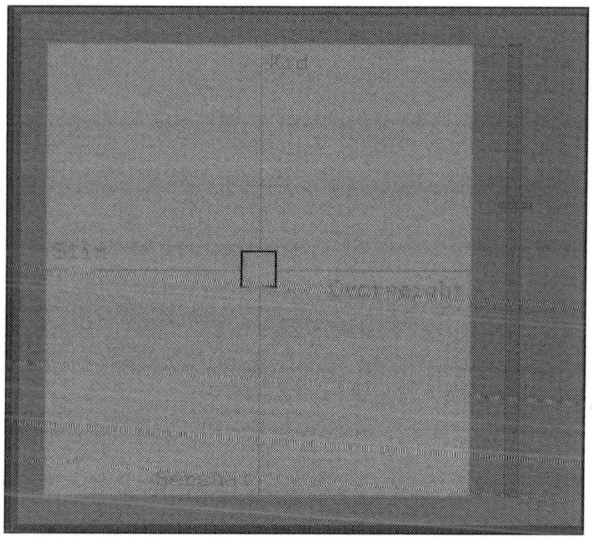

4. Click on the square in the center of the quadrants and drag it around to adjust the proportions of the character. For example, to make a character with the proportions of a child, drag the square into the quadrant marked **Kid**.
5. The slider to the right of the menu controls the height of the drawing doll. Adjust it as you like.

6. This method may not give you the fine control that you want. If so, click on the **Adjust body shape and size of 3d figure in detail** icon. The following menu will appear:

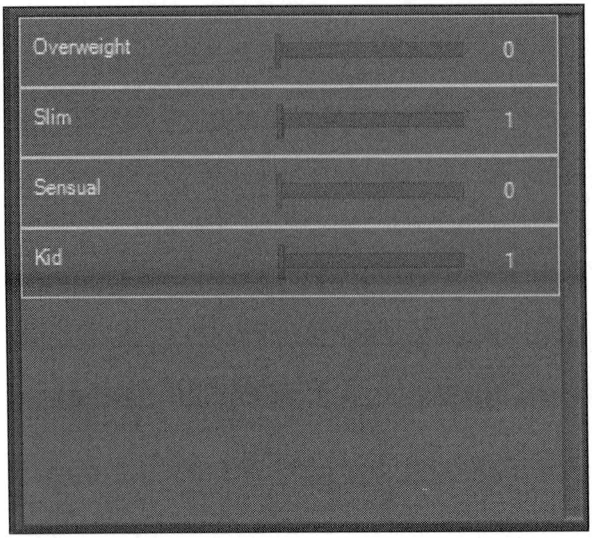

7. The sliders under this menu allow more fine-grained control over the proportions of the character. Move any slider to the right to apply more of the specific trait to the drawing doll model.
8. For even more control over the model, click on the **Adjust size of each part of 3D drawing figure in detail** icon. Then this menu will appear:

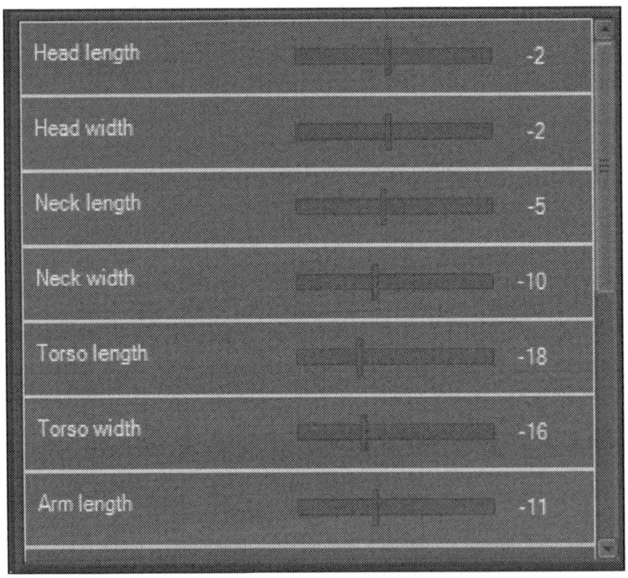

9. Each slider controls one aspect of the drawing doll, as they are marked. With these detailed controls, it is possible to make even "chibi" characters, as shown in the following screenshot:

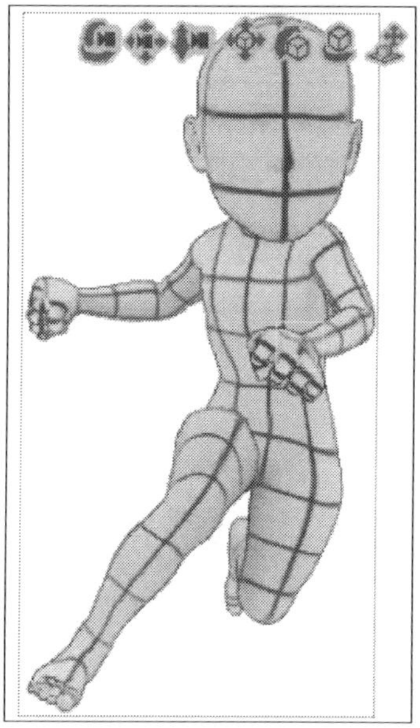

This "chibi" doll was made by increasing the width and length of the head and decreasing the torso, leg, and arm lengths. The arm width and torso width were also decreased.

After the doll had been posed, a new layer was created above the 3D doll. Then the doll was used as a basis for the drawing shown here:

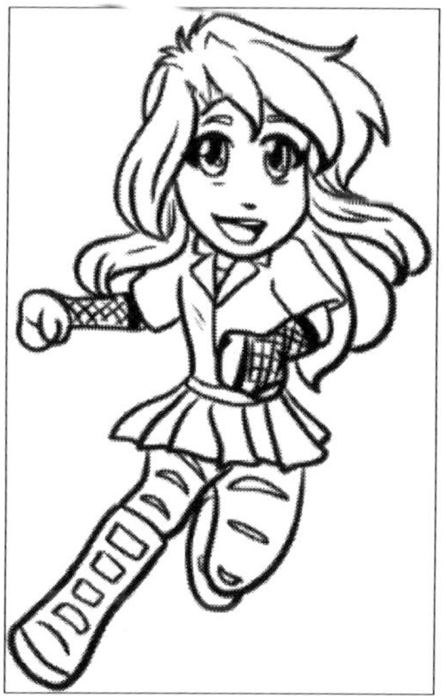

11
Exporting the Finished Product

In this chapter, you will learn the following recipes:

- Exporting for printing
- Adjusting the image quality and file size
- Resizing an image while exporting
- Exporting for web display
- Exporting pages in a batch (EX only)

Introduction

Now that you have your comic pages drawn, it's time to take them out of Manga Studio EX 5 and put them in print or on the Web. This chapter will teach you how to use all the exporting options, including how to resize pages during exporting and adjust the resolution.

Exporting for printing

Is there anything better than seeing your work printed in a book or magazine? I don't think so! Whether it's a full graphic novel or just a few printed illustrations, seeing your hard work on paper is one of the great things about being a digital artist. With these directions, you'll learn how to export pages to get a nice print, whether you're making them at home or sending them to a printer.

> When sending your work to a print shop to be printed, make sure that you research what file formats and resolution they accept as well as any restrictions that they may have. Adjust the steps in this recipe to fit them. Sending a batch of `.jpg` files to a printer that only accepts `.png` files will only waste time and cause headaches all around!

Getting ready

You will need a file open to export. In order for your illustrations to look good in print, they must have a resolution of at least 300 dpi. Anything lower than this may look pixelated or blurry when printed.

How to do it...

The following steps will walk us through the process of exporting a page for print:

1. Click on **File**, and then scroll down to **Export (Layered)** or **Export**. For this recipe, we will be exporting using a **Layered** option and saving as a `.psd` file.

> You should choose **Layered** or **Single Layer** based on your needs for the page after it has been exported. If you will be opening the image in another graphics program and will need to edit layers, then choose one of the **Layered** options. If you will simply be sending it to a printer or laying it out as a book in a layout design program, then one of the **Single Layer** options will likely work. When sending to an outsourced printer, remember to check out their guidelines for file formats.

2. Choose the desired file extension from the menu under the **Export (Layered)** or **Export (Single Layer)** option and click on it.
3. Name your file and choose where to save it. Then, click on **Save**.
4. The **Export** options for the file format that you're saving the file in will appear. The following are the options for saving it as a `.psd` file:

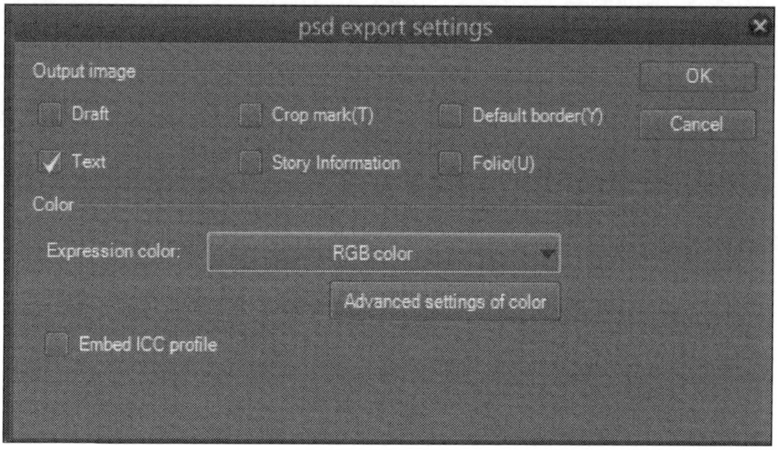

> Some file formats, such as the `.jpg` and `.png` formats, will have slightly different options, which will be covered in the *Adjusting the image quality and file size* recipe and the *Resizing an image while exporting* recipe in this chapter.

5. Check the boxes next to any of the options that you'd like to export. For example, if you need the crop marks or the default border to be shown, click on the boxes next to them to select them and they will be included in your export.
6. Choose the **Expression color** from the drop-down menu. Since we are sending this to be printed, we will choose the **CMYK color** mode. Manga Studio gives us a warning about saving layered files in CMYK mode, which is shown in the following screenshot:

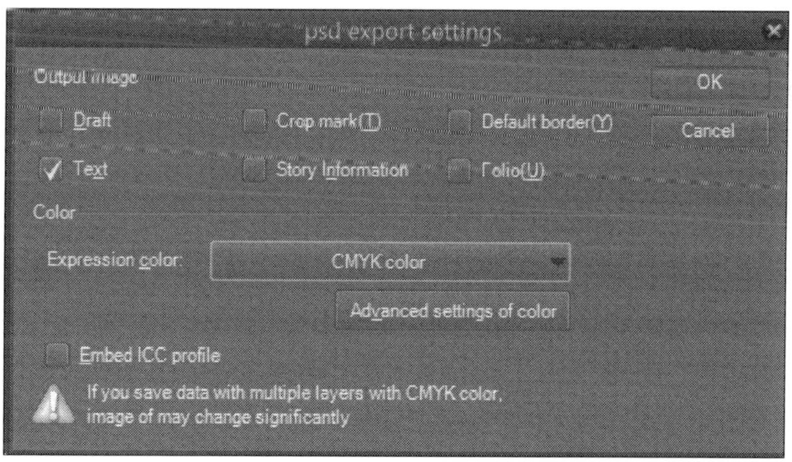

7. Once your options have been set, click on **OK** to complete the export.

Adjusting the image quality and file size

There are times when you do not need a full-resolution image. This recipe will explain how to export an image with compression so that the image quality is decreased, along with the size of the file.

Getting ready

You will need a file open to export.

How to do it...

The following steps will explain how to change the image quality:

1. Navigate to **File** | **Export (Single Layer)** | **.jpg (JPEG)**.

> This will only work for lossy file formats, such as `.jpg`. Other formats, such as `.png`, are lossless. To reduce the file size of a `.png`, `.bmp`, or `.psd` file, the image will have to be resized using the directions in the next recipe.

2. Name the file and choose a folder to save it in. Click on **Save**.
3. The **JPEG export settings** dialog box will appear. Click on the checkbox next to **Preview rendering results on output** at the top of the window.
4. Under **JPEG settings**, find the **Quality** setting. It is marked in this screenshot:

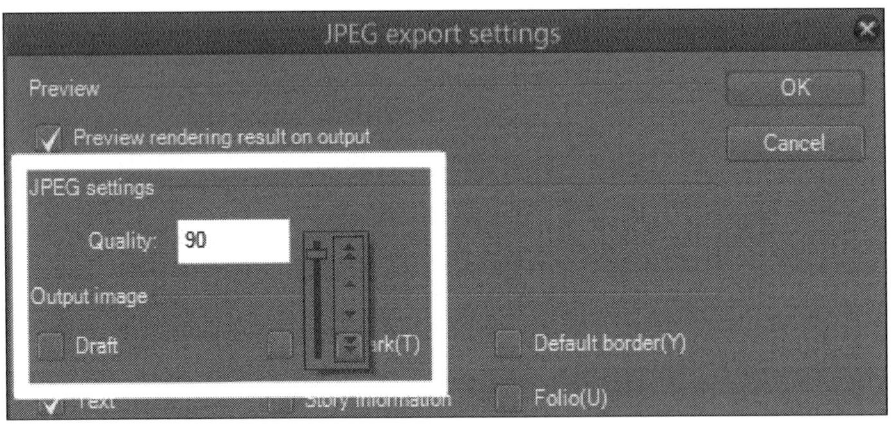

5. Click on the arrow next to the number box and adjust the slider, or use the up and down arrows to change the compression of the output file.

> Checking the **Preview rendering result on output** box will allow you to see and adjust the compression on the next screen, so don't be too concerned about getting it perfect just now. We can change the settings even after clicking on **OK**.

6. Click on **OK**.
7. The **Export preview** window will now appear. If needed, continue to adjust the quality using the setting in the bottom-right corner of the preview window.
8. Click on **OK**.

How it works...

The lower the number set in the **Quality** option, the lower the file size of the export. As shown in the following screenshot, the **Quality** option is set to `80`. Note the fairly large file size, at over 880 KB.

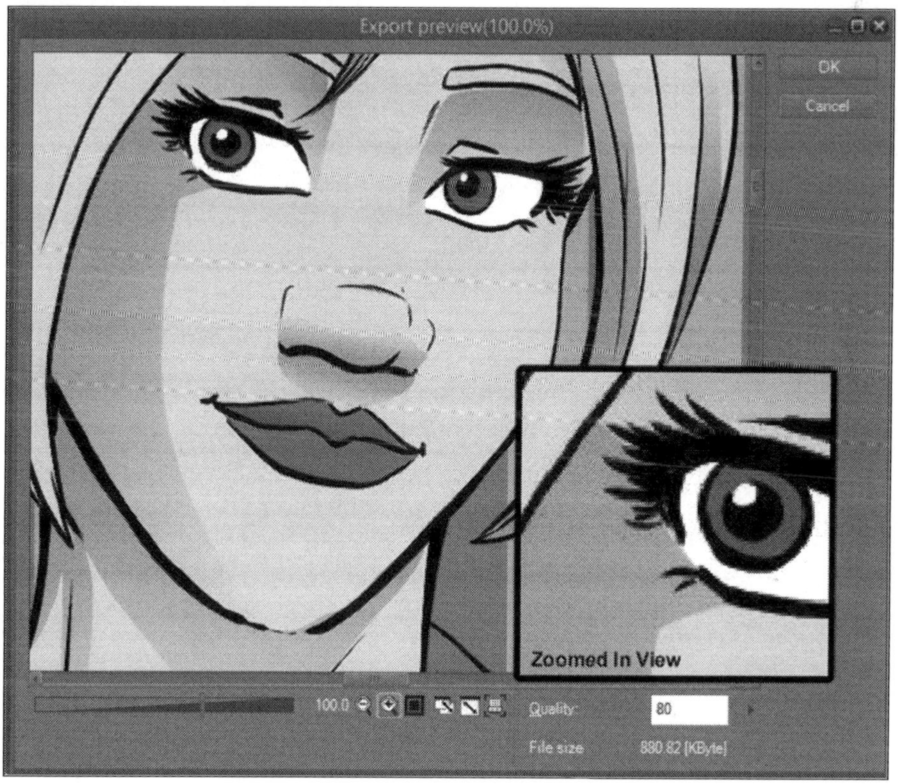

We can make the final file smaller by adjusting the quality down even more. By doing this, we sacrifice the quality of the image. Note how much the file size has gone down in the following screenshot, but also note how pixelated the image has become because of the low quality, especially around the gradients and the black lines:

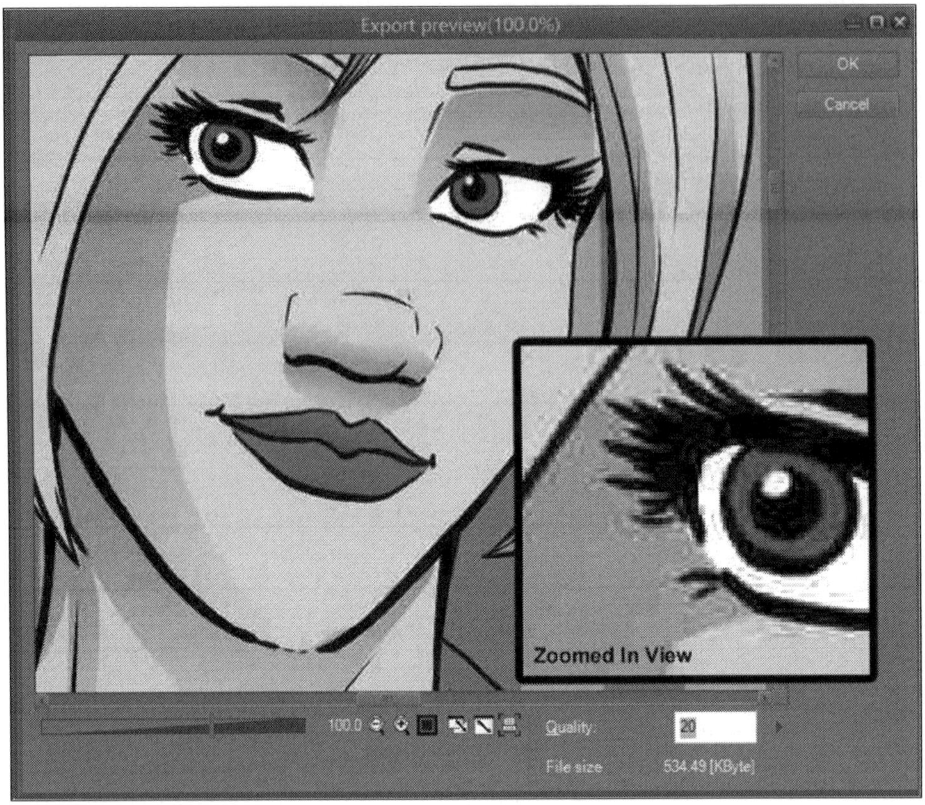

Resizing an image while exporting

Another way of changing the file size of the exported image is by changing the width and height of the image during export. This can be done on the fly without making any changes to your original file. Simply adjust the size during export and upload the image to the Web or to your e-mail, without being in danger of accidentally saving a 600-pixel-wide image over your full-size drawing ever again.

Getting ready

You will need a file open in order to export it.

How to do it...

Let's change the dimensions of an image with the following recipe:

1. Navigate to **File** | **Export (Single Layer)**, and then choose the desired file format for the exported file. For this recipe, we will be using the `.png` file format.

> Only the **Export (Single Layer)** options allow you to change the output size, but any of the file formats under this menu option can be used. Using **Export (Layered)** does not allow changes in the output size.

2. Name the file and choose a folder on your computer to save it in. Click on **Save**.

   The export settings for the file format you chose in step 1 will appear.

3. Locate the **Output size** options. They are marked in the following screenshot:

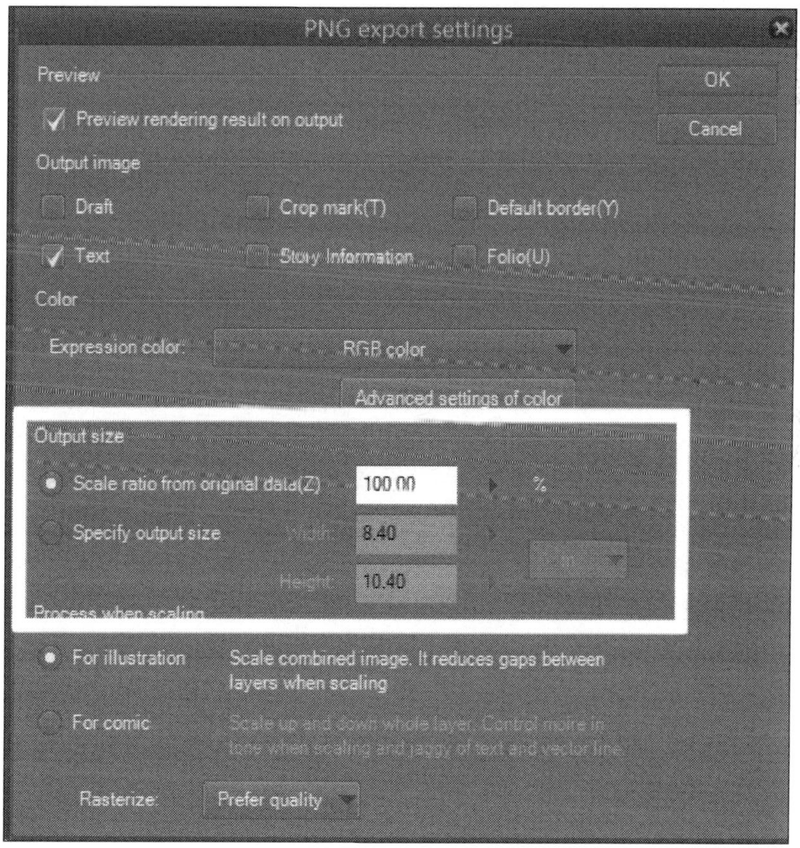

4. Select the radio button next to **Scale ratio from original data(Z)** to scale the image by percentage. In the following screenshot, the scale ratio has been set to **50.00%**. Note that **Width** and **Height** in the grayed-out boxes below the percentage box have changed as the ratio changes.

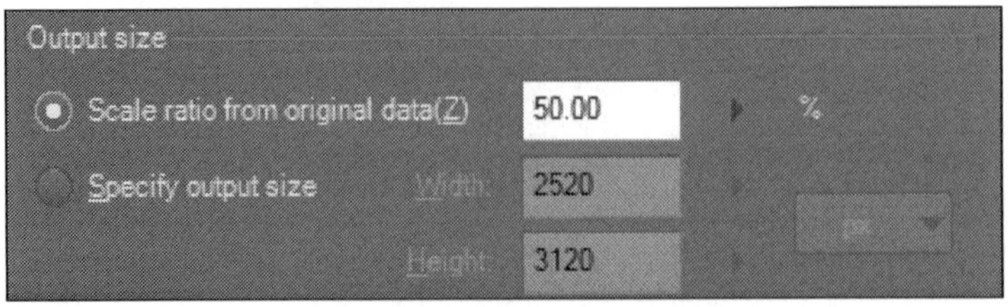

5. Select the radio button next to **Specify output size** to enter an exact **Width** or **Height** measurement. In the next screenshot, we have changed the drop-down menu to the right from **in** to **px** and entered a width of `800`. The height changes automatically as we enter a new width measurement.

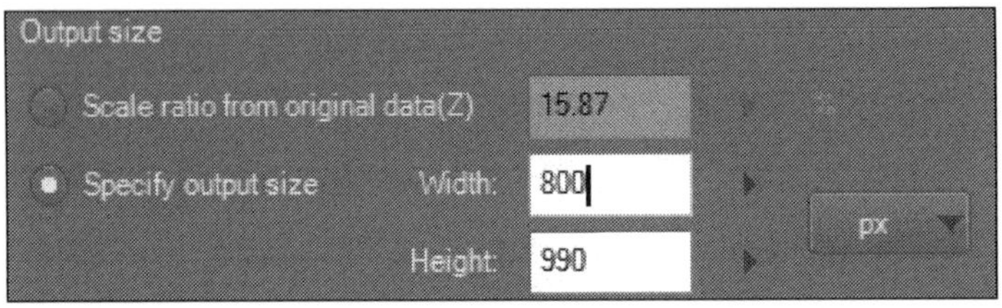

6. Click on **OK** to complete the export.

Exporting for web display

There are chances that you'll also want to share your comics or illustrations on the Internet. Whether it's on a personal portfolio site or whether you're making a webcomic, you'd want to be able to resize and compress your files to optimize them for the Web. Let's export a comic page for the Internet!

Getting ready

You will need a file open to export. It can be of any dimension and dpi; we will be adjusting these values as we export.

How to do it...

The following steps will show us how to export an image for display on the Internet:

1. Click on **File** and then scroll down to **Export (Single Layer)**. Choose any of the `.jpg`, `.bmp`, `.png`, or `.tif` file formats for your output file and click on it.

> Want to make your file sizes reasonable for fast loading times on the Web? Choose the `.jpg` file format and adjust the image quality to take advantage of file compression. The other file formats listed in this step are lossless formats and will be larger than `.jpg`.

2. Name your file and choose a folder to save it in on your computer. Click on **Save**.
3. Ensure that **Preview rendering result on output** is checked.
4. If you are exporting in the `.jpg` format, adjust the **Quality** option as explained previously in the *Adjusting the image quality and file size* recipe. As shown in this screenshot, we have adjusted **Quality** to `70`:

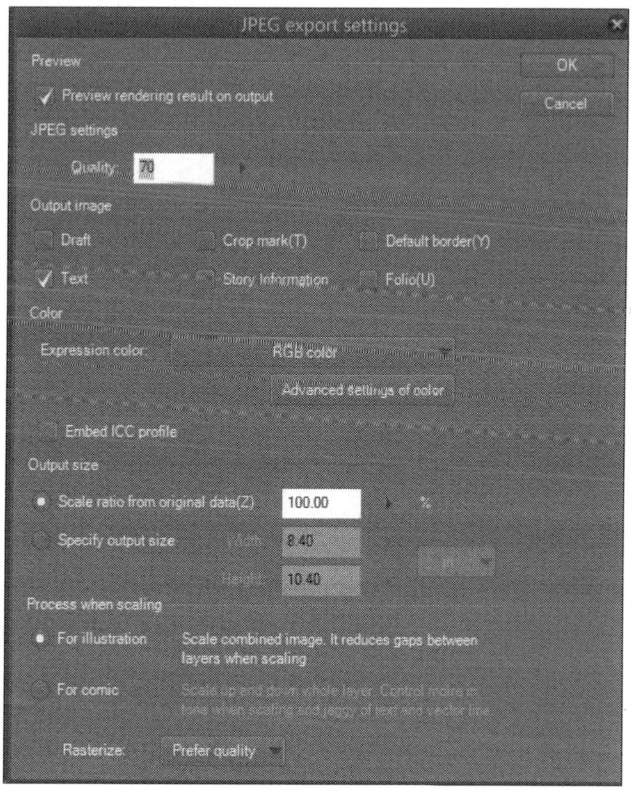

5. Adjust the **Output size** options to dimensions that are web friendly. Usually, this is 1000 pixels or less in width, but it may change depending on the format of the website that the image is being uploaded to (as an example, for my current comic website, I export my pages at 576 pixels in width and 700 pixels in height). In the following screenshot, we have used the **Specify output size** options to adjust the width to `1000` pixels. For more information on **Output size**, refer to the *Resizing an image while exporting* recipe.

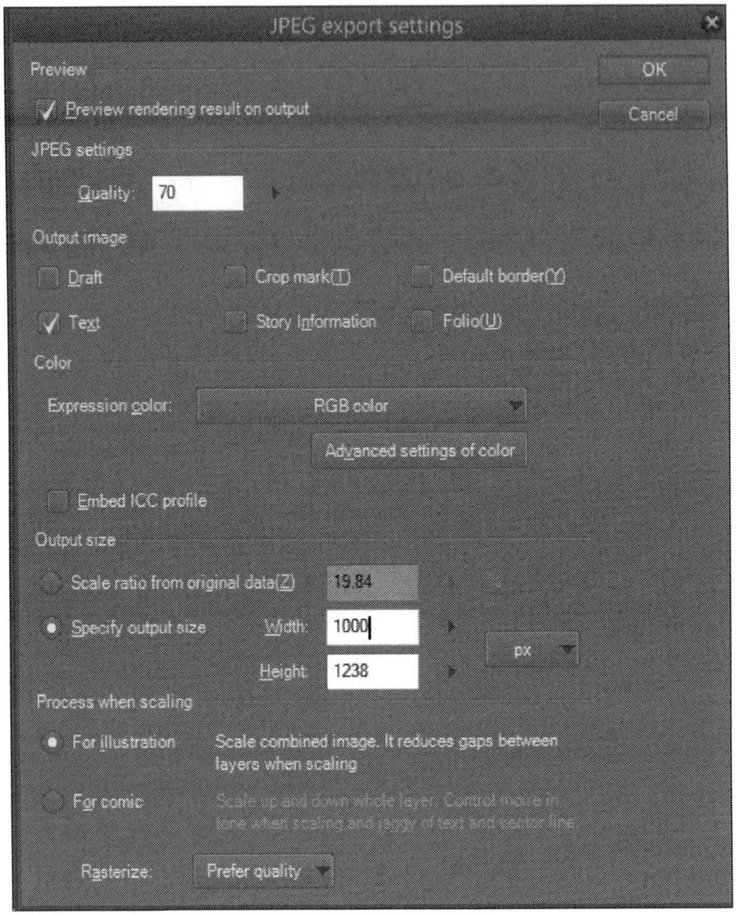

6. At the bottom of the export settings, we have the **Process when scaling** options. If you are exporting an illustration or something without tones, select the **For illustration** button. If the export image is a comic with vector lines, text, and screentones, choose the **For comic** option instead. These options are marked here:

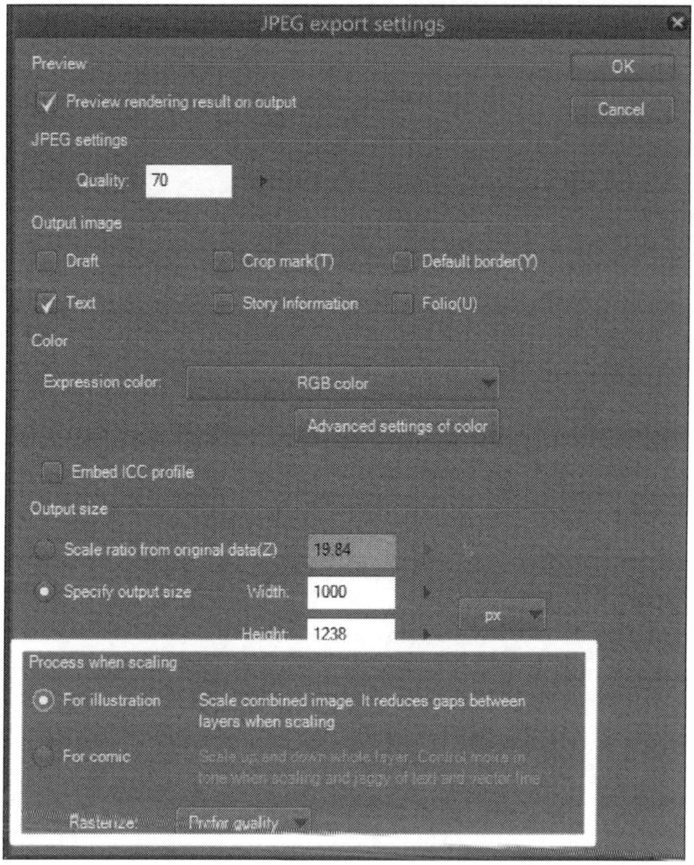

Using the **For comic** option will control the "moire" pattern that happens with screentones when they are scaled incorrectly. I highly recommend that you use it for black-and-white comics with tones!

7. Click on **OK**.

8. The **Export preview** window will be displayed once the image has been rendered. Use this preview to review the dimensions and the quality of the final exported file. Make any required adjustments to the file quality. In the following screenshot, we decided that `70` as the quality was too low, so we increased it to `80`. The result is still a fairly small file size, but it looks much better!

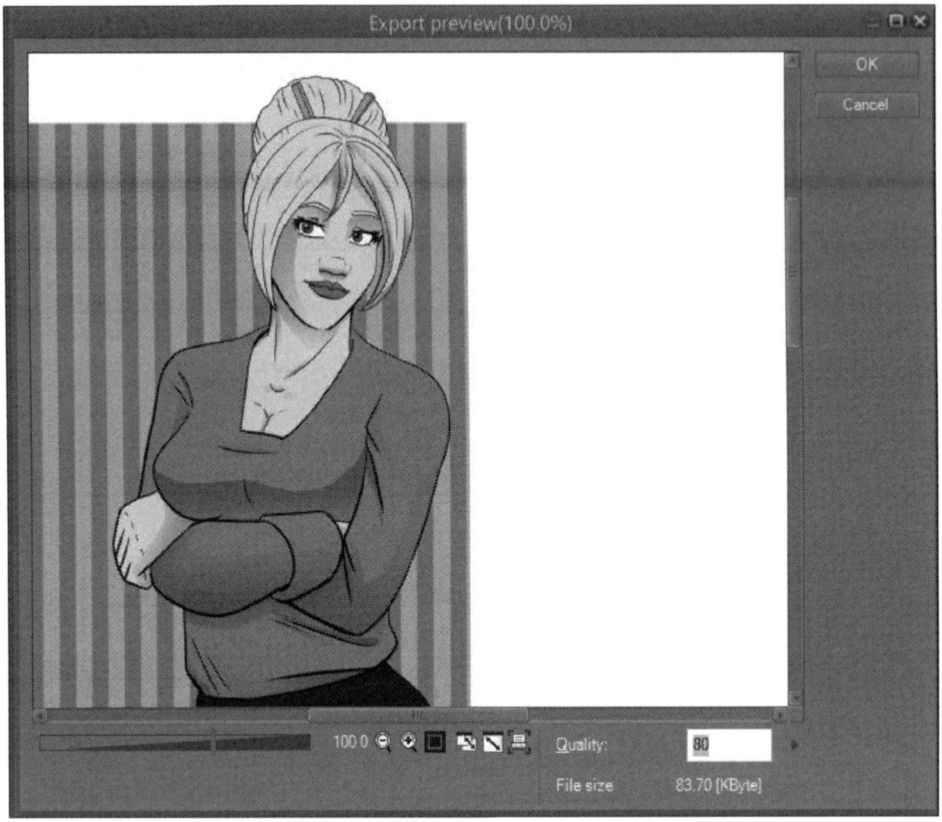

9. Click on **OK** to complete the export.

Exporting pages in a batch (EX only)

No need to export your entire graphic novel one page at a time as long as you have Manga Studio EX 5! We can do a batch export and save lots of time, saving all the pages in a story file for printing or sizing them all for the Web at once!

Getting ready

You will need an open story file to get started.

How to do it...

Let's export an entire chapter's worth of pages at once with the following steps:

1. Click on **Story** and then go to **Batch process** | **Batch export**, as shown in this screenshot:

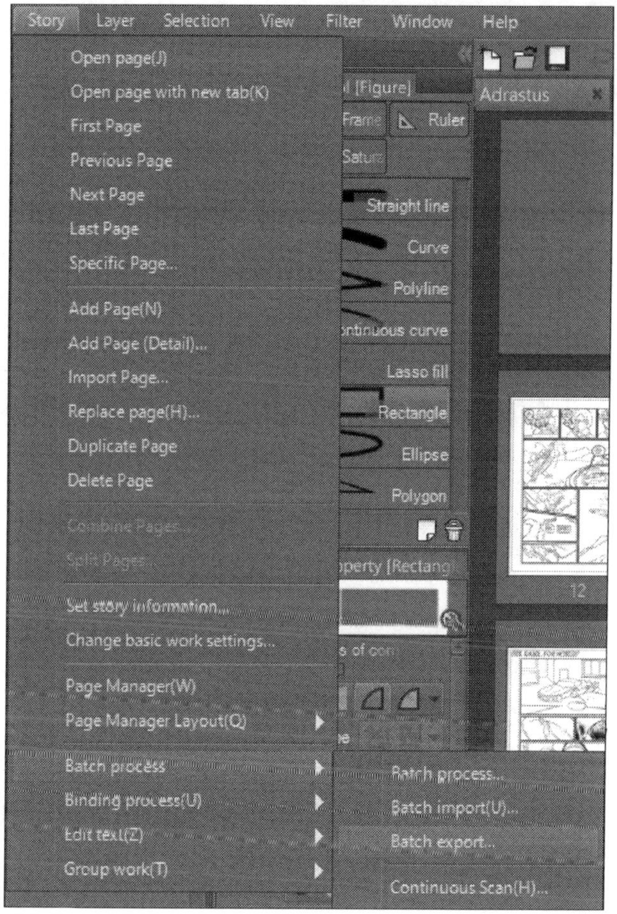

2. The **Batch export** options will show up on the screen. They are depicted in the following screenshot:

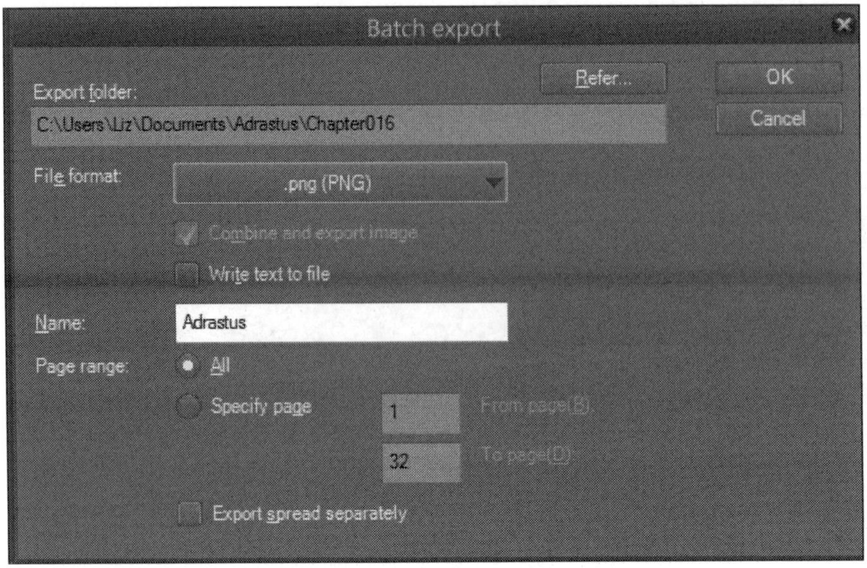

3. Use the **Refer** button to choose a file to save the exported batch in.
4. Select the **File format** option to save as from the drop-down menu.
5. In the **Name** box, type the name that all the exported files should be prefaced by (for example, `Page` or `Chapter01`). When the pages are exported, this name will be followed by the number of the page, such as `Page001.jpg`.
6. Select the page range. **All** will export all the pages in the story file. To export only a selected range of pages, click on the radio button beside **Specify page**. Then enter the page number to start at in the **From page(B)** box and the page number to end at in the **To page(D)** box.
7. To export each half of a two-page spread in a separate file, check the box next to **Export spread separately**.
8. Click on **OK**.
9. Manga Studio will now load the file and prepare for exporting. This may take several minutes, depending on your computer's speed and the size of the file. Be patient!
10. Now, the export settings for the file format chosen in step 4 will be shown. If the exported batch is for web display, use steps 3 to 9 given in the *Exporting for web display* recipe to complete the export.
11. Click on **OK** when all the settings have been adjusted in order to finish exporting.

Index

[PACKT] PUBLISHING

Thank you for buying Manga Studio Ex 5 Cookbook

About Packt Publishing

Packt, pronounced 'packed', published its first book, *Mastering phpMyAdmin for Effective MySQL Management*, in April 2004, and subsequently continued to specialize in publishing highly focused books on specific technologies and solutions.

Our books and publications share the experiences of your fellow IT professionals in adapting and customizing today's systems, applications, and frameworks. Our solution-based books give you the knowledge and power to customize the software and technologies you're using to get the job done. Packt books are more specific and less general than the IT books you have seen in the past. Our unique business model allows us to bring you more focused information, giving you more of what you need to know, and less of what you don't.

Packt is a modern yet unique publishing company that focuses on producing quality, cutting-edge books for communities of developers, administrators, and newbies alike. For more information, please visit our website at `www.packtpub.com`.

Writing for Packt

We welcome all inquiries from people who are interested in authoring. Book proposals should be sent to `author@packtpub.com`. If your book idea is still at an early stage and you would like to discuss it first before writing a formal book proposal, then please contact us; one of our commissioning editors will get in touch with you.

We're not just looking for published authors; if you have strong technical skills but no writing experience, our experienced editors can help you develop a writing career, or simply get some additional reward for your expertise.

[PACKT] PUBLISHING

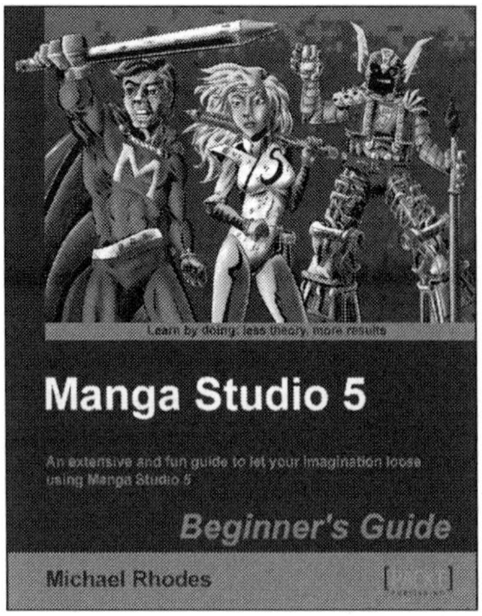

Manga Studio 5 Beginner's Guide

ISBN: 978-1-84969-766-8 Paperback: 400 pages

An extensive and fun guide to let your imagination on loose using Manga Studio 5

1. Illustrated with real-world examples, we embark on a journey of a comic's creation from initial idea to finished page.

2. Discover methods for emulating analog creation digitally and investigate ways of producing unique comics.

3. Full of examples and illustrations to make comic creation fun and easy.

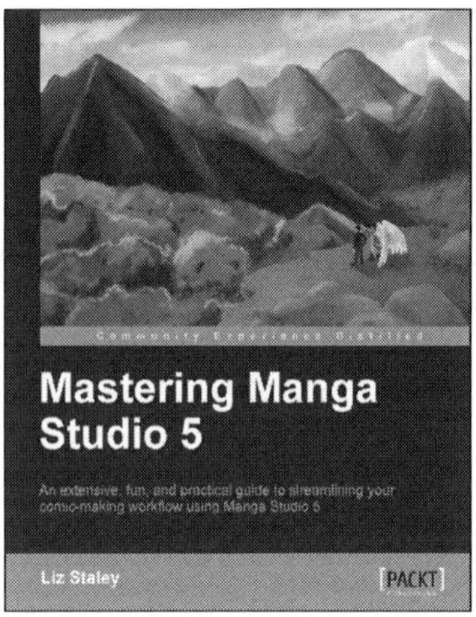

Mastering Manga Studio 5

ISBN: 978-1-84969-768-2 Paperback: 298 pages

An extensive, fun, and practical guide to streamlining your comic-making workflow using Manga Studio 5

1. Make Manga Studio 5 your own personalized software by creating your own workspace, tools, page layouts, and materials.

2. Explore using 3D models, actions, ruler tools, and creating projects to save you time.

3. Full of examples, illustrations, and tips with a lighthearted and fun style to make comic creation fun and easy.

Please check **www.PacktPub.com** for information on our titles

54202124R00168

Made in the USA
San Bernardino, CA
10 October 2017